pp 81-99

Churches and States:

The Religious Institution and Modernization

CHURCHES *and* STATES

AMERICAN UNIVERSITIES FIELD STAFF, INC.
366 Madison Avenue New York, N.Y. 10017

The Religious Institution

and Modernization

by VICTOR D. DU BOIS

LOUIS DUPREE

CHARLES F. GALLAGHER

WILLARD A. HANNA

JACOB NEUSNER

DENNISON I. RUSINOW

THOMAS G. SANDERS

STUART SCHAAR

Edited by KALMAN H. SILVERT

With a foreword by KENNETH W. THOMPSON

Library of Congress Catalog Card Number 67-22384

Sources of the quotations from the works of Max Weber appearing on the parts division pages are: Part I Judaism: *Ancient Judaism*, translated by Hans H. Gerth and Don Martindale, Glencoe: Free Press, 1952, pp. 206-7; Part II Catholicism: *The Sociology of Religion*, translated by Ephraim Fischoff and introduction by Talcott Parsons, Boston: Beacon Press, 1964, p. 223; Part III Islam: *ibid*, p. 199; Conclusions: *ibid*, pp. 124-5.

Chapter 7: "The Plateau of Particularism: Problems of Religion and Nationalism in Iran" by Charles F. Gallagher was published in AUFS Reports, Southwest Asia Series, Vol. XV, No. 2, 1966.

Design by Hugh O'Neill

Printed in the United States of America

Foreword

In his chapter on religion and nationalism in Iran, Charles F. Gallagher summarizes conversations with a broad spectrum of Iranian intellectuals on whether the ethical base of Iranian life is Islamic. He found that "although a minority made a vigorous defense of the proposition that it is—and practically none disputed that this is the case for the mass of the population—most either denied a close connection between Islam and modern Iran as a political entity or chose to ignore the problem as unimportant." In one sense, this reaction summarizes the central problem with which the authors of *Churches and States* seek to grapple. Religion as such espouses universal values which often seem remote from the particular concerns of politics. It is tempting, therefore, especially for skeptics and political realists to assume that religion at best is irrelevant to statecraft and at worst is confusing and misleading. Philosophers writing within the framework of Western civilization have made this point and have assumed, with little detailed knowledge, a similar limitation of organized religion in other societies. Churchmen in turn respond by pointing to the many areas in which religion has exercised influence on society. By claiming too much for their viewpoints, both political cynics and religious apologists are likely to allow their original premises to carry them beyond the facts. Many of us suspect that interrelationships between church and state are highly subtle and complex and that a host of contingent factors come into play in shaping patterns in widely divergent societies. Serious theologians and moral and political theorists have contributed to a growing literature that helps to clarify basic issues and general principles in this field.

The virtue of the present volume is to translate a general discussion into terms of historical and cultural concreteness. Successive authors

v

examine the relation of Judaism, Islam, and Catholicism to political systems that are varied and diverse. The spotlight focuses on African, Asian, European and Latin American societies separated in cultural time and experience. While there is less explicit comparison than in a volume by a single author, the writers explore a number of common themes. They approach their country or regional case studies with an unmistakably unified interest in bringing "methodological order" to the study of religion and national development. The unity of approach results in part from the fact that AUFS scholars comprise "a career service" of extraordinarily able practitioners of the applied social sciences and humanities seeking to evolve tentative theories about society. Evidently, the invited scholars who joined the AUFS cadre in this endeavor shared, or through conference and discussion came to share, this theoretical interest. More important, the organizing theme of religion and modernization, which at its core is a particular contemporary expression of the perennial problem of the relationship between church and state, imposed on the contributors across all their differences what emerges as a common focus and approach.

Modernization brings into sharp relief the facts of social change—facts that life in developing countries brings home to AUFS scholars as textbooks or library study can never do. Indeed, if AUFS literature has a single unifying theme, it is the impact and social consequences of modernization from North Africa to Southeast Asia and the Far North to South Africa. I hope it is not unfair to say that more has been written in AUFS Reports and books on modernization than on religion. If students of comparative religion find this book an invasion of their preserve, the response must be that two of the authors are drawn from religious studies. More importantly, the evidence multiplies that outsiders are sometimes more likely to throw new light on scholarly subjects than those who risk becoming mired in minutiae and detail. Thus Reinhold Niebuhr has spurred contemporary political philosophers to confront problems of theory and practice that might otherwise have been ignored. The historian Herbert Butterfield has challenged ethical writers and political scientists to reexamine questions that had been pushed aside. Or more significant still, outlanders like Lord Bryce and Alexis de Tocqueville have drawn in bold relief a portrait of American civilization more illuminating than the bulk of detailed studies by specialists born and bred in the nation's culture.

Beyond this, who can question that values today must be viewed in the context of change. The ferment which surrounds contemporary debates, say, between spokesmen of "situational ethics" and their critics is a measure of the concern with change. The "sacred texts" are being reexamined not alone from the standpoint of new historical and documentary evidence but as well for their relevance to the contemporary scene. In shifting the focus from doctrine to context, ethicists by definition are forcing themselves to come to terms with change.

The problem of change in values is highlighted in the present volume by its focus on "religious institutions." It will not do for students of contemporary religion or ethics to close their eyes to the status quo character of religious institutions through much of history. There is a double sense in which religious institutions may be a deterrent to modernization and social progress. On one hand, like institutions in general, they become fortresses of fixed doctrines and beliefs. They become a part of the social fabric sanctifying established religious and social practices. On the other hand, religious institutions are prone to isolate themselves from the immediate and the proximate, to set the eyes of believers on otherwordly concerns and to organize the life of the church around "a complex of absolutes of a supra-worldly nature." Identifying this tendency of the religious institution, Professor Silvert asks whether it can be "compatible with . . . constant extension of man's control over his environment, himself, and his future?" His question runs through the studies that comprise this volume. It quite properly remains in the mind of the reader as he follows the careful reviews of Islam, Judaism, and Catholicism in developing countries. In the end, the answer remains equivocal, for it seems intimately bound up with time and place.

The most profound reason for this historically bounded conclusion stems from the fact that for at least some religious traditions in some periods, religion's concern for the absolute is bound up with a perception of the relativism of social and political ethics. Jacob Neusner, whose chapter "From Theology to Ideology" is theoretically and analytically most suggestive, writes of the Jew, "He has always seen so diverse a world that he knew about the relativity of values, even while he affirmed his own." Neusner also links relativism with a framework of agreed general values or overall standards in the phrase, "Judaism knew that when all values were seen to be relative, men most needed the fellowship of congenial people to sustain them."

Translated into terms of American constitutionalism, this viewpoint has meant that certain objective principles of justice, equality, and freedom created the necessary framework within which social and political choices of a highly practical kind could be made. Or seen from the history of Christendom, the tradition of absolute values has not been incompatible with a growing corpus of prudential diplomatic and political practice. In short, proximate norms for the social and political order have derived from the ultimate precepts of religion. Often they are but pale reflections blended perforce with elements of expediency and compromise.

It is this middle realm of proximate rules and guiding principles discussed by contemporary Western ethical philosophers that needs elaboration. These guiding principles carry the prospects of success or failure for religious institutions as they confront change. It would be utopian to assume they can evolve in every culture and foolish to suppose they can survive in every state. Yet if mutual accommodation and reinforcement is to result, these middle principles and practices need review as to whether they are present or lacking in the changing context of church-state relations around the world.

KENNETH W. THOMPSON

New York
March 26, 1967

Preface

This volume grew out of a conference on "The Religious Institution and Modernism," sponsored by the American Universities Field Staff and held at Indiana University in October 1966.

The conference at Bloomington was a new departure for the AUFS and its member colleges and universities, as well as a further link in a continuing series of regular meetings held every autumn since 1953. For many years it had been the practice of AUFS associates, returning from abroad for an academic year of lecturing on member campuses, to make a general report on significant developments in their areas of specialization at these annual fall meetings. The gatherings also provided an opportunity for consultation on the needs and opportunities related to the AUFS program at the various campuses.

More recently, however, it gradually came to be felt for a variety of reasons that an informal, general meeting was insufficient for the increased needs of the times. For one thing, the deepening professionalization of interests among staff associates and the continuity developed after long periods of residence in their areas of competence meant that more information was available for analysis in a more systematic manner. For another, the much broader participation in many aspects of foreign area studies by almost all American academic institutions made it seem desirable to provide a more structured forum in which AUFS associates and their academic counterparts could participate and interact directly.

At the same time a tendency has been developing within AUFS in recent years toward greater integration of conceptualizing and working methods. This move arose spontaneously through the individual approach characteristic of much AUFS work, and was a result of the interplay of ideas among colleagues of more than a decade who were more and more turning their attention to the underlying structural problems of the societies they dealt with, rather than confining themselves to more cursory observation and information-gathering as had been usual in the earlier years of AUFS when underdeveloped and non-Western countries were relatively unknown and American interest in them less sophisticated.

In furtherance of this integrative trend, the AUFS, beginning a few years ago, undertook a series of collaborative endeavors under the stewardship of its Director of Studies, Kalman H. Silvert. The first venture was a study of nationalism and development published in 1963 under the title *Expectant Peoples*. The following year, a conference held through the kindness of The Rockefeller Foundation at the Villa Serbelloni in Bellagio, Italy, laid the groundwork for publication of *Discussion at Bellagio: The Political Alternatives of Development*, in which six AUFS associates were joined by academicians and political figures from the United States and eight other countries. Almost completed is the latest all-AUFS collaborative study, *Freedom and Development*, which pursues an inquiry into some of the major problems raised in the initial efforts.

In all its work the American Universities Field Staff has tried to harmonize the objectivity of the social sciences with the sympathetic understanding of the humanities by emphasizing the quality of human development above all else. Holding fast to this concept, we have sought to narrow and refine particular areas of study within a vast domain. Thus, *Expectant Peoples* was a broad survey of the role of nationalism and the idea of the nation-state in the newer nations of the world, based on the postulate that nationalism both as a social value and as an ideology is fundamental, in many variant forms, to the complications of human development through which emerging nations are passing. The Bellagio conference study concentrated on the politics of national development and surveyed the range of political alternatives available to these countries. That meeting led to a further sharpening of focus as the idea gained currency within AUFS that the freedom needed to make rational decisions in matters of development might be a "functional requisite for self-sustaining development" and a prerequisite for "the generation of the attitudes and values necessary for the chain reactions of the modern, empirical society." It was this idea which led directly to the examination of the relationship of public and civic freedom to the entire developmental process that is found in *Freedom and Development*.

Meanwhile, the first attempt to bring methodological order and substantive continuity into the annual fall meetings was taking place. At Harvard in 1964, AUFS panelists held a discussion centered around

Mediterranean cultural patterns and their relation to national development. Following that, it was agreed in 1965 that the annual meetings would be appropriate for formal, scholarly conferences, and for the first of these it seemed normal to proceed along those lines of inquiry which had already suggested themselves. Problems of free choice seemed to be particularly troublesome and poignant in religious and family behavior according to much of the research done for the study of freedom and development, and it was decided that an examination of the religious institution—from a historical, cultural, and sociological viewpoint—and its influence on development and modernization was the next logical step.

Readers familiar with past AUFS works will remember that they attempted to provide a combination of tentative theory, specific case studies, and empirical conclusions. It is a pleasure to note that, without suggestion or prodding, the papers presented at the Indiana Conference—both by associates of the staff and colleagues from member universities whose contributions have been of capital importance—follow this tradition. They have provided us with a conference framework which offers a broad compatibility in preliminary approach that is balanced by the diversified detail of personal interpretation.

As will be evident from the papers and discussion which follow, complete agreement cannot be expected in defining and using terms as multifaceted and elusive as religion and modernism. In fact this was not achieved at the conference, but a substantial area of accord was certainly reached. From the beginning, those in AUFS charged with planning the meeting were conscious of the need to clarify essential terminology, and it is useful therefore to refer briefly to the concepts which guided preliminary activity. The term "religious institution" was selected to underline our emphasis on viewing religion primarily, but not exclusively, as an institutionalized element in the social structure and to indicate that our treatment would aim toward a dispassionate study of the sociology of religion as one of the basic institutions of society. Religion may also be considered as a belief system dealing with absolutes employed as a moral guide and a theoretically ultimate arbiter for human behavior. Within the concept elaborated, then, we were also viewing religion as an instrumentality for putting order into the scattered symbols of reality in which the world abounds. We have also tried to keep in mind that religious belief is utilized as an underpinning to and justification for all kinds of individual and social action and behavior patterns which are interlinked with and harmonized with religious symbols, unless these symbols are to be replaced by others of ultimate value—an occurrence which has not yet taken place in any society at any time over a substantial period.

The concept of modernism which dominated the conference was expressed by Professor Silvert in the introduction to *Expectant Peoples*, where he has characterized it as: "Attitudes, social devices and traditions which permit orderly institutionalized change . . . and which assume in one or another degree that public decisions must be secular, pragmatically derived and subject to empirical test." And in the same work he goes on to suggest that: "The self-sustaining nature of change, supported by appropriate values and by other social institutions as well as by the State is probably the most important single characteristic of modern society."

Given the general acceptance of these two definitions of scope, the range of the papers presented was unusually wide, but the conference benefited from their having been circulated previously among the participants. Thus only a brief oral summation, sometimes elaborated by fresh additional ideas and last-minute thoughts, was necessary before the round-table discussions began. Manifestations of religious behavior were examined in lands ranging from Southeast Asia through the Middle East, Africa, and Catholic Europe to Latin America, but the principal emphasis clearly lay in the historically transitional religions—Islam, Christianity, and Judaism.

The conference was held in four sessions. Alan W. Horton served as chairman; Charles F. Gallagher gave the introductory presentation, outlining the topic in broad terms; and Kalman H. Silvert offered a summation at the close of the discussions. The guest participants and their topics were:

Kenneth W. Morgan, *Department of Religion, Colgate University*
"SOME HINDU AND BUDDHIST REACTIONS TO CHANGE IN THE TWENTIETH CENTURY"

Jacob Neusner, *Department of Religion, Dartmouth College (Department of Religious Studies, Brown University, 1968)*
"FROM THEOLOGY TO IDEOLOGY: THE TRANSMUTATION OF JUDAISM IN MODERN TIMES"

Thomas G. Sanders, *Department of Religious Studies, Brown University*
"RELIGION AND MODERNIZATION"

Stuart Schaar, *Department of History, University of Wisconsin*
"REBELLION, REVOLUTION, AND RELIGIOUS INTERMEDIARIES IN NINETEENTH-CENTURY ISLAM"

The AUFS Participants were:

Victor D. Du Bois
"Church-State Relations in French-Influenced West Africa"

Louis Dupree
"Traditionalism Versus Modernism in Afghanistan"

Willard A. Hanna
"The Malay-Muslim State of Kelantan"

Dennison I. Rusinow
"The Retreat from Josephinism: Austrian Catholicism Responds to the Twentieth Century"

The rapporteur was Bruce Berman, *graduate student in political science, Yale University.*

Others attending the sessions included:

Campus Committee Representatives:

University of Alabama	Charles G. Summersell
Brown University	Whitney T. Perkins
California Institute	
of Technology	Edwin S. Munger
Carleton College	Robert E. Will
Dartmouth College	Laurence I. Radway
Harvard Business School	***
Indiana University	John M. Thompson
University of Kansas	Clifford P. Ketzel
Louisiana State University	Quentin Jenkins
Michigan State University	***
Tulane University	John S. Gillespie
University of Wisconsin	Robert J. Miller
American Universities	Teg C. Grondahl
Field Staff	Richard D. Dodson

Guest Observers:

Hugh Barbour, *Earlham College*
Richard H. Nolte, *Institute of Current World Affairs*
Lawrence Olson, *Wesleyan University, Connecticut*
Don Peretz, *New York State Education Department*
Joseph Whitney, *Earlham College*

The American Universities Field Staff extends its thanks to President Elvis J. Stahr, jr. of the University of Indiana and to his colleagues and associates for the warmth of their hospitality and the ingeniousness of their anticipations of our needs. We also owe a most particular debt to our colleagues on member campuses who contributed their papers, their presence, and their enthusiasm to this joint work.

Tangier, Morocco   CHARLES F. GALLAGHER
March 15, 1967

Contents

Churches and States:

The Religious Institution and Modernization

INTRODUCTION

KALMAN H. SILVERT

American Universities Field Staff

Perhaps because of equalitarian embarrassment or academic reticence, analysis of the relation of the religious to other social institutions suffered a generation of neglect before the present emergence of interest in problems of development, modernization, and social change. As recently as 1959 it could be written, with particular reference to the United States, that

> Nothing is being done on the interrelationships between religious ideas and the values of the economic order, for example, or on church-state relationships. Studies along these lines are likely to come into vogue only if and when sociologists begin to think of religious ideas as having more than a historical relationship to the dominant values of the general society.
>
> . . . It is perhaps a mistake to think of the sociology of religion as the exclusive province of sociological specialists of religion. . . . Some of . . . [the important problems of the field] can be studied more appropriately from the points of view of other disciplines. Thus, as has been true to some extent in the past, contributions to the body of knowledge comprising the sociology of religion should be expected to come not only from the specialists but from social theorists, students of bureaucracy, sociologists of the professions, and from the general field of social psychology.[1]

[1] Charles Y. Glock, "The Sociology of Religion" in Robert K. Merton, Leonard Broom, and Leonard S. Cottrell, Jr. (eds.), *Sociology Today: Problems and Prospects*, New York: Basic Books, 1959, pp. 176-7. This book is an inventory of the state of the discipline as of the time of its publication.

It is with no particular pride, even in light of the foregoing statement, that we point out that no sociologists of religion have been involved in the preparation of this book. The reason is a function of the direction from which our interest in the theme came. This volume concerns modernization first, and second the role of the religious institution in that process. Thus all of the authors deal somehow with social change, either in the broad sense of shifts in belief systems and group behavior, or else in the narrower sense of specific changes involving the establishment of modern social organization and practice. Professors Neusner and Sanders, even though they are specifically identified in their academic lives with religion as discipline, here consider changing institutional and ideological matters and not theology as a special kind of philosophical thought.

This specific and thus exclusionist limitation of subject has given us pause, as has the fact that the chapters comprising this book are built around a common theme, but not a common theory. To educate ourselves in the subject matter is a legitimate undertaking. But to presume that we have enough of significance to say to publish yet another book in the very long line of collected conference papers may at the least be immodest. To be blunt, it may also be dishonest if we are merely pressing to put a title on a "non-book," as the sophisticates have it. We have no doubt that all of the chapters in this book are well worth publication, and that some will have a long and useful life. That judgment is not necessarily to the point, however, for as individual pieces they should find their way to the reader through appropriate journals. It also would be insufficient justification to argue, as we legitimately can, that there is a scarcity of published materials of a comparative nature on church-state relations in the developing world.[2]

The basic reason for thinking of this collection of chapters as a book is that there is a unity of themes, problems, and definitions running through all the studies which invites a confrontation of cases and a resultant comparative synthesis. We have not felt justified, however, in pushing the materials to an integrated conclusion, for no testing of common hypotheses has been undertaken. The state of this field of inquiry is sufficiently fluid to permit this hesitancy and to justify asking of the reader that he bring his own wit and training to bear on building bridges of generalization across the chapter divisions.

Three strategically placed religions are the only ones studied in this

---

[2] We are well aware that sensibilities may be ruffled by our referring to "church-state" relations in non-Christian cultures. The term, when here employed, refers to "church" in its generic sense, however, and should be so understood in the proper context in the body of this book. Conceptual considerations as well as stylistic ones have been permitted to govern in this usage.

book. They are Judaism, Catholicism, and Islam—organized, Western, monotheistic religions sitting precisely astride that critical line joining the grandly traditional to the modern. Judaism is the religious persuasion of the Ashkenazim, with their memories of the Eastern European *shtetl*, their attachment to the cultures of the areas spreading from Germany to Russia, and their continuing diaspora to new worlds in the Americas, South Africa, and even the Pacific. But it is also the religion of the Sephardim with their memories of Spain, Portugal, and the Netherlands and their actuality in North Africa and the Middle East. And now, of course, Judaism is also in a special relation to the world of politics in Israel. Catholicism, too, informs an extremely broad range of social occurrences. From the Gallican Catholicism of Western Europe to the ostensibly Catholic practices of Mayan villagers, that institution embraces a vast array of social adjustments, including accommodations to Italian, Spanish, Portuguese, Irish, Polish, Yugoslav, and other widely diverse secular practices from Europe to the Philippines, Africa, and Latin America. The equally large geographical area covered by Islam does not provide so much social diversity as the Catholic world, but the range remains enormous. The universe starting with the French-influenced Maghrib and ending with Malaysia and Indonesia includes nomadic tribesmen and worldly urbanites and an infinity of those other contrapositions so characteristic of the unevenness of rapid social change.

It is now a commonplace to argue that the stronger the institutions of tradition, the more difficult the transition to the kind of modernism characterized by the old industrial states classically suffused with the effects of Ascetic Protestantism—however those effects may appear in today's context. We do not wish to enter the controversy about the "Weber thesis" or the "Durkheim theory" or the various counter views pretending to discover the relationships among social ethic, individual thought and action, and public behavior. As has been said, this book stems from no specific theoretical commitment in that area, although the problem is freely discussed by several of the contributors. What we do wish to say is that we are studying three religions which help to define the ethos of as many highly complex cultures whose very degree of subtlety and elaboration enhances the effectiveness of their defense against the appeals and attacks of other world views. These institutionalized religions, with their highly articulated bodies of doctrine and their variety of patterns of religious adherence, exist in extraordinarily heterodox social situations.

We have then for our problem area a complex set of variables in shifting patterns of relationship among themselves: the heterogeneous institutional manifestations of the religions; not only the differing understandings of those religious beliefs in kinds of human communities varying from the urban industrial to the tribal, but also the differing understandings within societies in accordance with the class order; variations in relationships with the sources of external stimuli as well as variations in the nature of the stimuli themselves; and then, of course, there still always remain those problems of analysis connected with leadership, charismatic or otherwise, the accidents of personality and timing, and the other casual elements which enter into all social affairs, but become particularly important in analyses of change and conflict. This complexity of social situations plus the relative elaboration of traditional institutional structures are precisely the conditions making possible widely variegated patterns of change as well as the organization of many kinds of effective resistance to unwanted change, or to change itself. More primitive cultures are denied any such multiplicity of response. If there is a descriptive continuum to development, then it is here that one finds it in clearest relief: the effect of growing differentiation is to permit a broader array of alternatives for effective choice than before. Our cases concern cultures with more than a little power of self-defense; presumably, they thus also have more than a little power to innovate, if so they will it.

There is a grand question concerning religion, however, which we should face, despite an inability to face it down. Baldly put, are religious beliefs and religious institutions inherently antithetical to social change over any appreciable period of time? We know perfectly well that religious groups in their "cult" and "sect" phases often actively agitate for change even of a revolutionary nature. That is not our question. Is a belief system based on an extended view of a complex of absolutes of a supra-worldly nature, necessarily unsusceptible to validation and just as necessarily *commanding* men to action, compatible with a human dedication to a constant extension of man's control over his environment, himself, and his future? Such a continuing expansion of effective interaction with environment demands an ethos of changefulness and a commitment to controlled uncertainty. Thus social rules in the modern world become internalized not as commandments, but as built-in governors of "oughts." A secular "religion" of ethics develops, not a sacred religion of "musts." Whether the absoluteness of religion can be harmonized through extended time periods with the relativeness of science and a social ethic of human values, not eternal truths, is an old subject for debate, of course. The question is not answered in these pages, naturally, but it is well worth noting that none of the authors, with only one exception, questions that the existence of strong religious institutions is compatible with the emergence and maintenance of modern styles and institutions.

4

Such optimism is itself a recent phenomenon, and may well be an accompaniment to the increasing interest in the sociology of religion brought on by contemporary problems of development.

Whatever the implicit views of the authors, the cases they present all reveal the difficulties religious institutions encounter in adjusting to change; whether those institutions experience greater difficulty than others is left unanswered here. What is apparent, however, is a very broad feeling in Western, industrialized society that religious institutions and the practices of modern life do not easily and automatically mesh. Max Weber poignantly summed up the attitudinal difficulties of the modern man and, by implication, the social scientist, with respect to religion. "The modern man is, in general, even with the best will, unable to give religious ideas a significance for culture and national character which they deserve." [3] Even though anthropologists are a major exception to this generalization, they and the sociologists who have been in the forefront of the development of so-called functional theory have ascribed to religion functions that are responses to man's guilts and uncertainties and social difficulties rather than to any ambitions he may have toward betterment for himself and his world.

> Religion, then, in the view of functional theory, identifies the individual with his group, supports him in uncertainty, consoles him in disappointment, attaches him to society's goals, enhances his morale, and provides him with elements of identity. It acts to reinforce the unity and stability of society by supporting social control, enhancing established values and goals, and providing the means for overcoming guilt and alienation. It may also perform a prophetic role and prove itself an unsettling or even subversive influence in any particular society. [4]

In this description, even the unsettling role played by prophetic movements may be opposed to the growth of secular relativism, for such views become subversive only in attempting to establish "the transcendence of God, and his consequent superiority to and independence of established authorities in society." [5] Historically, for example, such opposition is often invoked specifically to counteract liberalizing political tendencies, particularly in the more traditional Catholic countries. To accept this statement of the general social functions of religion is also to presume that in most cases the religious insti-

[3] Max Weber, *The Protestant Ethic and the Spirit of Capitalism*, trans. Talcott Parsons, New York: Charles Scribner's Sons, 1958, p. 183.
[4] Thomas F. O'Dea, *The Sociology of Religion*, Englewood Cliffs, N.J.: Prentice-Hall, 1966, p. 16. This book is an excellent analysis of functional theory in the field and is highly recommended as an introduction to the subject.
[5] *Ibid.*, p. 14.

tution will oppose itself to any organic social changes, dedicated as it is to system-maintenance ends in its social manifestations. By this same token, once the changes introducing modernism have occurred, then the religious institution, to preserve its nature, should adjust and support the patterns of modern social life. Despite religion's ultimate premises and its intellectual style which is necessarily concerned with dogma, modern societies, in their functional specificity and structural differentiation, should be able to support a sector of absolutism within the generalized social ambiance of relativism. Let us turn once again to Weber who, taking rationalization as the keynote of the modern situation, shows how the empirical and pragmatic may be accommodated to the extra-worldly and dogmatic.

> Now by this term [rationalism] very different things may be understood. . . . There is, for example, rationalization of mystical contemplation, that is of an attitude which, viewed from other departments of life, is specifically irrational, just as much as there are rationalizations of economic life, of technique, of scientific research, of military training, of law and administration. Furthermore, each one of these fields may be rationalized in terms of very different ultimate values and ends, and what is rational from one point of view may well be irrational from another. Hence rationalizations of the most varied character have existed in various departments of life and in all areas of culture. To characterize their differences from the view-point of cultural history it is necessary to know what departments are rationalized, and in what direction.[6]

As we have said, Judaism, Catholicism, and Islam are all highly rationalized bodies of religious thought in situations of widely varying institutional differentiation. The empirical problem is to discover the kind and quality of the several differentiations, implying the necessity of comparing and contrasting the religious to other social institutions. The theoretical problem is to discover the significances of one or another set of relations, and to project these sets of relationships into situations of change. In selecting what part of this task to undertake, the authors of the chapters in this book have all taken essentially the same path: they have described the relationship of the religious institution in their areas to the political institution; and they have examined valorative, ideological, and power aspects of that relationship as revealed through situations of conflict and conciliation associated with generalized developmental trends or specifically modernizing ones. Here is the essential unity of theme of the volume. As is evident, it is an approach of strategic significance. The reason is not the commonly

[6] Weber, op. cit., p. 26.

advanced one that in modernizing settings the state often competes with the religious institution by advancing its own "secular religion," which leads to such discussions as whether Communism, for example, is but a cheapened religion.[7] Much more importantly, this relationship is significant because the polity is often the starting point for social change, and inevitably the citadel to be stormed by any groups desiring to seize control of the means for leading development. And once through that difficult passage to the modern situation, it is the public mechanism which insures that the differentiation permitting complex and varied rationalizations "in terms of very different ultimate values and ends" may proceed in support of the total system. Religion in a modern setting must somehow come to terms with a pluralistic society if the necessarily absolutist beliefs of religion are not to destroy the equally necessary relativistic beliefs of societies dedicated to the institutionalization of change. The necessity for this kind of separate togetherness, so to speak, has been put as follows:

> . . . our working hypothesis will be that there is a correlation between economic underdevelopment, social extremism, and ethical-religious Latin American spirituality. In a somewhat more developed form, our hypothesis is that Latin American Catholic spirituality seems to be characterized by an undue projection of the ethical-religious categories, and their corresponding attitudes, into the profane world of economic development and social change.
>
> In our opinion, a sort of profanation occurs in the Latin American world. The religious categories stray from their valid orbit, and begin to direct the profane world. And here we make bold to state a value judgment: We believe that this undue projection of that which is specifically religious into the economic and social areas is a true adulteration of the profane. . . .
>
> It seems to us that the Latin American world is marked culturally by a scheme of authority that is essentially vertical. This world tends permanently toward a dictatorial scheme. Even in its "formal democracies" there are shades of totalitarianism—in other words, some degree of statism or acceptance of the Providence State. The cause, in our judgment, is that the Latin American tends to project a vertical scheme of authority that is valid and legitimate in the ethical and religious realm into the profane world.[8]

[7] For an excellent treatment of this subject, see J. Milton Yinger, *Religion, Society and the Individual*, New York: Macmillan Co., 1957, esp. pp. 118–20 for his treatment of Communism.

[8] Roger Vekemans, S. J., "Economic Development, Social Change, and Cultural Mutation in Latin America," in William V. D'Antonio and Frederick B. Pike (eds.), *Religion, Revolution, and Reform: New Forces for Change in Latin America*, New York: Frederick A. Praeger, 1964, pp. 136–7.

The very fact of the transitional nature of the cases studied in this book highlights this unity-diversity dialectic and shows its critical role in the modern world. In his study of the movement of European Jewry in modern times "from theology to ideology," Professor Neusner turns the problem inward to the Jewish community itself in order to control for the many polities to which Judaism has reacted. He begins by reminding us that the very concept of "tradition" is a modern one—for distinguishing the "modern" from the "traditional" is itself only possible to cultures analytically divided as well as synthetically joined. He then proceeds to an examination of how four streams of the Jewish tradition—theology, messianism, social ethics, and scholarship—have fared in adjustment to the modern world. This chapter is placed first not only out of respect for chronology, but also because it provides a leitmotiv for the book. Professor Neusner also reminds us that an interaction implies changes in the internal structures of the elements in play, and not merely in their respective physical or power relations one to another. And like the other authors, he demonstrates how the tradition came to look out from itself and espouse such worldly causes as socialism and Zionism as logical consequences of antecedent and coincident religio-ethical styles and habits of thought.

Three cases from three continents illustrate the problems of the Catholic Church in accommodating to change. Dr. Victor Du Bois examines the problems of the Church in three new nations cut out of former French West Africa. The theme here as in the remainder of the chapters clearly concerns the determination of spheres of influence between secular and religious authority, and at least as importantly, the nature of the ideology to be espoused for the public legitimation of public acts. His cases are divergent and introduce us also to the problems of accident—the role of circumstance and personality within the situational frame. We then move across the South Atlantic to Brazil, where Professor Sanders describes in intimate detail the emergence of what may be called cultist politics inside the Church in the attempt to create a progressive Catholicism of revolutionary social content—not as answer to Marxism, but as attempt to accomplish what Marxism failed to do, yet embraced within the fullness of religious commitment. The contrast of the very underdeveloped with the intermediately developed and the almost modern is completed with Dr. Dennison Rusinow's analysis of Josephinism in Austria; that is, the close identification of state and established Church in traditional Austria as it is slowly being modified by the new social doctrine emanating from Rome. He takes us on a historical tour from the Church's support of monarchy to the corporativist stand characterizing it still in some Mediterranean countries to the new restiveness of ecumenism and progressive social involvement. But the scene is Europe, and not Africa or Latin America, and so the modifications within both Church and state, as the mutually but differently experienced mixes of the eternal and mundane work themselves out, are qualitatively different from the processes in the less developed examples.

The last block of cases concerns Islam. Professor Stuart Schaar starts his analysis in the 17th and 18th centuries, beginning with the historical emergence of modernism as do Neusner and Rusinow. His concern is not with ideological religious change, but rather with structural change as it affected religion, especially in terms of the role of intermediaries between elites and masses. By taking this view, Schaar brings to the fore what in the Catholic cases was a sub-theme: the relationship not alone between religious institution and state, but in addition interaction between centralized and local authority. The Catholic African cases are insufficiently articulated to make this problem significant enough to be included in a short study; and national integration has already proceeded so far in Austria as to make the case somewhat moot. But in Brazil and all the Islamic examples, central-local controversy comes to the fore as an important source of irritation, dislocation, and policy confusion. Dr. Willard Hanna provides a case study of a state in Malaysia which reveals in exquisite detail how religious and ethical differences affect economic and political development. If his case is at the other end of the Islamic world from Mr. Schaar's, it also reveals an opposite pattern in local-central authority relations. In Kelantan, Malaysia, it is the state government which lags in development and stubbornly defends a theocratic order. In Mr. Schaar's analysis of the Western regions of Islam, it is the *mullahs* who abandoned their function as intermediaries for the peasants. In turning to representatives of the central political authority for amelioration of their social problems, the peasants also made themselves mobilizable into integrated and quasi-national organization.

These subjects are then further elaborated in two other opposed cases—highly national Iran, and the predominantly village culture of Afghanistan. Mr. Charles F. Gallagher flatly counterposes nationalism and religion in Iran, a confrontation made possible because the country with which he is dealing "stands apart as a mature entity resting on the tripodal base of a long and distinguished history, a shared endurance through many evil eras, and the persistence of a prestigious cultural tradition with solid and ancient roots in the national soil. It is by any measure a nation . . ." Dr. Louis Dupree emphasizes the distance between the religion of the literate and the religion of the pre-literate. He carefully relates the village to the national level of politics, underscoring the role of religion as an artifact

9

employed by developers and their opponents alike. Indeed, his chapter title indicates that he has driven this central theme all the way: it is "The Political Uses of Religion." [9]

Here, then, are the common analytical directions and points of contact among all the articles. The theoretical commitments are more implicit, as has been said, but the conclusions will attempt to bring some of them to light. Certainly, however, all the authors in their papers and more so in discussion revealed some of that discomfort mentioned before, the unease caused whenever the relative and the absolute, the spiritual and the material are confronted simultaneously. Perhaps we should content ourselves with the admonition from one of the leading students of religion in its social manifestations:

> . . . if one really thinks about the core of religion . . . and . . . economic and political developments, that they may not be capable of complete harmonization, that there may be an intrinsic tension between the spiritual needs of man, which can never be completely done away with no matter how clever one is or how much one manipulates institutions or anything else. The real problem in any state or in any religious tradition is to decide first what is spiritually essential to it and what is not. And second, how to preserve the spiritual values the religion is directed toward, and how, on the other, to get economic and political development—how to keep these two different things in balance. . . . I think we might reflect more about this intrinsic dynamic tension, which must exist in human life and which is not necessarily to be deplored.[10]

The author of that statement invites us to a dynamic balance—which in itself is an invitation to libertarian modernism. The relativistic secularist will content himself with that formulation because he can see the possibility for human innovation and enrichment within it. The socially tolerant religious believer will also see therein the possibility for him and his co-religionists to worship in their own convictions. Indeed, the secularist and the believer may be the same person under those conditions. But the dogmatist on either side must necessarily reject such a construction. The confrontation between sacred and secular values may well most clearly reveal how necessary a pragmatic, experimental, relativist, plural approach is to modern social life—and how absolutely it must be held if faith is to support reason, and not drown it.

[9] Prof. Kenneth W. Morgan's study of contemporary Hinduism and Buddhism has been regretfully omitted from this volume because those cases present special theoretical problems which would have broken the continuity of the problem area here treated.
[10] Clifford Geertz, transcript of discussion in Robert N. Bellah (ed.), *Religion and Progress in Modern Asia*, New York: The Free Press, 1965, pp. 166-7.

I *Judaism*

Rarely have entirely new religious conceptions originated in the respective centers of rational cultures. . . . The reason for this is always the same: prerequisite to new religious conceptions is that man must not yet have unlearned how to face the course of the world with questions of his own. Precisely the man distant from the great culture centers has cause to do so when their influence begins to affect or threaten his central interests. Man living in the midst of the culturally satiated areas and enmeshed in their technique addresses such questions as little to the environment as, for instance, the child used to daily tramway rides would chance to question how the tramway actually manages to start moving.

Max Weber
Ancient Judaism

1.

FROM THEOLOGY TO IDEOLOGY: THE TRANSMUTATION OF JUDAISM IN MODERN TIMES

BY JACOB NEUSNER

Dartmouth College

INTRODUCTION: SHABBATAI ZVI AND THEODOR HERZL

When the Messiah comes, he will sound a great trumpet to call the scattered people of Israel out of the four corners of creation and bring them back to Mount Zion. In the past three hundred years, the Jews have looked hopefully toward two Messiahs, and the contrast between them provides a striking symbol of how classical Judaism has changed, while remaining constant, in the process of modernization. The first was Shabbetai Zvi who, with his apostle Nathan of Gaza, proclaimed a Messianic mission. Though in a crisis he renounced Judaism for Islam, his movement had already spread like wildfire throughout the entire Jewish world with the result that, in the words of G.G. Scholem, "An emotional upheaval of immense force took place among the face of the people, and for an entire year [1665–6] men lived a new life which for many years remained their first glimpse of a deeper spiritual reality." [1] The second was Theodor Herzl who in 1897 convened at Basel a world Zionist congress, there predicting that within fifty years a Jewish state

[1] G. G. Scholem, *Major Trends in Jewish Mysticism*, New York: Shocken, 1961, p. 288.

13

would become a reality, as indeed was the case. What is striking about these two movements is their universal impact within Jewry: both evoked a broad and international experience, and set the issues for discussion among Jews from the Vistula to the Atlantic. Sabbateanism was the last such international movement before Zionism, and since the fulfillment of Zionism, no similarly ecumenical call has reached Jewish ears. The contrast between the two is instructive. Sabbateanism phrased its message in strictly theological, Kabbalistic terms. Shabbatai Zvi was not merely "the Messiah," but rather played a central role in the metaphysical drama created by tensions within the Godhead itself. Zionism spoke in political and thoroughly worldly terms, identifying the Jewish problem with sociological, economic, and cultural matters. Herzl was never "the Messiah," though Zionism unhesitantly utilized the ancient Messianic scriptures and images of Jewish Messianism. The contrast is, therefore, between theological and ideological Messianism, and it is rendered significant by the fact that the spiritual experience, apart from the verbal explanations associated with it, in each case exhibits strikingly similar features: an emotional, millennarian upheaval, dividing friend from friend, leading some to despair and others to unworldly hope, and leading a great many to act in new ways.

What we understand by the process, or phenomenon, of modernization is here, therefore, illustrated, yet we must not be bound by the limitations of our illustration. The passage from theology to ideology marks one way only, among many leading in much the same direction. Similar contrasts of tradition and modernity may be drawn between sacred revelation and secular enlightenment; between revealed law guiding every action from Heaven, lending supernatural significance to workaday behavior, and simple rules of accepted conduct; between prophecy and research; between the life of the corporate community and that of the anomic town. One may likewise point to the internationalization of "culture," in which appeals to singular revelation carry less weight than the demands of reason, and in which parochialism, tribalism, and self-sustaining realms of discourse and meaning are set aside in favor of a single, universal language of thought and technology.

If, however, one accepts these qualities as significant aspects of modernization, then he must wonder just how *modern* the process truly is, for it seems, upon reflection, to be as old as the Greeks. To be specific, in the process of Hellenization of the Near East, which took place between the 5th and the 3rd centuries B.C., one may discern many of the traits we associate with modernization. For example, we commonly contrast the "modern" city with the "traditional" countryside, and only now are beginning to recognize how exaggerated is this contrast. Similarly, Morton Smith[2] speaks as follows: "The contrast commonly drawn between the Greek cities and the Semitic countryside has been exaggerated. The countryside was permeated by Greek elements and influences . . ." We refer to the internationalization of culture. Smith states, "Typically Greek artifacts and techniques were everywhere in use [in Palestine]. The country had a monetary economy, foreign trade was a major concern, the frame of thought had ceased to be the land of Palestine and become the civilized world, and Greek had become the normal language of business and politics." One need only substitute "English" for "Greek" to have an approximate description of any of the newly modern countries of Africa or Asia. We may, therefore, derive considerable insight from Smith's warning: "The forces which produced the changes called Hellenization were not universally or even primarily Greek . . . Hellenization cannot be described simply as adoption of Greek ways by peoples of the Near East and Oriental ways by Greeks. Instead we have a vast tissue of change in which innumerable strands of independent but parallel development are interwoven with a woof of influence and reaction to produce a single new culture, the Hellenistic, which is no less different from classical Greek culture than from the cultures of the more ancient Near East." These modulations, from the classical Greek to the Hellenistic ambiance, include change in classical land tenure patterns, from the small-holding form to the development of vast estates of king or temple; change from the small and homogeneous city-state to the absolute monarchy holding vast territories and governing various peoples; change from a way of life governed by local custom and tradition to the growth of explicit, written laws, derived not from revelation or tradition but from legislation and rational assessment of current needs; change from a religion in which the cult of the gods of the city was the center for petition and patriotism to the universal cult of a divine ruler without political affiliations; change from a situation in which private individuals mattered and politics was an important concern to one in which political units were so enormous that non-political arts and philosophy, centering upon the private affairs of radically isolated individuals, became the focus of the individual life; and, finally, change from civil administration by amateurs to the development of professional bureaucracies. The passage from theology to ideology may similarly find a parallel in that from cultic religion to metaphysical philosophy, which historians of Greek thought, including its Jewish variant, discern. One can hardly avoid the conclusion that there is nothing particularly "modern" about modernization. Nor does

[2] Morton Smith, *The Formation of Palestinian Judaism*, New York: Columbia University Press; in press for 1968.

Hellenization provide the only historical instance of a similar phenomenon, for the economic, social, and intellectual environment of 9th-century Baghdad exhibits similarly striking parallels, and doubtless others can locate additional examples.

Religion provides nonetheless a particularly useful focus for students of the process, for while in such other areas as politics and economics that which is "modern" may meaningfully be set apart against that which is "traditional," it is in religion that the complexities of the process of social change become most evident, the certainties less sure, the subtleties more inviting. Even the very definition of the problem to be studied poses difficulty. We facilely refer, for instance, to "the impact of cultural modernization upon traditional religion," as though religion is a given, "a compact entity inherited from the past in a particular form," and as though modernization is also a given, a process with a fixed direction.[3] So, according to the "impact theory," it is *modern* culture that acts upon *traditional* religion, just as economic and political patterns are "modernized." As Wilfred Cantwell Smith points out, the "impact theory" is altogether too "externalist," for it minimizes the "*interiorization* of modernity in the religious life of all communities," a process that takes place from within as much as from without. It underestimates the dynamism of the so-called tradition, ignoring its own evolution. Its usefulness as a metaphor is therefore limited. Morton Smith's description of "Hellenization," quoted above, provides a similar warning, that we speak of "the impact" of one thing upon another only at the risk of vast oversimplification. The dynamic is *within*, as well as *upon*, the tradition. W.C. Smith further asks, can we speak of "traditional religion *and* modern culture?" and finds difficulty in so doing. He points out that the supposed dichotomy between "religion" and "culture" emerges uniquely in the West, which "not only conceptualizes, but institutionalizes the two separately." "Traditional religion and modern culture" is not only a Western concept, but a Western *phenomenon*, Smith says, and, one may add, *if* Judaism is a Western religion, then the dichotomy fails even here. Smith raised, in his *Meaning and End of Religion*,[4] and again in the lecture quoted here, the broader issue: Is it meaningful to speak of "religion" at all in non-Western contexts? "Hinduism is a modern Western concept, which formulates in Western cultural terms what can more accurately . . . be characterized as Hindu culture," Smith says, and the same may be said of Judaism. "Judaism" poses two

[3] Wilfred Cantwell Smith, "Traditional Religions and Modern Culture," Address at the XIth Congress of the International Association for the History of Religions, Claremont, California, September 9, 1965. This entire analysis follows Smith's paper, and all quotations are drawn from it.
[4] New York: Mentor Books, 1963.

problems: the first is that Hebrew has no abstract word for "religion," the modern Hebrew equivalent, *Dat*, being a Persian loan-word originally signifying law; and second, that even the concept "Judaism" emerges only in contact with an alien civilization, forcing upon the formerly unselfconscious tradition a need to define itself over against something else. We first find the word not in Hebrew but in Greek, "Judaismos." These facts reinforce W.C. Smith's conclusion: "In non-Western societies, there is no such thing as religion, there is only culture." Many of the specifically Jewish identity problems we shall consider derive from that fact. What makes Judaism especially interesting, however, is its possibly unique combination of non-Western with Western traits.

We are led, therefore, to affirm W.C. Smith's chief emphasis, that the very concept of a "religious phenomenon" existing apart from culture is one of the very *significations* of "modernization." Hence, the isolation of something called "traditional religions" is similarly a byproduct of modernization. The very recognition of the category of tradition represents the first step toward the disintegration of that tradition, in al Ghazali's sense: "There is no hope in returning to a traditional faith after it has once been abandoned, since the essential condition in the holder of a traditional faith is that he should not know he is a traditionalist . . ." Smith seems to be offering a paraphrase: "The emergence of Hinduism and Islam as 'traditional religions' is itself a symptom of modern culture." So, too, he states, "Curiously, this modern-cultural phenomenon of something called 'traditional religions' turns out to be not only not traditional, but also not religious." By "religious," W.C. Smith refers to two qualities—first, timelessness, and second, a sense of daily presence: "If religion is anything at all, it is something that links the present moment to eternity." So long as religion is a "living reality," immediately present in the lives of the communicants, so long as the law is practiced, not merely obeyed, so long as society represents the corporate stage for living out the divinely ordained duty—so long is "the religious tradition" fully *traditional*.

The issue is, therefore, more adequately stated by W.C. Smith as follows: "To discern and to delineate what is happening to man's religiousness in the flux and turmoil of the modern world." A corollary, peculiarly modern issue, which will be of special concern here, is: What is happening to the "religiousness" of men who, in Smith's words, "either do not express their religiousness formally at all, or, if they do, express it in new untraditional ways?" The question is a broad one. Religious phenomena in the past expressed an inner orientation in the personal lives of men. If so, what is today happening to the qualities of life that those traditions used to represent and to foster?

What, in other words, is happening to man? It is this investigation that is here subsumed under the narrow and yet exemplary rubric of Judaism: What has happened to Jewish-men?

Two points come clear from the earlier illustrations. First, Jewish-men persisted in an extraordinary belief, rooted not in reality but in their own fantasies, that some day things would be better, that somehow problems would find solutions, that men were not fated to repeat their old mistakes forever and ever. They retained the faith that times would change for the better, and that faith called forth from them extraordinary changes in their normal patterns of behavior—in 1665–6, requiring them to sell all their possessions and await the great day and, in the years after 1897, demanding that they leave their homelands for a Mediterranean country previously known only in prayer, dream, and Scripture. So the very substance of the "tradition" continued unchanged, and the psychic realities embodied in it seem, in retrospect, to have endured amid all kinds of changes. On the other hand, Jewish-men so fundamentally changed that they could no longer talk about reality in the arcane metaphysics of the Kabbala, but had rather to adapt for their own use the—to our eyes—equally arcane and Kabbalistic language of democratic socialism and 19th-century romantic nationalism. Shabbatai Zvi and Theodor Herzl could not be more different, and yet, had they met, their followers may have seen in the sparkle of one another's eyes, in the willingness to act, in the hopeful, even frenzied optimism, something not wholly unfamiliar.

From such a perspective, one may readily perceive the unreality of the "impact theory" and of formulating the issue in terms of "modernization *and* religion." What one wants to know is not how matters *progressed* to their present state, but rather what changed, and what remained the same? What is constant in man's experience, and what has been altered in the passage of time, in the movement of men from one place to another, and in the alteration of inherited patterns of economic, social, and political behavior? And of greatest interest in the Jewish paradigm: how has the inherited tradition shaped, as much as it has been shaped by, the processes of change we call, for convenience's sake, modernization?

FOUR CASES OF MODULATION OF TRADITIONAL STRUCTURES: THEOLOGY, MESSIANISM, SOCIAL ETHICS, AND SCHOLARSHIP

We turn, then, to examine four significant themes within the Jewish tradition. In each case we shall ask how the tradition has changed, and how it has preserved continuities with the past. In no instance shall we be able to locate simple or obvious examples of "modernization." In each we shall see that much has changed, much has remained the same, but nothing standing by itself is an adequate instance of "pure, one-way modernization." The four structures are not easily compared one to another. The first, theology, comprehends the ways in which thoughtful Jews have explained to themselves the central propositions of Judaism as a religious tradition. The modern consequences, in reform and orthodoxy, were superficially intellectual, and are here treated as mostly so; yet the social results of changes of mind are at least as significant. Different theological affirmations produced different social, economic, and cultural ideals, and hence, styles of life. These consequences are at best merely hinted at. The second theme, Messianism, produced the Zionist movement which was a chief formative factor, though obviously by no means the only or most important one, in creating the State of Israel. So the direct consequence of the new Messianism lay in political rather than in religious or cultural life. Yet here, too, we shall see important theological and cultural results. The third, social ethics, produced the most "secular" of all movements in modern Judaism, Jewish Socialism in Eastern Europe and the United States, but that most secular movement seems to me to have preserved the most profoundly religious themes of Jewish tradition, and hence to reveal the most ambiguous result. The fourth theme, scholarship, is peculiarly Jewish, for the traditional impulse, which so dominated Jewish life, was to study the Torah. The highest virtues were those of the master of the Torah, and no value more deeply informed Jewish culture. Yet, as we shall see, traditional learning and modern scholarship are by no means congruent with one another. These four facets of the Jewish tradition reveal changes in religious, political and historical, social, and intellectual ways of "being Jewish." In the past century and a half the Jews have endured a lingering crisis of identity, for they have not agreed since the 18th century upon the most basic propositions of self-definition. Some Jews have found it possible to exhaust the meaning of "Jewishness" in religion, narrowly construed as the Protestant West defined it; some in nationalism, equally narrowly defined in terms of sovereignty, state, and flag; some in socialism, the new homeland for an international folk; and some in scholarship, understood in the university way as the detached and open-minded, non-protagonistic study of a past long dead and gone. These are not the only options, for as is well known, vast numbers of Jews have found a satisfying expression of "their" Judaism through philanthropic, non-sectarian enterprises; others through clinging close to an ethnic group, in ghettos of the assimilated in all but name; and still others in intense participation, largely with other Jews for company, in the most advanced cultural enterprises of the day. And of course, one cannot ignore the fact that for many Jews, modernization signified the end of "Jewishness" altogether. The cases we shall survey do, I think, reveal striking ambiguities and engaging complexities. That is why I have chosen them.

In *Tradition and Crisis*,[5] Professor Jacob Katz provides a comprehensive account of "traditional Judaism" on the threshold of modernization. Defining "traditional society" as "a type of society which regards its existence as based upon a common body of knowledge and values handed down from the past" (p. 3), Katz stresses the commonalities of religion, nationhood, and Messianic hope, and the disintegrative effect upon them of religious charisma in Hasidism, and of rationalism in the Jewish Englightenment. To the end of the 18th century, when the "modern period" of Jewish history begins, Jewish society was corporate, segregated, and collective in emphasis. Jews in Europe—with whom we are here chiefly concerned—spoke a common language, Yiddish, and regarded themselves, as they were seen, as a separate nation living within other nations, but awaiting, as we have noted, their ultimate return to their own land. The central social ideal was study of Torah, which would result in heavenly reward. The obligation to study the Torah, leading to an intense appreciation for intellectualism, prevented the "sanctification" of economic activity as an ultimate goal, and insured effective control over the people's value structure for the tradition, study of which was the chief purpose of living. The community itself was governed by its own classical legal tradition, with the rabbi as judge and community official. The *kehillah*, or structure of community government, controlled economic activities, relations with non-Jews, family and social life, and matters of religion, including of course all aspects of culture, and education. It was the structural embodiment of the corporate community. How did this community disintegrate, so that the focus of Judaism came to center upon the individual, and the emphasis of Jewish thought to locate upon the individual's personal religious needs and convictions? *It was not the result of external catastrophes.* Jewish society was badly shaken by the massacres of 1648–9, but the response of the community, as Katz points out, did not deviate from the traditional pattern. "There is no record of any program of action being instituted to prevent the recurrence of such an event . . . no political or social conclusions were drawn from the historical experience. As a matter of fact, the realistic explanations were overshadowed by the traditional view of

[5] New York: The Free Press, 1961.

divine providence, so that the lesson that emerged from the stock-taking was a religious-moral one." [6] It took the form of fasting, prayer, severe sumptuary laws, and rededication to study and observance of the Torah. Katz stresses that it was Hasidism in Eastern Europe, and Haskalah, or the Enlightenment in the West, which undermined traditional society. These movements shattered the framework of the community, which had formerly been able to reconstitute itself following banishments and migrations, in the several localities.

Hasidism, a pietist movement recalling the contemporary Methodism of Britain and the Great Awakening of mid-18th-century New England, weakened the fidelity of the people to the rabbinic-lawyer's leadership by stressing the importance *not* of learning in the law, but of religious charisma, the capacity to say particularly effective prayers, tell evocative stories, and engage in acts of theurgic character. Katz states, "The historical and social conditions . . . must be regarded as anomic, abounding in lost souls whose attachment to existing institutions was insufficient to bind them to the common activity sponsored by those institutions. In such circumstances, the situation was ripe for the creation of new social alignments between individuals whose attachment to the old institutions had been weakened." [7] But, Katz emphasizes, it was not social conditions which gave rise to Hasidism, but rather Hasidism, in its content, values, structure, and history, which "represented such an innovation that all that went before did no more than pave the way." [8] A movement within the community, Hasidism created sects which split the traditional corporate society into two parts, those who followed the charismatic leader, and those who did not. This is not the place to summarize the doctrines and policies which led to the destruction of the earlier social structure, but it suffices to note the consequence of these doctrines and policies, which was a religious and social revolution based upon a new requirement for leadership, not learning but charisma, and resulting in the formation, within the body of the old community, of new and limited sects, or societies, and in consequence, the destruction of the traditional *kehillah*.

The second force for "modernization" of traditional society was the Enlightenment which, working in France and Germany, altogether revolutionized the basis of Jewish society by destroying its legal and philosophical foundation. External rather than internal in its impact, the Enlightenment withdrew the political basis of Jewry by extending

---

[6] *Tradition and Crisis*, pp. 214-15.
[7] *Ibid.*, p. 229.
[8] *Ibid.*, p. 230.

to Jews the rights of citizens, and at the same time denying Judaism the authority over Jews it had formerly exercised. It furthermore encouraged the development within Jewry of a new type of person, the *maskil*, or illumined man, who mastered areas of human erudition formerly thought to be irrelevant to Jews. So the Enlightenment's processes of dissolution reinforced one another. The *kehillah* lost its legal standing, and some of its subjects opted out of it at the same time. The turning point, Katz says, was "when individual members of Jewish society transferred their social goals to the context of the surrounding non-Jewish milieu." [9] Had Jews merely converted to Christianity, it would hardly have affected the traditional society. What is of special consequence is that many left that society but chose to remain Jews, and hence plunged into a crisis of identity which has yet to find resolution. As part of the Jewish community—though perhaps on its fringes—the *maskilim* held up to the tests of reason, intelligence, and nature the artifacts of the tradition which had formerly been accepted as part of the given, or the revealed reality, of the world. And they did so aggressively and derisively. The values they projected were those of the neutral society, which they saw as the "wave of the future." They criticized the economic structure of Jewish society, its occupational one-sidedness, the traditional organizations, whose compulsory authority they rejected, and the traditional system of education, which did nothing to prepare young people to participate in the new world then seen to be opening up. They did not, as I said, propose to abandon society, but to modernize it. Values formerly held to be ends in themselves now came to be evaluated in terms of their usefulness and rationality, a usefulness measured not within the Jewish framework at all. The synagogue came to be seen as the assembly of the faithful for prayer, rather than as the focus for administration, society, and culture, as in former times; and the content and language of prayer, the architecture of the synagogue and its ritual—all these were among the earliest objects of a reformation. Most significantly, the traditional modes of social control—denunciation, excommunication—ceased to operate effectively. The "deviant" was no longer a sinner, but an opponent who, as Katz says, "felt that his deeds were justified by his own system of values." [10]

Katz's account helps us to understand the specifics of "modernization" within the Jewish setting, though we should err if we think he describes a broad phenomenon. The striking fact is that "modernization" as we have here considered it mattered in only a very few places, and even there unevenly, to almost the present time. Though the

[9] *Ibid.*, p. 251.
[10] *Ibid.*, p. 258.

kehillah in its late medieval form underwent vast changes, the traditional personality and pattern of living of Jews in many places did not, or did not change in quite the ways Katz describes. The Enlightenment's impact, even in Germany, was limited to the upper classes until well into the 19th century. Hasidism was mostly a regional phenomenon, and after two generations, its fervor was directed into more or less traditional channels, so that today, while remaining highly sectarian, it has become a bastion of "the tradition" in its least malleable forms. More broadly still, the Jews in Muslim countries, apart from the Gallicized urban upper classes, remained deeply a part of the traditional culture, not so much affirming intellectual reasons for remaining so as practicing the faith in its classical forms, into the 20th century. For many, arriving in the state of Israel also signifies arrival into the 20th century as we know it. The political changes we associate under the title Emancipation never reached Polish, Rumanian, and Russian Jewry before the Holocaust of 1933 to 1945. Furthermore, for many Jews in Western countries the experience of "modernization" was objectionable, and as we shall see many rejected it. If a "tradition" changes, it is only for some; it never disintegrates for all. Katz provides us with a useful ideal type, rather than with a comprehensive description, which he never claims to offer, of the passing of traditional Jewish society.

Indeed, it would be impossible to offer a fully adequate delimitation of the "modernization" of Judaism for three reasons. First of all, as I have said, substantial parts of the Jewish people never underwent such a process, these being not only the Jews in Muslim countries, but also very large segments of Eastern European Jewry, extending as far westward as Hungary. Second, even in the great cities, to which the majority of central and Western European Jews had come by 1900, significant populations of traditionalists existed to the time of the Holocaust, and, in the Western countries, to the present day. Whether *they* are traditional in the way in which the 17th-century Jew was traditional is not the issue. The fact is that those qualities we have associated with traditionalism apply without qualification to parts of Jewry, and therefore to significant segments of Judaism in the State of Israel, the United States, Great Britain, continental Europe, and elsewhere. Third, as W.C. Smith makes clear, the inner dynamism of a living tradition is such that at no point may we arbitrarily arrest its development for purposes of definition, and conclude that a given form is "*the* tradition" from which all that changes thereby deviates and therefore constitutes modernization. Within the circles of the most traditional Jews, cultural phenomena are today accepted that a century ago would have been regarded as unacceptable, and yet, as I have implied above, should we call such Jews "modernists" the term would be deprived of any denotative meaning whatever.

Within these almost paralyzing limitations, I shall consider in a fragmentary way four kinds of modernization within Judaism: theological, Messianic, ethical, and scholarly. In each instance I shall try merely to provide some of the factual data and a few observations to make possible a broader consideration of the issues at hand.

THEOLOGICAL MODERNIZATION. The history of modern Jewish thought ought, rightly, to be offered under this rubric for, from the 19th century forward, the efforts of Jewish theologians (I use the term in the Protestant sense) have been devoted almost exclusively to formulating a "modern" statement of the faith, the enterprise itself being the most striking exemplification of modernization. The chief issue faced by these thinkers has been: having abandoned what I conceive to be "the traditional faith," do I thereby cease to be a Jew? It is a very slight step from such a question to a sociological, rather than a theological, reply, and many have not hesitated to take it: your "Jewish identity" remains valid, for the following reasons. One may supply whatever reasons he chooses. It is not my task to report or to evaluate them. I can conceive of no more striking transformation of theological into ideological language than the very question with which discourse begins. The issue of "identity" is, after all, sociological, and not theological either in intent or in reality, nor are the concomitant ones: survival, consensus, commitment. The very issues of Judaism have, therefore, taken on a secular character in the hands of theologians. Even distinguished protagonists of Jewish orthodoxy could anachronistically say, in the words of Rabbi Walter S. Wurzburger, "It was out of a sense of *personal religious commitment* that individual Jews remained within the fold" [11] [italics supplied] in past generations, thus focusing discussion upon the private person rather than upon the corporate community, where the emphasis ought to be for historical discussion, as we have seen. The two most interesting cases of theological modernization are, most obviously, reform Judaism, and least obviously, orthodoxy. It is upon these that we shall concentrate, though numerous individual thinkers would well have supplied interesting paradigms.

Reform Judaism, as its name implies, began as an effort to create a reformation of Jewish tradition. The Jewish reformation proceeded on two levels, that of the virtuosi and that of the masses. Large numbers of Jews in the great cities of Germany and, later on, in France, Britain,

[11] Rabbi Walter S. Wurzburger, "Meaning and Significance of Jewish Survival," *Journal of Jewish Communal Service*, Vol. XL, No. 3, 1964, p. 307 ff.

and the United States responded to the new situation by acculturation, thereby meeting the requirements of the world to which they were invited. Accepted as citizens, they abandoned any pretense of separate nationality. Granted full economic equality, they shaped their own economic ideals to conform to those of the city. They were desperately eager to deserve the promises of cultural emancipation, and so, like the *maskilim* a generation or two earlier, they examined their cult to discover those elements that were alien to the now interested world, and determined to do away with them. These were not Jews who would choose the road of assimilation through conversion, perfunctory or otherwise, but who chose to remain Jews and to retain Judaism. One might say, they wanted to be Jews but not too much, not so much that they could not be men, achieving a place in the "undifferentiated society." This they wanted so badly that they saw and eagerly seized upon a welcome that few gentiles, if any, really proffered. The religious virtuosi, those who had a better education, a richer family experience, a deeper involvement in the tradition to begin with, had the task of mediating between "the tradition" and the changes they saw about them and enthusiastically approved. For them, change became *reform*, and the direction of the people became providential. As Solomon Freehof wrote [12]: ". . . it was the Reformers who hailed the process and believed in it." [13] They founded their reformation upon the concept that "essential Judaism" in its pure form required none of the measures that separated the Jew from other enlightened men, but consisted rather of beliefs and ethics—beliefs which were rational and destined in time to convince all mankind, and ethics which were universal and far in advance of any available from other sources. Again Freehof: "Reform Judaism is the first flaming up of direct world-idealism in Judaism since the days of Second Isaiah."

Isolating the prophets as the true exponents of Judaism, and within the frenzied messages of the prophets those texts which served as useful pretexts for the liberalism of the age, the reformers looked back upon the "golden age" of that time when Judaism spoke to all mankind of the obligations of justice and mercy. It was that message which they saw to be essential, and all else was expendable. So the social ideals of the masses, who yearned for a liberal society in which even Jews would find acceptance, and those of essential Judaism, were identical. The necessary changes would indeed constitute a reformation, and a return *to that time* of the true and unadorned faith. But more than this, the reformers turned not only back to a golden age, but also forward

---

[12] Solomon Freehof in his preface to W. Gunther Plaut, *The Rise of Reform Judaism*, New York: World Union for Progressive Judaism, 1963, p. viii.
[13] *Ibid.*

to a golden age in the future, to that time when bigotry and injustice would cease. They exhibited an idealism and an almost other-wordly confidence in mankind that suggest a radical disjuncture between their fantasies, on the one hand, and reality on the other. The Jews were Europe's Negroes, and Germany was their Mississippi. They were excluded from the universities, ridiculed in the pulpits, libeled in the newspapers, shamed in private life, and yet they saw men as God's partners in the rebuilding of creation. They had the effrontery even to see themselves as bearers of a mission to mankind: God's Kingdom would be realized only through Judaism, that most rational and ethical of all religions. The Jews had, they believed, an inherited, innate ability to give the world an ethical consciousness. In the symphony of the nations—so common a metaphor in these decades—they would play the ethical melody.

Orthodoxy is a creation of the reformation, as much as the spirit of Trent three centuries earlier was born in Wittenburg. Chronologically, orthodoxy comes to self-conscious formation within a half-century after the reform movement took shape, not only in Germany, but, three-quarters of a century later, in the United States. It, too, accepted the premises of the reformation, that the Jews were going not only to live *among* gentiles, but *with* them, and that therefore they had better learn the languages and adopt the culture, in its broadest form, of the West. Underlying this presupposition is a vast reformation in "traditional" attitudes. Before the Jews could conceive themselves in such a new situation, they had to accept it as a good thing, and affirm it as the will of Heaven, in a way in which they never accepted or affirmed the high cultures of medieval and ancient times. "Modernization" long antedated both the modernist movement *and its opposition.* But the opposition was at a deep disadvantage, for it had to debate the issues already set by the reformation, and take a negative view where, in a more congenial situation, it would have found the grounds for affirming change.

Favoring the orthodox party were three factors. First, the natural conservatism of religious men who, within Judaism, followed not only the path of the fathers, but the ways of the *father (paterfamilias)* himself. These ways were, in many instances in this generation, traditional ones, and lent powerful psychic support to the orthodox viewpoint. Second, when all was said and done, the reformers had to argue that they were of the true Judaism, while the orthodox were deviants from its spirit, an argument that was weakened by incontrovertible facts. These facts were first, that the orthodox were surely more like the preceding generations than they, and, second, that the virtuosi's rigor was in behalf of a diminishing lay concern for authenticity. That is to say, whatever the virtuosi's intent, for the lay follower the reform movement was a vehicle of his own convenience, used by the passenger to reach a point quite outside the intention of the driver. The third factor favoring orthodoxy was that, as the orthodox claim to constitute the one legitimate form of Judaism and to measure by itself the "authenticity" of all "deviant" forms developed, orthodoxy came to offer a security and a certainty unavailable elsewhere. Its concept of a direct relationship between the individual's conformity to the tradition and the will of the Creator of the Universe bore a powerful attraction for those seeking a safe way in the world, and less concerned with the golden age to come, though they still hoped for it.

Just as not all Europeans were liberals, but preferred another way, so too not all Jews, probably not even most Jews in some places, responded to the liberal message of the reformation. And many who did were in time won back to the "tradition"—in its central European, "cultured" form to be sure—when orthodoxy addressed itself to them in good German, rather than in good Yiddish, for what some wanted was merely that: to dress like gentiles and speak like them, but to live, nonetheless, by patterns believed to be revealed at Sinai. The achievement of the orthodox thinkers was to offer reassurance that certain parts of life were truly neutral. But in so saying, they accomplished the grandest reformation of all.

Of greatest interest here is Samson Raphael Hirsch (1808–88), the chief spokesman for orthodoxy. He was raised in Germany, and his knowledge of the traditional sciences was acquired mainly through his own efforts. The chief influence on his thought about contemporary Judaism was Jacob Ettlinger, who stated, "Let not him who is engaged in the war of the Lord against the heretics be held back by the false argument that great is peace and that it is better to maintain the unity of all designated as Jews than to bring about disruption." Such an affirmation of the sectarian option represents a strange attitude indeed among those who would lay claim to "sole legitimacy." Hirsch, by contrast, in his *Nineteen Letters*,[14] issued no threats of excommunication, but stressed the affirmative requirement, to study the Torah, with the rationalistic, perhaps ironic, certainty that knowledge would yield assent, an optimism different in form but not in substance from that of the reformers. When he settled in Frankfurt, he found a community dominated by the reformation. At his death, he left in it a bastion of orthodoxy, originally established in separation from the "community" —that is, from the government-recognized *Gemeinde*, which was reform. Hirsch accomplished this change chiefly by founding a school. He designed the curriculum so that the next generation would con-

[14] New York: P. Feldheim, 1960.

27

form to the ideal by which he lived: "Torah and *Derekh Eretz*," that is, traditional science combined with general secular enlightenment. Judaism, he held, "encompasses all of life, in the synagogue and in the kitchen . . . To be a Jew—in a life which in its totality is borne on the word of the Lord and is perfected in harmony with the will of God—this is the scope and goal of Judaism . . . In so far as a Jew is a Jew, his views and objectives become universal. He will not be a stranger to anything which is good, true, and beautiful in art and in science, in civilization and in learning . . . He will hold firmly to this breadth of view in order to fulfill his mission as a Jew and to live up to the function of his Judaism in areas never imagined by his father . . . " Hirsch therefore proposed a model of "the Jewish man" who fears God, keeps the commandments, and looks at the "wonders of the Lord in nature and the mighty deeds of the Lord in history." He added, however, that "Jewish-man" brings about not only the redemption of Israel, but also the redemption of all mankind. No less than the reformers', Hirsch's reformation spoke of a "mission of Israel," and aimed at the "redemption of mankind," both the hallmarks of the liberal, enlightened German of the day.

Both reform and orthodox Judaism represent, therefore, modes of response to modernization. For both, the constants were Scriptures, concern for a religious dimension of existence, concentration upon the historical traditional sciences, though in different ways, and concern for the community of Jews. These persisted, but in new forms. Hirsch's "Torah and *Derekh Eretz*," no less than the "science of Judaism" produced within the reform movement, constituted radical new approaches to the study of the Torah; the rhetoric of Israel's mission, now focusing in both movements upon the private person, revealed the new social datum of Jewish living, and concealed, in both cases, the utter decay of the traditional social forms. For both, concentration upon the community and its structures, policies, and future involved considerable use of sociological language, and for neither were the traditional categories of covenant and sacred community any longer characteristic of a broad and catholic concern for all Jews in a given place. Both addressed themselves, because the times required it, to German- or French- or English-speaking Jews, though Hirsch quite openly said that it was a matter of necessity in the 19th century, as it was not in the 2nd, for Judaism to learn humane and natural sciences. Neither could conceive of a parochial and self-sustaining language of Jewish discourse. Both spoke of a "mission of Israel" to the world, and conceived of redemption in terms at least relevant to the gentile. This is not to suggest that the tradition in its earlier formulations was here misrepresented, as we shall see below, but one needs to keep in mind how very different both orthodox and reform Judaism were from contemporary, pre-modern Judaism in the east, in North Africa, and elsewhere.

W.C. Smith's contention that one cannot fruitfully speak of "the impact of cultural modernization upon traditional religion" requires reassessment at this point. If one is able to regard "traditional Judaism" as a fixed and completed structure, then the changes we have touched upon do indeed represent the "impact" of a new political, social, and cultural situation upon a stable "tradition." Our review of Katz's description of the disintegration of traditional society suggests otherwise. The processes he traces had, by the middle of the 18th century, completed the destruction of an earlier social religious phenomenon. Those we have considered here came to fruition only after the turn of the 19th century, and in some instances, considerably afterwards. Both the religious virtuosi and their audience were already prepared for a new formulation of the tradition long before reform and orthodoxy made their appearance. Indeed, in significant ways, both represent a very considerable lag. The very rigidity of orthodoxy, moreover, is peculiarly modern, and was called forth by changes in the quality of Jews' way of living. One can hardly locate, in earlier times, an equivalent rejection of contemporary learning (in this respect, Hirsch must be seen to be far more historical than those to his "right" who rejected all forms of Western science). One can find only few pre-modern examples of such paralysis in the face of need to update legal doctrines. Quite obviously, it was a fearful inability to cope with change which produced the claim that change was, for the most part, undesirable and even impossible. Change was not only not reform, it was the work of the devil. Similarly, the sectarianism of both reform and orthodox groups, their abandonment of the ambition to struggle with all Jews for the achievement of universal Jewish goals, constitutes a failure of nerve in the face of the diversities and inconstancies of the modern situation. Modernization called forth many changes indeed, but these were produced by a tradition very much in flux, and by men who had come a long way toward the modern situation before the challenges of modernization in political, cultural, and religious matters had to be faced. Nor, as Smith emphasizes, is it a consistent matter, for modernization ought to have produced one response only, and that is the reform one, while in Germany the responses were in significant measure a reaffirmation of what men conceived to be the tradition. Modern culture acted upon traditional religion, but the contrary proved also to be the case: the modern Jew was surely as much shaped by his inherited culture as that culture was shaped by modernization, and that modern Jew had a significant impact indeed upon the formation of what subsequent generations understood to be modernity. This becomes self-evident when we consider the modernization of Messianism.

MESSIANISM. Unlike the Bombay Parsees, the Jews sustained a hope of return to the homeland, and the very heart of their Messianic belief was shaped by that hope. Some Jews always remained in the land, but all Jews, until the 19th century, expected to witness the resurrection of the dead there. Jewish Messianism was, as Joseph L. Blau emphasizes,[15] invariably supposed to be a political phenomenon by contrast to the restorationism of non-Jews, in which Zion was in heaven, not on earth. William Blake's "Jerusalem" could be built in England. The Zion of Jewish piety could only be the earthly, specific place. For this reason the early reformers found traditional Messianism an embarrassment. When Napoleon asked the French Sanhedrin of 1807, "Do those Jews who are born in France . . . regard France as their native country," the answer of the rabbis could only have been in the affirmative, and that answer could not possibly constitute a true one, except in the reformation. Ludwig Philippson wrote, "Formerly the Jews had striven to create a nation . . . but now their goal was to join other nations . . . It was the task of the new age to form a general human society which would encompass all peoples organically. In the same way, it was the task of the Jews not to create their own nation . . . but rather to obtain from the other nations full acceptance into their society."[16] Similarly the West London Synagogue of British Jews heard from its first rabbi in 1845, "To this land [England] we attach ourselves with a patriotism as glowing, with a devotion as fervent, and with a love as ardent and sincere as any class of our British non-Jewish fellow citizens." One could duplicate that statement, and with it, its excessive protest, many times. So the reformation emphasized that Judaism can eliminate the residue of its nationalistic phase that survives in traditional doctrine and liturgy. The reformers saw Messianism not as a Zionist doctrine, but as a call to the golden age in which a union of nations into one peaceful realm to serve their one true God would take place. The happy optimism which underlay these hopes and affirmations survived among some even after Auschwitz, but for the assimilated Western Jews of Paris, Vienna, and London the rise of virulent scientific and political anti-Semitism during the last third of the 19th century raised significant doubts. Nor did the political situation of Eastern European Jewry, characterized by pogroms, repres-

[15] Joseph L. Blau, *Modern Varieties of Judaism,* New York: Columbia Univ. Press, 1966, p. 121.
[16] Quoted by Blau, *op. cit.,* p. 124.

sion, and outright murder, provide reassurance that mankind was progressing very quickly toward that golden day.

Modern Zionism represented a peculiar marriage of Western romantic nationalism and Eastern Jewish piety. The virtuosi of the movement were mostly Western, but the masses were in the East. Fustel de Coulanges' saying, "True patriotism is not love of the soil, but love of the past, reverence for the generations which have preceded us," [17] at once excluded Jews, who were newcomers to French culture and could hardly share love for a French past that included banishment of their ancestors, and invited some of them to rediscover their own patriotism. The Jews could not share the "collective being," could not be absorbed into a nation whose national past they did not share. The Dreyfus trial forced upon the Viennese reporter, Theodor Herzl, a clear apprehension that the "Jewish problem" could be solved only by complete assimilation or complete evacuation. (It occurred to no one in the West that extermination was an option, though the Russians thought of it.) In 1896, Herzl published *Der Judenstaat,* from whose appearance we conventionally date the foundation of modern Zionism. One can hardly overemphasize the secularity of Herzl's vision. He did not appeal to religious sentiments, but to modern secular nationalism. His view of anti-Semitism ignores the religious dimension altogether, but stresses economic and social causes. Modern anti-Semitism grows out of the emancipation of the Jews and their entry into competition with the middle classes. Nor could the Jews cease to exist, for affliction establishes their cohesiveness. Herzl's plan was wholly practical—to choose a country, perhaps Argentina, or Uganda, or Palestine, and to colonize it. Herzl espoused Uganda, which was made available by the British government a few years later. But what was important was a plan, the poor to go first and build the infrastructure of an economy, the middle classes later to create trade, markets, and new opportunity. The first Zionist Congress was not a gathering of Messianists, but of sober men. Herzl's statement, "At Basel I founded the Jewish state," was not, however, a sober statement, nor was his following one, "The State is already founded in essence, in the will of the people of the State." All the rest were mere practicalities. Herzl's disciple, Nordau, held that Zionism resulted from nationalism and anti-Semitism. Had Zionism led to Uganda, one could have believed it.

But when Herzl proposed Uganda, he was defeated. The masses in the East had been heard from. To them, Zionism could mean only Zion, and Jerusalem was in one place alone. It is hard to convey the excitement Herzl himself created when he visited the East, the

[17] Cited by Blau, *op. cit.,* p. 140.

emotional outpouring accompanying the movement and its slogans. As I said, the classical language, much of which was already associated with Zion in the Messianic era, was taken over by the Zionist movement, and evoked a much more than political response in peoples' hearts. Zionism swept the field, and in the 20th century even the reform movement affirmed it and contributed some of its major leaders. Small groups within reform and orthodoxy alone resisted, the latter because they saw Zionism as an act of hubris, contravening the hope in supernatural Messianism. Calling a land-colonization fund, known in English as the Jewish National Fund, by the Hebrew words, *Keren Kayemet Le-Yisrael*, that is, the *Eternal Fund of Israel*, was a deliberate effort to evoke the Talmudic "Keren Kayemet le-Olam HaBa," *Eternal Fund for the World to Come*, which consisted of acts of merit, piety, or charity, destined to produce a heavenly reward. To the doggedly religious ear such a title was nothing less than blasphemy, for it made use of sacred language in a secular sense. But that, it seems to me, was the very ambiguity of Zionism, a strange marriage between Western assimilated leaders, on the one hand, and Eastern traditionalists on the other. The history of Zionism has not here been adumbrated, let alone exhausted, but for our purposes, its peculiarity had become clear. As Arthur Hertzberg stated, "Zionism cannot be typed, and therefore easily explained, as a 'normal' kind of national risorgimento . . . From the Jewish perspective, messianism, and not nationalism, is the primary element in Zionism . . . Writers too numerous to mention here have characterized the modern movement as 'secular messianism,' to indicate at once what is classical in Zionism —its eschatological purpose; and what is modern—the necessarily contemporary tools of political effort . . . " Hertzberg rejects this characterization as too simple. Rather he sees as the crucial problem of Zionist ideology "the tension between the inherited messianic concept and the radically new meaning that Zionism, at its most modern, was proposing to give it." [18] Hertzberg's analysis is very searching, but I believe it is precisely this tension which is meant by those who have, as we have, seen Zionism as a modernized, if not wholly secularized, Messianism. But Hertzberg greatly deepens the discussion when he says that the crisis is "not solely in the means but in the essential meaning of Jewish messianism . . . it is the most radical attempt in Jewish history to break out of the parochial molds of Jewish life in order to become part of the general history of man in the modern world. Hence we are face to face with a paradoxical truth: for the general historian, Zionism is not easy to deal with because it is too

[18] Arthur Hertzberg, *The Zionist Idea*, New York: Doubleday, 1959, p. 14 f.

'Jewish'; the Jewish historian finds it hard to define because it is too general."

SOCIAL ETHICS.   Among the most influential ideologies in late 19th- and 20th-century Judaism in Eastern Europe and the United States— and in the Zionist movement in both places—was Jewish Socialism. If reform and orthodoxy are heirs to the traditional theology, and Zionism to the traditional eschatology, then one must see in Jewish Socialism a deeply secular movement by conviction and orientation, the heir of the ethical and moral idealism which had, in traditional society, found expression in the vast legal enterprise at the heart of Jewish existence. No less than Zionism, we find in Jewish Socialism the many ambiguities and eccentricities of a modernized tradition, the psychic and emotional continuities and the formal differences. Zionism chose to restore the Hebrew language, Jewish Socialism to explore Yiddish. Zionism turned to the ancient land; Jewish Socialism saw all lands as equally sacred in the struggle for humanity. Zionism's impact proved significant mainly in the Middle East. Jewish Socialism has left behind the vast American Jewish community, a product far more directly the heir of Jewish Socialism than of any other single force in modern Judaism.

The liberalism and socialist sympathies of American Jewry in former days, which produced a Meyer London and a Samuel Gompers, have become less stylish today, when for various reasons religion in a rather narrow sense had come to constitute the vehicle for Jewish separatism. It is no accident, however, that the New Deal is partially a product of New York's Democracy, or that the Jews, even in this age of their affluence, still constitute the highest economic bracket in the voting population overwhelmingly to support the measures of "socialist" Democratic administrations since Roosevelt. American Jewry looks back upon the putative orthodoxy of its grandfathers, but the life of the ghettos, which the current generation would like either to idealize or to forget, was not orthodox, but Socialist. Charles S. Liebman makes this quite clear.[19] The immigrants, he says, did not give their children a classical religious education. In 1908, only 28 per cent of the Jewish children in New York City received any Jewish education at all. "The immigrants flocked instead to the public schools, to night classes, and to adult-education courses, not only for vocational purposes but for general cultural advancement . . . " It was only in the 1920s, after the wave of emigration from Eastern Europe spent

[19] Charles S. Liebman, "Orthodoxy in American Jewish Life," *American Jewish Yearbook 66*, Philadelphia: Jewish Publication Society, 1965, p. 27 ff.

itself, that traditional Judaism revived in Eastern Europe. Those who migrated before then were the least traditional, whose piety Liebman calls situational or environmental, rather than personal and theological, or traditional. They came to a country which, they had been told, was simply not *kosher:* yet they came, and one can hardly turn back now and praise their piety. Renowned rabbis warned them against emigration. If they were not orthodox, nor, quite evidently, reform, then what were they? The obvious answer is that they were, in their masses, residually pious, but actively Socialist. The synagogue meant less, even to those who attended it, than did the union hall, the Socialist party centers, the cultural clubs. For many, Socialism replaced Judaism, and the radicals, seeing in "religion" the opiate of the masses, and in its exponents agents of reaction, could not but conceive of themselves as more truly heirs of prophecy and ethical rabbinism than others who made more vociferous claim to the legacy. What is it, then, that they affirmed, and how shall we assess it by "the tradition?" A poem by J.L. Kantor provides a testament to the radicals' faith:

We believe

—that misdeeds, injustice, falsehood, and murder will not reign forever, and a bright day will come when the sun will appear . . .

—men will not die of hunger and wealth not created by its own labor will disappear like smoke

—people will be enlightened and will not differentiate between man and man; will no longer say, 'Christian, Moslem, Jew,' but will call each other 'Brother, friend, comrade'

—the secrets of nature will be revealed and people will dominate nature instead of nature dominating them

—man will no longer work with the sweat of his brow; the forces of nature will serve him as hands.[20]

Many of them marginal figures, the radicals harbored sentiments which bore so strong an affinity to the eschatological visions of Isaiah and others of the prophets that one hardly knows how to interpret them. Quite obviously, they did not set out to paraphrase prophetic visions, and did not do so. Yet how far away have they strayed from a tradition which saw in a starving man an affront to heaven, and which contained a grand variety of proof texts for precisely the kind of social revolution espoused by the radicals? It is here that the complexity of

[20] Quoted in Melech Epstein, *Profiles of Eleven,* Detroit: Wayne State University Press, 1965, p. 17.

our problem poses the severest challenges, and my own prejudices are not the least of them. These prejudices lead to an instinctive approval of democratic socialist idealism, of its optimism, of its anger. I deeply want, therefore, to identify radicalism with the elements within Jewish tradition that seem so obviously to call for such an identification. Had the radicals offered a Jewish equivalent to Christian Socialism, the problem would be far simpler, or had it access to a Leo XIII, the tradition would have posed fewer problems in its modern formulation. But the exponents of "the tradition" remained rooted in medieval concepts of charity (which were not the most sophisticated parts of medieval Jewish economic and social thought) and the radicals delighted in conducting dances on the evening of the Day of Atonement, to the consternation of precisely those who, in their time, were held to be "religious" to the exclusion of others.

Our problem is not simplified, moreover, by the Jewish secularist ideologists, who, at their most inviting, offer a statement of the secularity of the socialists which is hardly irreligious. The secularists to whom I refer are the so-called Yiddishists; that is, those who seek to preserve and enhance the Yiddish language as a major vehicle for Jewish creativity. In "Who Needs Yiddish? A Study in Language and Ethics," [21] Joseph C. Landis describes the Yiddish language as the embodiment of the ethic of European Jewry. "Jewish value and Jewish sense of life are embodied in the repatterned sentence style and structure, in the altered pronunciation and word order, in the reshaped inflectional forms and their derivatives, in the enlarged vocabulary, in the created folk expressions and sayings, in the metaphors and allusions." Its capacity to express man's obligation to be his brother's keeper, to convey human relatedness, to express tenderness and endearment, sentimentality and more than that, morality—these render a language, surely the most secular of all phenomena, into the instrument, as Landis says, "in which Jewish *mentschlekhkayt* [humanity] expresses its religious *yidishkayt* [Jewishness, Judaism]." Yiddish, he adds, "is . . . the voice of Jewish ethic, the voice of Judaism as a religiously centered pattern of life . . . the voice of Jewish loyalty and self-acceptance, the voice of Jewish rejoicing in Jewishness." Even addressing himself to the secular Jewish values of a language, therefore, an exponent of the secular viewpoint returns very unashamedly to the religious core of Jewish existence. Religious ethics and morality became embedded in a language. The secular proponents of that language—even as they firmly oppose piety and religion in the commonplace forms—cannot for one instant truly divorce themselves from a religious tradition, and in the end, do not really want to.

[21] *Judaism*, 13, 4, 1964, pp. 1–16.

It is this fact which renders our inquiry so delicate and tentative. On the one hand, religious spokesmen have been willing to argue that religion has functional value because it contributes to the survival of the Jewish people, or is the bearer of certain values or ideas. On the other, secularists affirm values and ideas which in any other context would mark them as deeply pious men. It is only by referring again to W.C. Smith's statements that we can begin to make sense of such paradoxes as these. In modern times, Jewish "tradition" seems to have evolved into an exceptionally complex phenomenon, so that an ethnic religion, apparently dividing like an amoeba, became an ethnicism and a religion in the Western senses, with the "religious" part of the tradition, narrowly construed, focusing upon the theological component, and the "ethnic" part upon the Messianic and ethical, if our understanding of Zionism and Jewish Socialism makes sense. As a concept, "Judaism," understood to mean "the Jewish religion," a phenomenon to be studied by reference to creed, cult, liturgy, and even law, thus appears as the most modern phenomenon of all, and the disintegration of "Jewish tradition" into "Judaism," on the one hand, and "Jewishness," or "culture," on the other, similarly is the direct consequence of the modern experience. It is not, however, that "the tradition" thus revealed the impact of "modernization," as Smith emphasizes, but rather that the tradition thus grew and changed in a growing and changing universe.

What has happened to "the religiousness" of men who "either do not express their religiousness formally at all, or, if they do, express it in new, untraditional ways"? In so stating the question, Smith provides a clear response for Judaism. The tradition persisted in the very same patterns of the past. Its emphasis upon learning was secularized, so that the Jews who at the end of the 19th century were believed to be unable to produce mathematicians and physicists, by the middle of the 20th century had produced at least a few significant names. More broadly, the intellectual devotion was very present, but it had entered new channels. Study remained central, but *Torah* became a narrow corpus of books, and intellectualism applied everywhere else. The Messianic hopefulness persisted, but in new ways. The strong stress upon ethical and moral conduct of society received renewed emphasis. The theological suppleness continued, the traditional hesitation to spell out in great and rigid detail what, precisely, it had to say about God characterized modern religious thought as well. Theology, Messianism, and ethics—the three pillars of Jewish tradition in earlier ages—continued strong and firm.

But with substantial differences! In Jewish Socialism, the ethical and Messianic impulses were divorced from theology. In reform and orthodoxy alike, theology parted company from Messianism, by so reconstituting the Messianic hope as to render it something else entirely from what it had been, now constituting a rather secular 19th-century optimistic affirmation of this world and its infinite perfectibility. In Zionism, as Hertzberg so trenchantly argued, the name remained the same, but all else changed. So, depending on how one reads it, one sees the persistence of forms with changed content, of attitudes with a drastically reshaped rationale and, even, focus. If from one perspective nothing seems to have changed, from another nothing is the same.

SCHOLARSHIP. The fourth case proves the most subtle. In the earlier ones, what was really modern and what was traditional seemed fairly clear. One could isolate the classical forms and the modern substance, however tentatively. In the realm of Jewish intellectualism, by contrast, both the powerful impetus of the tradition (which laid tremendous stress upon the study and transmission of sacred texts as an act of religious consequence, and by extension, upon all forms of intellectual endeavor) and the equally powerful influence of modern Western culture never ceased to play one upon the other. Had one stood at the threshold of the 19th century with a prevision of what was to come, he would have been able to predict one thing: this people is going to remain literate. Learning was so important in the lives and values of the Jews that whatever would happen, they would continue to place the highest value upon the educated person. So it would surely have seemed likely to any observer that whatever else would change, Jewish learning would remain a vital enterprise.

What actually happened would not have been foreseen: the Jews remained as a group deeply devoted to all forms of learning, *except* to Jewish learning. They entered each field of modern science and scholarship as it was opened to them, from natural and social science, to classics, Romance languages, and finally English. Their children and grandchildren occupied a disproportionately high number of university places, and entered the free professions if they were able. Their great-grandchildren became professors in the very universities which one hundred or fifty years earlier—or less—excluded Jews. At the same time the "traditional" devotion to learning so changed that the one thing Jews ceased to study was the Jewish tradition. In the history of Judaism one cannot locate a comparable situation in which the Jews so resolutely studied everything but their own sacred texts. The great Jewish physicians of the Middle Ages were also noted doctors of the law. The Jewish astronomers of Babylonia were also and mainly teachers of Torah. The masses of every age could at least read the

37

Hebrew Bible in the original language, could recite their prayers and understand the meaning of the Hebrew and Aramaic original, would read a book of Jewish thought, broadly construed, and look respectfully upon those who wrote it. In the Jewish communities of the West today, the "people of the book" has long since forgotten the language in which it is written, and in the libraries of the people of the book are represented the great literatures of the world, but, if at all, only the most banal and Philistine examples of Jewish writing. The expansion of taste came to everything but the Jewish tradition which was rendered trivial and bourgeois. Experts in many subjects hardly even comprehended the profundity of their ignorance of Judaism in its historical forms. So one may suppose that the tradition of scholarship exhibits, in the end, the most striking phenomenon: the perfect and continuing viability of the intellectual tradition, along with absolute deJudaization.

But that is not the whole story of what has happened to Jewish scholarship. If among the masses the tradition of learning directed itself away from Judaism, among the virtuosi a more interesting change took place. To understand it, we must first assess the traditional foundation and forms of Jewish learning. Traditional Jewish learning found a central place in Jewish piety because of the belief that God had revealed his will to mankind through the medium of a written revelation, given to Moses at Mount Sinai, accompanied by oral traditions which were preserved in a specific party within ancient Judaism, the Pharisees. The text without the oral traditions might have led elsewhere than into the academy, for the biblicism of other groups yielded something quite different from Jewish religious intellectualism. But belief in the text was coupled with the belief that oral traditions were also revealed, and with the claim, never successfully challenged once it was issued, that it was specifically in the Pharisaic and later rabbinical academies that these traditions were preserved and handed on. In the books composed in these academies as much as in the Hebrew Bible itself was contained God's will for man. The act of study, memorization, and commentary upon the sacred books was holy, and the study of sacred texts therefore assumed a central position in Judaism for which it is hard to find an equivalent in other traditions. Other traditions had their holy books, but few required, as did Judaism, that piety be measured by knowledge of them. Other traditions had their religious virtuosi whose virtuosity consisted in knowledge of a literary tradition, but few held, as did Judaism, that everyone must become such a virtuoso, or at least, see to it that his sons did.

Traditional processes of learning were discrete and exegetical. Creativity was expressed not through abstract dissertation, but rather through commentary upon the sacred writings or, more likely in later times, commentary upon earlier commentaries. One might also prepare a code of the law, but such a code represented little more than an assemblage of authoritative opinions of earlier times, with a decision being offered upon the few questions which the centuries had left unanswered. The chief glory of the commentator was his *hiddush*, a word meaning "novelty." The *hiddush* constituted a thoroughly scholastic disquisition upon a supposed contradiction between two earlier authorities chosen from any period with no concern for how they might in fact relate historically, and upon a supposed harmonization of their "contradiction." Or a new distinction might be read into an ancient law, upon which basis ever more questions might be raised and solved. The focus of interest was, quite naturally, upon law, rather than theology or history or philosophy or other sacred sciences. But within the law it rested upon legal theory, and interest in the practical consequences of the law was decidedly subordinated. And, one cannot stress too much, the devotion of the Jews to study of the Torah, as here defined, was held by them to be their chiefest glory, a sentiment repeated in song and prayer, and shaping the values of the common society. The important Jew was the learned man, and his learning consisted not only of what he actually knew, and least of all of what he could "do" with what he knew, but even more, of who regarded him as a learned man, of who had taught him and praised him, and of how he was received in the circles of the pious. I can think of no more striking parallel to the spirit of Mandarinism.

Modern Jewish scholarship emerged, first of all, in Germany, where the nascent reform movement for essentially theological reasons committed itself to *Wissenschaft*. As I have said earlier, the motive of the reformers was originally to substantiate their claim that if one could discover the "essence" of Judaism, if one could reach back to that golden time in which the faith was pure and unembellished, then one might find the true authority for a reformation—namely, historical precedent. Against the legal precedent of the orthodox, it was a powerful argument, and one which powerfully motivated the adoption of German science and its methodologies in the service of Jewish theology. Zunz made this point quite clear, in a letter to M.A. Stern, December 8, 1857: "I have discovered the one correct method which will both pave the way for historical insight and truly initiate a continued development based on firm foundations." [22] A second motive was the eagerness of the reformers for gentile acceptance, which was so powerful a concern of their followers. That

[22] Cited in Max Wiener, *Abraham Geiger and Liberal Judaism. The Challenge of the Nineteenth Century*, Philadelphia: Jewish Publication Society, 1962, p. 121.

acceptance seemed to them more likely in the universities, supposedly centers of reason and enlightenment, and hence the adoption of university methods of study seemed important. Zunz never complained that the orthodox did not read his books, but he did write to Theodor Nöldeke that it was strange that the Christian scholars of Germany did not cite his works, that the *Zeitschrift* he edited was not even received by the University of Göttingen library. Zunz saw this as "startling evidences of the narrowest kind of prejudice." [23] Whatever tension characterized the early generations of reform scholars, however, had resolved itself by the end of the 19th century to be replaced by a phenomenon persisting even to this day, the transit from classical Yeshiva to university.

That transit, at first characteristic of the reform movement alone, persisted through the whole era of modernization, and became *the* shaping force in the sociology of modern Jewish learning from about 1880 to the end of World War II, as one generation after another of Yeshiva-trained students underwent the spiritual crisis of deciding that the Talmud did not encompass all worthwhile learning, that there were other things worth knowing and doing, and better ways to do them. Of course many who made such a decision went into other areas of learning entirely. But some—and these are most interesting for our purposes—sought to add to their Yeshiva training the methods and sciences of the "West," and to achieve a synthesis between the tradition and the "modern world" as they understood it. These came so to dominate modern Jewish scholarship in the United States, Israel, and Central Europe before World War II that the absence of a traditional training, and with it, one supposes, the spiritual initiation provided by a crisis of faith and conscience in abandoning the Yeshiva, were regarded as insuperable obstacles in the path of a Jewish scholar. If one did not study in Slobodka—*and leave*—then he had no prospects whatever. I know leading Jewish scholars today who have no doubt whatever of that fact, which leads to some reflections on the "normalization of alienation," or the elevation of a temporary crisis into a situation of permanent and normative value best left unarticulated. That such scholars see no prospects whatever for Jewish learning in the United States seems to me a symptom of the onset of cultural rigor mortis. But enough of polemics.

We have so far concentrated upon broad social structures, movements and ideal types. We may usefully consider, finally, how a significant individual exemplified the process of "modernization"—and suffered it. He was Louis Ginzberg, Professor of Talmud at the Jewish Theological Seminary of America for the first half of the 20th cen-

[23] Letter, August 28, 1865, cited in Wiener, *op. cit.*, p. 127.

tury, a highly regarded Yeshiva student in his youth, and then a Doctor of Philosophy in Semitic Philology in a German university. Ginzberg's magnum opus, his commentary on the Palestinian Talmud, was both modern and traditional—modern in its choice of text, for the traditional academies neglected the Palestinian Talmud in favor of the Babylonian one; but modern in little else. While, to be sure, Ginzberg's extensive philological training led to a new range of questions and interests, the commentary remained just that, a *commentary*, mostly exegetical but always compendious, in which texts were brought to contrast with one another, not in order to make the traditional *hiddush*, but to make something much like it in a modern mode. Stress was laid on finding the right "reading," but traditional doctors of the law were not indifferent to variant readings. As in traditional literature, no serious effort was made to organize the data, to spell out in a clear and abstract language the consequences of the author's research. *The only framework of organization was the traditional text itself.* No index was provided, nor was any very substantial introduction prepared to what the author had contributed, though an elaborate statement about the Palestinian Talmud—in English, unlike the commentary itself—was included. It was paradigmatic, exemplifying the divisions between the traditional and the modern modes in Ginzberg's mind.

Nor should it be thought that the man himself exhibited a more soundly integrated personality. As reported by his son,[24] Ginzberg never fully achieved a separation from the attitudes and affirmations of the Yeshivot of Eastern Europe, by the best of whose products he was trained—and even fathered. He is quoted as saying, or believing, that a Jew should eat *kosher* and think *tref*: that is to say, that he should conform to the traditional laws, but preserve the freedom to think in new ways. The recommendation of orthopraxy is hardly new in Judaism. What is new, I believe, is the suspension of intellectual endeavor to unite traditional practice with a new way of understanding the tradition, to integrate faith and practice. The failure to find some sort of an integrated perception of the faith is most dramatically illustrated by two facts. First of all, toward the end of his life, he grew increasingly concerned about the breach which his approach and method had caused between his father and his father's father and himself. His son reports, "He told me regretfully that he could never have published his *Commentary* during his father's lifetime." [25] Second, his reaction to a poison-pen letter seems so utterly out of proportion that a

[24] Eli Ginzberg, *Keeper of the Law: Louis Ginzberg*, Philadelphia: Jewish Publication Society, 1966.
[25] *Ibid.*, p. 265.

deep-seated ambivalence, resulting in psychosomatic manifestations, became revealed. Within twenty-four hours after reading a perfectly routine piece of vitriol, Ginzberg fell ill with an acute case of shingles and, his son says, "although the acute infection subsided after a time, he was left with an aggravated neuralgia which plagued him every day and night until he died." [26] The despair he felt at the death of his father four decades earlier seems an appropriate foil: "My father was the embodiment of all the noble and great Rabbinical Judaism has produced and his death takes away from me the concreteness of my 'Weltanschauung,' " he wrote,[27] and he later said, "I know my poor father did not die peacefully on account of my becoming a scholar instead of a gaon [Talmudical sage] and on account of my bachelorship. . . . " [28] Shortly afterward he married, but he was never able to retrace the path that had led him from the East. Ginzberg wrote: "The vitality of an organism is shown in its power of adaptation. Judaism in modern times . . . was confronted with the almost insurmountable difficulty of adapting itself to modern thought. . . . Judaism passed from the fifteenth century into the nineteenth, and thus could not take place without a formidable shock. That it withstood this shock is the best proof of the power and energy inherent in Judaism." [29] Ginzberg himself, making the transition from the scholarly modes of one world to those of another, required by the facts of psychology and the affirmations of theology not to give up the one in the acquisition of the other, more nearly absorbed that shock in his person than others of his day. He seemed more aware of it, suffered more deeply from its affects, and in the end proved unable to preserve health within the tensions it imposed. Those who preceded him, like those who followed, accepted the given as normal. It was he who had to make his way across the abyss between traditional and modern scholarship.

THE REASSESSMENT OF IDENTITY. What then has happened to Judaism, and what has the Jew become? That which we have referred to as "the Jewish tradition" has become, in the felicitous phrase of Ben Halpern, "the Jewish consensus." [30] Halpern says, "If certain laws, rituals, linguistic and literary traditions, together with the myth of Exile and Redemption, were the universal values that bound Jews together, then with their loss the Jewish people should have disintegrated. But these values *were* lost and the Jews did *not* fall apart. In

[26] *Ibid.*, p. 266.
[27] *Ibid.*, p. 121.
[28] *Ibid.*, p. 121.
[29] Louis Ginzberg, *Students, Scholars, and Saints*, Philadelphia; Jewish Publication Society, 1928, p. x.
[30] Ben Halpern, "The Jewish Consensus," *Jewish Frontier*, September, 1962.

the 19th century, values which had been universal among traditional Jewry still continued to be shared—but only by part of the Jews. There were some who no longer shared them, yet these dissenters continued to be regarded as Jews by the remainder who preserved the old values. . . . Apparently there must have been a different 'consensus' binding them together—that is, a set of values that were *universally* shared among all the Jews." What were these values? Halpern denies that it is necessary to define them for, he points out, "What was the most striking thing . . . about the cohesion and the survival . . . of traditional Jewry? It was the fact that they were united and survived without many of the shared values that are generally believed to hold a normal people together and constitute essential parts of the consensus of comparable groups." Judaism had few dogmas, and Jewish law and courts were backed by little power or hierarchial authority. What constituted this inchoate consensus? Halpern sees it in a "community of fate," rather than of "faith." "Only because they are constantly involved in the consequences of each other's acts need each care what the other wants." It was a consensus, too, of shared sensitivity. The Jews thus remained what they had been in earlier times, a singular people, not quite like any other, and "Judaism," instead of positing a Providence receptive to the prayers, and responsive to the deeds, of Jewry, became instead the repository of those experiences which Jews could share in common, however much they differed. What were they? The Holocaust was one, the astonishment at the rise of the State of Israel another, the unexpected persistence of Jewry beyond the time when it ought to have faded away still a third: in sum, the very fact of *being Jewish* constituted the experience uniting so hopelessly divided a society—that, and the concern that the experience of being Jewish persist into the coming generations. Though most no longer express their religiousness in traditional ways, and many no longer in formal ways at all, the Jews retain, not only in the specific instances we have considered but in a more general way as well, very real bonds to the classical tradition.

JUDAISM AND SECULARITY

Given both Judaism's and the Jews' astonishingly successful transition from the pre-modern to the modern situation, one must ask, Has the tradition prepared the Jews for the modern situation? Has it even in pre-modern times carried within itself the qualities we now associate with modernization? I think the answer to both questions is mostly affirmative.

43

In *The Secular City*,[31] Harvey Cox provides a helpful definition of secularity, by which we may find answers to these questions. He stresses the worldliness of secularity ("The world has become man's task and man's responsibility" [32]), its cosmopolitanism, and its relativity ("It has relativized religious world-views. It has convinced the believer that he could be wrong, and persuaded the devotee that there are more important things than dying for the faith." [33]). In the new age, religion provides for few an "inclusive and commanding system of personal and cosmic values and explanations." [34] It is urbanization which represents the context for secularization. "Urbanization means a structure of common life in which diversity and the disintegration of tradition are paramount . . . It means that a degree of tolerance and anonymity replace traditional moral sanctions . . . " [35] In the secular city, nature becomes disenchanted, politics desacralized, and values deconsecrated. Nature plays no great role in life. No one rules by divine right. And no values are seen to be ultimate. The shape of the secular city exhibits these qualities, Cox says: anonymity, an increase in the range of possibilities for communication, free choice, mobility, pragmatism, and profaneness. In a word, Cox describes the situation of pluralism, of a universe in which values are no longer obvious or self-fulfilling, in which men no longer verify one another's prejudices.

Jewish tradition provided Jews with two significant advantages for the new era, which in a measure account for their spectacular adjustment to it. First of all, as a persecuted minority, Jews have never seen a world in which their particular values and ideals were verified or substantiated by society. They always found the world a challenge to faith. They never ceased to be cosmopolitans, living under an international law and in communication with men living under widely disparate cultures. Theirs was an international tradition even before the rise of nation-states. For centuries they accepted the setting of their local life without losing touch with the community of faith that transcended local settings. When not persecuted, they were ignored by the great world beyond. Christianity taught—and continues to teach—that Judaism died at the mountain of Calvary. Islam regarded it as an incomplete version of truth. So the Jews' particular religious world view never received full and affirmative support from the world. Christians, seeing mainly other Christians, may not have perceived the possibility that they could be wrong. But Jews could never escape it. Diversity and disintegration were, therefore, experiences for which the

[31] Harvey Cox, *The Secular City*, New York: Macmillan Co., 1965.
[32] *Ibid.*, p. 1.
[33] *Ibid.*, p. 2.
[34] *Ibid.*, p. 4.
[35] *Ibid.*, p. 4.

Jew was well prepared. His Bible never regarded nature as enchanted, but only as neutral; he never had a sufficiently constructive experience of politics to take seriously the "divine right" of kings or anyone else. He has always seen so diverse a world that he knew about the relativity of values, even while he affirmed his own.

The Jew moreover aspired to the present situation. He spent close to two hundred years in the effort to encourage the secularization of politics, so that he might participate in it, so that, at the very least, politics would cease to be an instrument of Christian persecution. Whether or not the biblical sense of the mystery and awesomeness of creation was phrased in narrowly religious terms, the Jewish intellectual, unfettered by traditional attitudes and always an outsider, knowing the meaning of alienation as he knew the streets of his city, found it possible to speculate about the unthinkable, to investigate the forbidden, to reconsider the commonplace—and so to reshape reality. If, moreover, the Jew advocated the secularization of common values, it was so that he might find a place within the common life. He not only advocated pluralism because of his historical situation; he created a situation of pluralism by his very presence.

Judaism denied the need of men to judge all values, all history, by their particular self-authenticating system of thought. Denying, in specific, theological terms, that the Messiah had already come, the Jews saw as transitory and useful the artifacts of the world which others understood to be absolute and perfected. Judaism told the world it was not yet redeemed and preserved a thoroughly skeptical attitude toward the perfections of the hour. It perceived reality—the immutable truths of others—as something to be criticized, to be elevated, to be transcended. Judaism differed from those who affirmed that the world is saved, or can be saved, through one or another gnosis. It was the task of the Jews through their very presence, through their very fate, as Halpern tells us, to remind the world that it does not yet exhibit the stigmata of salvation, and whether it was the Christian world or the Communist world hardly matters. All who see the status quo—"tradition"—as absolute must, therefore, have been offended. For all their Messianic fervor, which we have traced here, the Jews advocated only a realistic assessment of what other men were prepared to see as Messianic; it was, therefore, an open-ended Messianism, affirming what must come, denying the finality of what was already present. This denial of a present redemption contained within itself the affirmation of an other-worldly hope. The Jews have said "no" to the achievements of this world, because they preserved the hope for an ultimately correct affirmation. The tension of an unrealized Messianic situation, imposed by Jewish tradition, resulted in the insistence that times

45

would change, and nothing is absolute; also that times *could* change for the better. Judaism welcomed the relativization of values precisely because it always kept alive the vision of a greater perfection than that of the present. It welcomed the desanctification of time, politics, culture, because it perceived a higher holiness, a more complete, just politics, a sounder and more appropriately modest assessment of culture. At the same time, Judaism was an activist tradition, which told men they were partners in the task of perfecting the world under the dominion of God. If the world was insufficient and incomplete, it was man's task to help complete it. If men saw values as in a measure relative to the situation of specific men and groups, Judaism held that men have as their chief task the duty to criticize and purify their ideals by criteria at once most ancient and still unrealized. It is this which accounts for the secular activism of Judaism in modern times, for its capacity to contribute one group of enthusiasts after another to the struggle for "a better world," to shape the "mission of Israel" in such extraordinarily immodest, and yet commonplace, workaday terms.

Confronted by a plurality of choices in an uncertain world, Judaism taught that men must choose, in the end, affirming a tentative and austere selection among the many truths available to men. That choice indeed needed to be cautious, as the tragic lessons of Shabbatai Zvi in the 17th century, and the disappointed optimism of German Judaism in the 19th and 20th centuries, suggested. But Judaism knew that men must end up somewhere in the city, and as some thing in society. Values may be relative, but men must have some ideal by which to guide their lives. Politics may be profane, but political life must go on, and within it, men must choose their parties. Men may have the right to anonymity in the secular city, but anonymity is not enough. Men may have the right to be nothing in particular, but Judaism saw men as needing to form more than anonymous cyphers in a valueless world. The Jews who saw the world in all its complex plurality also choose to form the most vivid, clannish of all groups, to sustain the most particular of all traditions, though they knew that their group was not coextensive with society, and their tradition was surely not the only right way of living life. Judaism understood, therefore, that men may face a relativity of values, but in the end men live in some specific place among some specific group of people, and the values that shape their lives are not relative to the conditions of those lives. Judaism found the possibility, even before the modern situation, to live within those circumstances we now see to be peculiarly modern, affirming community and fellowship within the disparate city. Judaism knew that when all values were seen to be relative, men most needed the fellowship of congenial people to sustain themselves. In a multiplicity of choices, men needed more than ever the brotherhood of some who will choose and sustain one another in their choices. In the end anonymity is a gift but also a deprivation.

Jews similarly were prepared by their tradition to welcome the increase in the range of possibilities for communication, in the range of cosmopolitanism. Living among many kinds of men, they tried to learn something from each. But they knew too that in the end, one talks to someone in particular who is neither "the world" nor "mankind." Communication requires a particular language, mode of expression, set of mutually comprehensible symbols, responses, expectations. These are not formed in an hour or day, nor do legislatures create them. They are the product of centuries of common culture. Jews spoke all the languages of the Western World, and learned their truths, but they spoke, whether Reform, or Zionist, or Socialist, to their own group. They did so not because of special sanctities, but because of the realities of communication, which impose the need for community and commonality, for a "community of fate" if no longer of faith.

Judaism kept alive the memory of ancient eternal cities, thought to be grand and permanent, and Jews knew that they alone, and those who read their Scriptures, kept alive the memory of world empires. They knew, therefore, that it is not the place, but the quality of life within it, that truly matters. No city is holy, but men must live in some one place, and have therefore grave responsibilities to the profane city with all its impermanence. Though no city is holy, men have, in theological language, the task of sanctifying the place in which they live. The very intrinsic profaneness of place stood as a challenge to the Jews, to shape any place to conform to a decent pattern of life, to build even though all one has for mortar may be slime. Judaism was not confounded by the possibilities for movement, by the desacralization of place, because Jews knew that they must love each place with open arms.

Pragmatism and profaneness are, Cox says, the style of the secular city. What shall we say of a tradition which laid its greatest stress upon deeds, upon a pattern of actions and a way of living, but that it is pragmatic? What shall we say of a perspective upon the world that focused, within it, upon worldly potentialities for sanctity, but that it is worldly? What shall we conclude of a "religious language" which called honesty or charity a *kiddush hashem*, a sanctification of God's name, but that it is secular? A faith whose highest commandments concerned love for one's fellow man and the practice of deeds of loving kindness is one which saw long ago that "the world was man's task and man's responsibility." The Jew was taught by his tradition to see it just so. But, as I said, the Jew could never stop with the affirma-

47

tion of the world. He found it incomplete and impoverished, the given to be criticized and elevated. The Jews' this-worldliness is of a different sort. He affirmed the world because God made it and left him tasks to do within it. He affirmed the relativity of world views because he understood the insufficiency of human achievements. Worldliness, cosmopolitanism, diversity, pluralism, the "internalization of values" —these have characterized the Jews' tradition even though they spoke of them, formerly, in theological terms, and may speak of them today in wholly secular ones.

The central and integrating fact, I believe, is this: Judaism preserved the capacity at once to assess the unredemption of the world, and to hope, and work, for its salvation. It is this unfulfilled yet very vivid evaluation of the world and all its works which, I think, provides the explanation for the Jew's capacity to love so much, and yet with open arms to affirm the world; to engage realistically in its tasks with a whole heart, and yet without the need to regard those tasks as the threshold of a final and completed fulfillment of history. It has permitted him to take seriously the range of worldly problems without the fatuous expectation that in solving them, he would save the world. His situation, once described in uniquely theological language and today in common ideological terms, imposed upon him a singularly fruitful tension, preventing him from taking too seriously what he so earnestly accomplished, requiring of him a hope so strong that workaday worlds came under its illumination, imposing upon him the affirmation of his own humanity, wholly man and yet "partner of God" in the perfection of the world. If, as I suppose, the Jew was uniquely ready for the modern situation, it was in part because he created it by his presence, in part because the worldly consequences of his tradition prepared him for it, but, I think, mainly because he found the modern situation congenial and congruent to his humanity.

With your indulgence, I shall close with a brief sermon, my prerogative as a rabbi. This is a world we Jews know well. Indeed, from my perspective, it seems that today, many men have entered the situation we Jews think of as peculiarly Jewish. If so, then men may well learn from us the lesson that pluralism and a free and open society represent an absolute gain for man, precisely because he may now freely choose. But in the end freedom of choice constitutes not completion but challenge: *in freedom actually to make a choice.*

48

II *Catholicism*

Every religiously grounded unworldly love and indeed every ethical religion must, in similar measure and for similar reasons, experience tensions with the sphere of political behavior. This tension appears as soon as religion has progressed to anything like a status of equality with the sphere of political associations. To be sure, the ancient god of the locality, even where he was an ethical and universally powerful god, existed merely for the political interests of his followers' associations.

Even the Christian God is still invoked as a god of war and as a god of our fathers . . .

Max Weber
The Sociology of Religion

2.

NEW STATES AND AN OLD CHURCH

BY VICTOR D. Du BOIS

American Universities Field Staff

In the French-speaking states of Black Africa, the determination of the role proper to the church in a developing society has provoked a great polemic. African governments, newly freed from metropolitan control, are reappraising the privileged position which the Christian church, especially the Roman Catholic, has so far enjoyed in their countries.

In most cases the debate has not been provoked by the presidents of the new nations themselves (most of whom have remained sympathetic to the goals and methods of the church), but by younger, more volatile elements in African society. Many of them are recently returned graduates from abroad, labor union leaders, and junior functionaries who tend to see the church as a vestige of a colonial past and as an obstacle in the path of national economic and social development.

The definition of the church's role is part of a larger reappraisal that is being made of other institutions brought to Africa by the white colonizer. But urgency is lent to the problem of church-state relations by the fact that, since 1960, the Catholic Church has been confronted with a challenge to the influence it wields and, in certain countries, with a threat to its very existence. Local Church leaders have had to make complex decisions on the possibility of concessions to the demands of nationalists while safeguarding their own principles and the interests of their followers in religion.

The demands of the nationalists are essentially two: that the Church be Africanized, and that it submit to the dictates of the state. By and large, Rome has been able and willing to comply with the first. Africanization, in its broadest sense, has come to mean not only replacing white prelates and clergy with Africans, but also making the Church more meaningful to Africans in style and substance. The reforms recommended and approved at Vatican Council II—celebration of the mass in vernacular tongues, the introduction of native traditions into marriage and funeral ceremonies, and the tolerance of native music and dance in connection with certain sacraments—all are attempts to satisfy these demands, recognized as legitimate by Church authorities.

It has been much more difficult for the Church to comply with the second demand; that is, that it submit to the will of the state. Over the years the Roman Catholic Church in Africa has acquired power and influence in the temporal domain through institutions which it controls —chiefly schools, labor unions, and newspapers—and which it is loath to surrender. It has thus at times come into conflict with the state, a conflict from which it has never emerged the victor.

Not everywhere in independent Africa, however, have the Church and state been at odds. Indeed, antagonism between the two has been the exception rather than the rule. In most of the former French territories, relations have been harmonious. Especially in the new states ruled by an older generation of national leaders well disposed toward France, the Church is looked upon as an ally, not an antagonist, of the new society in the making. Its services in education and civic training are regarded as a useful contribution to internal cohesion and national progress.

In this analysis, after briefly tracing the origins of Christianity in Black Africa, I shall examine the development of relations between Church and state in three nations south of the Sahara formerly ruled by France: Guinea, the Congo-Brazzaville, and the Ivory Coast. The first two are self-proclaimed members of Africa's "revolutionary" block of states whose relations with the Catholic Church have been extremely tense. The third country, the Ivory Coast, is the leading member of French-speaking Africa's so-called "moderate" bloc in which Church-state relations have been much more cordial, though by no means entirely free from strain.

THE ESTABLISHMENT OF CHRISTIANITY IN BLACK AFRICA

North Africa received Christianity in apostolic times, and for centuries was the home of flourishing Catholic communities. Saint Augustine, it will be recalled, was an African bishop. Yet nearly all traces of this spiritual conquest were washed away by the tidal wave of militant Islamism which rolled over the entire northern rim of the continent and was halted only by the natural barriers of the Sahara, the Atlantic, and the mountain fastnesses in which the Ethiopians preserved their ancient Coptic Church. South of the Sahara, Black Africa's primitive paganism remained largely untouched by these great religious phenomena.

In the mid-15th century the formidable land barriers were circumvented by the persistence and daring of the Portuguese. The islands off Africa—the Azores, Madeira, and the Cape Verde group—were colonized and became the scene of Franciscan missions. Dominicans thought a foothold had been secured in Senegambia when, in 1489, a few local notables were taken to Lisbon for baptism. And before the century was closed a Benin chief was converted. For the next several centuries many European religious orders strove to establish missions for the faith along the coast, but their successes, while occasionally spectacular, proved ephemeral. The Portuguese did not have the necessary resources of men and money to undertake extensive colonization. A lack of adequate supplies, disease, and attacks by local African tribes also took their toll.

Any summary of the introduction of Christianity to the western coast of Africa should make at least passing mention of the amazing if short-lived Christian triumphs in the Congo. In the early 1480s the Portuguese came upon the great river which they still call the Zaire. In accordance with established practice, a few natives of the region were taken back to Lisbon for interrogation and baptism. Missionaries were quickly dispatched, and they converted the paramount chief, known as the "Manicongo." Although he was himself lukewarm in the faith and eventually a backslider, his son and successor, known in Portuguese annals as Dom Affonso, was a zealous Catholic and actively supported a growing number of missionaries in their work of conversion.

The European clergy set up schools and Dom Affonso dispatched a personal envoy to the Pope in 1513. Five years later one of the king's sons, Dom Henrique, was consecrated a bishop. Several Africans were ordained and a flourishing Catholic community, with strong indigenous roots, seemed to be in the making. In 1534 the Diocese of São Tomé (including the Congo and West Africa) was established, and in 1597 the Diocese of Congo and Angola. These were entrusted to European prelates, however, as the native aristocracy became involved in disputes over the succession to the throne and many opposed the alien faith.

European rivalry with the Portuguese and internecine wars among the tribes spelled the doom of Christian beginnings in the Congo, nonetheless significant for providing the first known case of a native bishop and clergy in Black Africa—in the early 16th century. Several hundred years were to pass before the rebirth of Catholic missionary endeavors on a large scale. The Christian establishments in the Congo today, as everywhere along the west coast, trace their origins to the great burst of religious activity that was so marked a feature of the 19th century.

France was the home base from which the great Catholic missionary movement of the 19th century radiated to Black Africa. Lesser contributors were Germany, Belgium, Italy, Portugal, and Spain. France, however, had established contacts with the peoples along the Senegalese coast as early as the 17th century. Although at first concerned with the spiritual care of Frenchmen in posts or trading centers, the Church soon manifested a missionary interest in the indigenous peoples which increased rapidly in the 19th century. In 1863 the Vicariate Apostolic of Senegambia was erected, and by 1902 a seminary had produced ten native priests. In 1878 the *Pères du Saint Esprit* had opened a mission among the Soussou along the Pongo River in what is now Guinea.

French Catholic missionary interest in the Ivory Coast dates from 1687 when a French priest, Father Gonsalvez, founded a mission in Assinie. The *Société des Missions Africaines* of Lyon sent missionaries into the region in the 19th century and achieved some success in the face of a colonial government strongly anti-clerical—reflecting the tension in Church and state relations in France itself at the time.

In Togoland both Protestant and Catholic missions had a precarious existence until, in the late 19th century, Imperial Germany secured possession. German Protestant organizations naturally met with favor on the part of the colonial regime, and Rome soon assigned Catholic responsibility for the region to a missionary organization (the Society of the Divine Word) most of whose members were German.

In neighboring Dahomey, where Capuchins from Spain had established a temporary mission in the 17th century, French influence finally triumphed. For a time, in the late 19th century, Dahomey was the scene of one of the strongest French Catholic missions in Africa.

While the Portuguese had reconnoitered the Cameroun coast in the 15th century, Christianity was not introduced until the 19th. English Protestants were the pioneers here but transferred their responsibilities to German-speaking Swiss when (in 1887) the German Empire acquired title to the coast and a vast hinterland. In the closing years of the century German Catholic missionaries entered the field and achieved comparative success.

During the late 19th and the first half of the 20th centuries, Christianity in Black Africa naturally reflected the sectarian character of the metropolitan churches which directed, staffed, and financed the missions. In French West Africa such missionary enterprise as existed was chiefly Catholic. It made its most notable progress in Dahomey and Senegal where colonial authorities, having neither the funds nor the personnel, left to the missionaries the task of organizing an educational system for the colonies. In the Ivory Coast an agreement in 1895 between the fathers of the *Société des Missions Africaines* of Lyon and Governor Binger opened the way for similar developments in that territory.

The anti-clericalism of the republican government in France, under Jules Ferry, in the 1880s was carried over to the colonies where it was a strong deterrent to further Catholic expansion. As a result in Senegal, France's oldest colony, Catholic influence began to decline. Only in the Ivory Coast and in Dahomey, where the missions had preceded the establishment of the colonial regime and had become virtually self-sufficient, was the Church able to hold its own.

Relations between Church and state in French West Africa, as in France itself, were strained throughout the latter part of the 19th century and into the early part of the 20th. Misunderstandings often arose between Church authorities and colonial officials over purely local matters such as ownership of mission property or the treatment accorded African converts. It was alleged that missionaries sought special favors for their catechumens at the expense of the pagan peoples, and that their opposition to the institution of polygamy threatened to upset the social order. Conflict arose, too, from the lack of congruence between religious and political administrative units.

The African environment itself presented difficulties. The sparseness of the indigenous peoples in many parts of the land, their nomadic habits, and the almost total absence of any but the most rudimentary means of communication, hampered the growth of Catholicism during those early days. Many missionaries fell victim to malaria and other then mysterious diseases. Finally, fetishism and Islam proved formidable competitors for the minds and souls of the recently conquered peoples. Yet despite all these obstacles, the Church made steady if fitful progress. By 1921 Catholics numbered some 695,000 in French Black Africa; by 1933 the number had risen to 1,400,000. Today there are some 4,500,000 Catholics [1] in the countries comprising the former federations of French West and Equatorial Africa.[2]

[1] These and other Church statistics are taken from *Annuaire des Diocéses d'Expression Française, Délégations Apostoliques pour l'Afrique Occidentale, l'Afrique Centrale et Madagascar* (Paris, 1965).
[2] In former French West Africa, the states of Senegal, Mauritania, Mali (formerly French Soudan), Guinea, Upper Volta, the Ivory Coast, and Niger; in former French Equatorial Africa, the states of Gabon, the Central African Republic

A territory under French rule was commonly spoken of as Catholic, and one under British or German rule was called Protestant. Although convenient terms, these were highly inaccurate simplifications.[3] Even in a colony where Christianity was considered to enjoy great success, Christians were but a small part of the population. The majority was still true to animism, in varying degrees of primitiveness, while in some areas Muslims far outnumbered Christians. Yet it was inevitable that the Christian missionaries, being Europeans and the purveyors of education and health and social services, enjoy an influence entirely out of proportion to their own number and that of their converts.

As has been said, the introduction of Christianity was made possible and its growth facilitated by the establishment of European colonial rule. Independence, when it finally came, brought about something which had long been a theoretical aim of all Christian missionary work, but one which was generally long postponed, often to such a point that there were sometimes serious doubts as to the sincerity of those who professed to be working toward it. This goal was the establishment of a truly indigenous Christian church staffed by native priests and prelates. For a very long time—except for a few historical precedents which proved exceptions to the rule—there was a general reluctance to entrust the direction of Church affairs to Africans.

Once the colonies were transformed into sovereign states, the accession of Africans to positions of authority in the Church could not safely be delayed. Many factors, however, conspired against this move: the scarcity of vocations to the religious life and to the priesthood, the lack of seminaries, and the greater rewards promised by careers in law, politics, and business. There were few human and natural incentives for an African to become a priest. As a parish pastor he could look forward only to a life of unremitting toil, hardship, and poverty amongst the poorest and humblest inhabitants of tragically under-developed lands. And with a constant succession of European prelates appointed by Rome there seemed to be, in the colonial church, literally no room at the top.

But just as independence guaranteed the Africanization of the highest political cadres, it tremendously accelerated the Africanization of the Church. The appointment of African bishops and archbishops

(formerly Ubangui-Chari), the Republic of the Congo (formerly Moyen Congo), and Chad. The former mandated territory of Togo is included for statistical purposes.

[3] In much the same way, vast areas of Africa are referred to as "French-speaking" or "English-speaking." This is a convenient way of indicating the official languages of the countries. In fact, the vast majority of the people speak only their indigenous tongue and perhaps one or two other languages of neighboring tribes. In "French-speaking" Black Africa, for instance, scarcely 10 per cent of the population speaks French.

not only conformed to an historic policy of the Catholic Church, but it also demonstrated that the Church ought not to be regarded, at least any longer, as a bulwark of colonialism. The spread of Christianity throughout the Middle East, North Africa, and all of Europe had proved, over the centuries, that the strength of the Church lay precisely in its traditional accommodation to local requirements. When patriarchs and popes sent missionaries to Goths and Slavs, to the German tribes, to Britons and Gauls, their success was signified by the rise of a native clergy and hierarchy. But all that lay in a far distant past, and there were many persons—among them some missionaries— who doubted that the African clergy was mature enough in the faith to repeat that historical pattern. Nevertheless, the great landslide of independence forced the issue.

There were, likewise, many doubts about the Catholic laity themselves. While thousands of them were but simple peasants clustered around mission stations in the remote interior, hundreds of them belonged to the native elite and after independence occupied positions of the highest authority. Could they be relied upon to be dutiful sons of the Church and, if not actually protect it, at least remain neutral toward its legitimate interests? Or might they become—like so many of the nominally Catholic French administrators before them—bitterly anti-clerical, and circumscribe the action of the Church? Was there really any reason to think that under an African government a Church headed by Africans would fare better than one headed by Europeans? That is, was Africanization really a crucial factor for the prosperity of the Catholic Church?

While the time span of independence has not been long—still less than ten years—it is nonetheless rewarding to try to answer these questions on the basis of developments in three countries, all of which were French colonies in Black Africa, gained their independence at about the same time, and in which the Catholic Church had been established for at least half a century.

CHURCH AND STATE IN INDEPENDENT AFRICA

When the French colonies in sub-Saharan Africa became sovereign nations, delicate questions concerning Church-state relations inevitably arose. In a number of states (e.g., the Ivory Coast, Niger, Upper Volta, Gabon) a majority of the indigenous population was pagan, and in others (notably Senegal, Mali, Guinea, and Mauritania) it was Muslim. Yet the questions which arose usually involved the Christian—more specifically, the Roman Catholic—minorities. Since the establishment of European domination, the Catholic Church had enjoyed a privileged position in French Black Africa. Its missions were given great latitude in educating the young, setting up medical stations in the interior, and proselytizing the indigenous populations. Catholic churches invariably occupied the most favored sites in the territorial capitals and in the towns up-country.

With the advent of independence, the transfer of power to Africans provided the occasion for a re-examination of this traditional policy. Nationalist leaders, many of them Catholic, did not hesitate to broach the issue. The Church was an inviting target, for its progress toward Africanization had been perilously slow. Since the overwhelming majority of its bishops and priests still were Europeans, it was easy enough to accuse the Church of being a bastion of colonialism and reaction even though a few individual members of the clergy had courageously championed the cause of African nationalism against the colonial regime, sometimes at great personal risk. And as early as 1955 the bishops of French West Africa publicly affirmed the "legitimacy of aspirations to independence"—at a time when practically nobody else dared speak of the subject.

The notion that the Catholic Church was a pillar of the colonial regime was a belief held by many West African intellectuals—a belief more often picked up in idle conversations in Left Bank cafés than based on an objective examination of the facts. The truth of the matter is that the Catholic Church had much less foreign character in West Africa than elsewhere. Far from being supported and subsidized by the colonial governments, it had often been the object of their attacks, precisely because it had taken the side of the African against the colonial establishment. Yet this misconception concerning the relationship of the Church to the colonial regime was tenaciously held by African intellectuals, and invariably figured prominently in their indictment of the Church.

However liberal the European clergy were in a particular territory, however much they had contributed to building up the country, the very fact that they were white put them at a disadvantage with the new African civil authorities. Their presence was an unpleasant reminder both of the alien origins of the Church and of white authority. Part of the antipathy toward the white clergy was a reaction to the ultra-conservatism of some of its early leaders. Some of it emanated also from the anti-clericalism inherited from the French residents. French teachers and government officials were notoriously anti-clerical at home. It is not surprising that when they went to Africa to live and work they brought old prejudices with them. These they eagerly inculcated in their African colleagues who often took them as their own.

58

The question of Church-state relations became much more complicated once Africans themselves came to occupy high positions in the
Church's hierarchy. It was difficult to accuse a bishop or archbishop of
being a colonialist when he was an African who had fought as hard and
believed as strongly in the cause of independence as some of the nationalist leaders themselves. Other grounds had to be found for com-
batting what was thought to be the undue influence of the Church.
The Church and state polemic provided the ideal issue for this purpose.

Ample grounds existed for a conflict of interest between the two.
The Church's influence over the education of youth through the
schools it controlled; the influence it wielded through certain action
groups such as labor unions and youth organizations; and finally its
power to mold public opinion through its newspapers, parochial, or
devotional publications as well as from the pulpits of its churches—all
of these impinged on prerogatives which the state considered its
own.

The African bishops, anxious to avoid conflict with the new leaders
of their states, hastened to allay any fears the latter might have regarding the Church's ambitions. On occasion they themselves brought up
the question of Church-state relations, assuring the government that
the Church sought freedom only to carry out its religious mission.
From 1960 onward, as each new African archbishop was enthroned, he
made it a point to stress this fact in his first pastoral letter. The forth-
right declaration of Monseigneur Luc Sangaré, Archbishop of Bamako
[Mali], is typical of those made by other African prelates:

> While we are citizens of the family of God and of His kingdom,
> we do not cease to be citizens of our earthly country. But this
> creates no problem. Belonging to a Church is not a brake on politi-
> cal or social plans. Rendering unto Caesar what is Caesar's in no
> way prevents one from following God's way in rendering unto
> God what is His due. . . . This is a happy opportunity for me to
> assure the highest public authorities of the cordial and loyal collab-
> oration of the Archbishop of Bamako with regard to their legiti-
> mate functions and powers . . .[4]

CHURCH AND STATE IN GUINEA

Nowhere was conflict between Church and state more likely to occur
than in Guinea. Ever since 1958 when Guinea gained its independence
in a bitter break with France, its President, Sékou Touré, had been at
odds with the Roman Catholic Church. Like many other nationalists of

[4] "L'Archeveque de Bamako Parle . . . " *Afrique Nouvelle*, Dakar, No. 774, June
7–13, 1962.

his time, he was convinced that the Church was an appendage of the colonial regime. Now that this regime had been repudiated, he felt the time had come to give a distinctive Guinean tone to the Church as well as to other national institutions.

Two features of the Church were particularly objectionable to Touré: (1) the Archbishop of Conakry and many other members of the clergy in Guinea were French; and (2) the Church, even in a now sovereign Guinea, still expected the favored treatment it had received from the colonial administration. During the French tenure, the Church was allowed to have its own youth groups, labor union, and periodicals, and even to broadcast over Radio Conakry. Touré was most distressed, however, that through its schools the Church had an important means of influencing the nation's youth. To the President the lingering European flavor of the Church and its privileged institutions were incompatible with the brand of nationalism with which he intended to mold Guinea's future. Touré resented what he interpreted as the Church's competition with his own efforts to control his people's destiny completely. Accordingly, he set out to rectify the situation.

Shortly after independence, Touré initiated a series of moves designed to reduce progressively the influence of the Roman Catholic Church. In March, 1959, the *Parti Démocratique de Guinée* (PDG), Guinea's sole and ruling political party, abolished all youth groups not directly controlled by the state. Among those affected were some organized by the Church. Henceforth only the *Jeunesse Rassemblement Démocratique Africaine* (JRDA), the officially sanctioned youth wing of the Party, was tolerated. Similarly, the government ordered the disbanding of all labor unions, including that supported by the Church, in favor of its own newly created national labor organization. The Church also was denied permission to broadcast over the Guinean radio.

Debilitating as these measures were to the Roman Catholic Church in Guinea, much more serious was the Party's decision to nationalize the Church's primary schools. A gradual phasing out of Church control over these schools was scheduled for completion within three years. Church schools were at once forbidden to enroll any more pupils during this transitional period. Although unhappy over the prospect of seeing their primary schools taken over by the state, Church authorities bowed to the government's will and were grateful at least to retain supervision over their few secondary schools.

In August, 1961, however, shortly before the three-year phasing out period was to end, Sékou Touré announced at a Party conference that the government had decided to nationalize not only the primary schools but all of the schools in Guinea. This decision brought cries of alarm from the clergy, who felt that the Party had violated its pledge. Some of them put up a spirited, if merely verbal, resistance to the plan. On August 20, 1961, Monseigneur Gérard de Milleville, the French Archbishop of Conakry, ordered read from the pulpit of every Church in his archdiocese a pastoral letter in which he took the Government severely to task:

> You have no doubt learned of the great difficulty which at present confronts the Church in Guinea as the result of treatment which is to be meted out to private education and which especially affects our mission schools.
>
> A circular from the Ministry of National Education provides that, as of the next academic year, recruitment of students for the lower grades no longer will be undertaken by us but by state inspectors headed by someone appointed by the Ministry . . .
>
> . . . We are aware of the gravity of this situation and have intervened in order to save this liberty which is threatened.
>
> During the last few months, under the cloak of secularization, the Church has found itself forbidden to conduct religious broadcasts over the radio; its youth movements have been reproached for allegedly wishing to compromise the unity of the country, and today it is its schools that are threatened.
>
> Know that if tomorrow the Church is forbidden to accept your children in its schools it is against its will that it will abandon this work.[5]

Archbishop de Milleville next addressed himself to the problems of Africanization and the conflict between Church and state, issues which had been raised by Touré:

> The Church has never ceased to work for the promotion of a native clergy and has always been concerned with becoming an African Church in Africa. The Church did not wait until 1961 to name not only African bishops, but an African Cardinal.* However let us make no mistake: The Church has never done this under external pressure. The Church is, and must always remain, entirely independent of all temporal power. The Church cannot be compared to any other social institution. It cannot force its faithful to become priests and from this fact alone one can understand why there are differences in advancement and delays in various countries.

[5] Berthe Ameillon, *La Guinée, Bilan d'une independence,* Paris, 1964, pp. 176–7; author's translation.
* Cardinal Rugambwa, Bishop of Bukoba (Tanzania), created in 1960.

> While always urging its faithful to assume their full civic duties, the Church has received its mission to lead and to teach from God, from an eternal truth, not merely from one useful for the time being.[6]

For three days after the Archbishop's pastoral letter was read from the pulpit, no word was heard from the government or the PDG. But their silence did not signify acquiescence. The Archbishop's words were regarded as virtual sedition by the more radical members of the Party. And on April 23, 1961, the Party's fury roared down on the Church in full force. On that day, over Radio Conakry's *Voix de la Révolution*, Sékou Touré launched a vitriolic attack upon the Archbishop. Ignoring the Archbishop's ecclesiastical title, Touré sneeringly referred to him as "Monsieur de Milleville," and warned that he would face expulsion from Guinea if he did not retract his statements.

The following day, August 24, Archbishop de Milleville requested an audience with Touré to clarify his remarks. When Touré refused to receive him, the Archbishop sent the President a letter in whch he explained his stand:

> There is no doubt that I oppose the abolition of the Catholic schools. However, I did not say that the Church would not submit to this measure, nor that it felt it had a right to impose its will on the State.[7]

The Church's role in education, de Milleville continued, had been an aid to the state. He stressed that this aid had never been given with the idea of making of the Church a state within a state:

> If I explained to the faithful that the Church was, and would remain, independent of temporal power, it was to make them understand that a State cannot impose a national character on a religious institution—be it Islam or Christianity. The Church respects the State and constantly urges its communicants to fulfill all of their obligations toward it. Inasmuch as the Church recognizes all of the rights of the State in the civil domain, it, in turn, asks the State to recognize the Church's authority in the religious domain. The citizen looks to the State for his civic duties; and to the Church as a believer. I am too attached to Guinea to be at the origin of a spirit of revolt. I desire only that there be good relations established between Church and State so that they may continue to work together for the good of the country.[8]

Although Touré received the Archbishop's letter, neither he nor any of his ministers consented to receive the prelate in person to let

[6] *Ibid.*
[7] *Le Monde,* September 1, 1961.
[8] *Le Monde,* August 29, 1961.

him explain his position. Instead, on the afternoon of April 26, officials of the Guinean *sûreté* called on the Archbishop and politely but firmly suggested that he prepare to depart on the evening plane for Dakar. De Milleville replied that he could not leave his post without an order from the Vatican. At five o'clock that evening, the *sûreté* men appeared once more at the Archbishop's residence, this time stating that they had orders to escort the Archbishop to the airport where he would be put on the plane bound for Dakar.

Realizing that resistance would be futile, the Archbishop let himself be escorted to the airport. Several hours later he disembarked at Dakar where he was met by Monseigneur Maury, Apostolic Delegate to West Africa.

In a statement to the press in Dakar the following day, de Milleville said:

> I was expelled for having protested against several conclusions reached by the PDG conference concerning the Church, notably those regarding the nationalization of the Catholic schools and especially those concerning the imposition of a national character on all religious organizations in Guinea.[9]

On August 28, 1961, before a meeting of the Central Committee of the PDG, Touré expounded further on what he meant by nationalization of the Church in Guinea:

> Henceforward no official of the Catholic Church will be accredited to us if he is not an African. Let him come from any African state they may wish, for it is not an issue of racism that we wish to provoke.[10]

Touré insinuated that the Catholic clergy in the country, like the Archbishop, were out to drive a wedge between the Government and the people:

> Yesterday, again, in his sermon, a priest told his communicants to attend in large numbers the mass to be held on Friday because at this mass "We are going to bless the Archbishop and curse his adversaries." [11]

Touré warned Guinean Catholics to weigh their actions: "Militants of the PDG will not fail to note those who attend the mass on Friday to curse the country." [12]

[9] *Ibid.*
[10] *Le Monde,* August 30, 1961.
[11] *Ibid.*
[12] *Ibid.*

On August 29, 1961, Monseigneur Maury, the Apostolic Delegate to West Africa, flew to Conakry and met with Touré. Also present at this meeting were Diallo Saifoulaye, President of the Guinean National Assembly, and the Ministers of National Defense, Interior, Education and Foreign Affairs. No communiqué of any sort was issued after this meeting by either side. From what followed, however, it was soon clear that Touré had succeeded in intimidating the Church.

Many Catholics confidently expected that, at a meeting in Dakar on October 6, 1961, of the Catholic bishops of West Africa, the bishops would demonstrate their solidarity with Monseigneur de Milleville by rallying to his side and condemning outright the action of the Guinean Government.

The bishops did no such thing. They adopted the much more prudent course of issuing a vague, platitudinous statement imploring "that God permit the Church in Guinea, in new found serenity, to continue without restraint, its work of peace and evangelization." [13] Eight months later Monseigneur Raymond Tchidimbo, a native Guinean, was named Archbishop of Conakry. Monseigneur de Milleville offered his services to the Archbishop of Fortaleza in a remote part of Brazil where there is an acute shortage of priests.

The appointment of Monseigneur Tchidimbo as Archbishop of Conakry was an important test case of how well the Church could fare under a totalitarian regime supposedly bent on its destruction. The new Archbishop was well equipped to conduct this test. Not only was he a native Guinean and a personal friend of President Touré, but he was reputed to be a fervent nationalist. During the colonial era he had spoken out against social injustice and openly consorted with known nationalist elements.

Catholics in Africa and abroad wondered, therefore, how Touré would greet the Tchidimbo appointment, and how the native prelate would acquit himself of his new responsibilities. The very existence of the Catholic Church in Guinea might well depend on the outcome. Both questions were soon answered.

On being informed of Tchidimbo's elevation to the See of Conakry, the Guinean Government immediately expressed to the Vatican its approval and gratitude. For the Archbishop's enthronment on May 31, 1962, the Political Bureau of the PDG put several villas and a fleet of official cars at the Archbishop's disposal to accommodate the religious and civil dignitaries who came from throughout Africa and Europe for the occasion. The administrative region of Conakry was granted an official holiday (with pay) so that its residents could attend the

[13] "L'épiscopat d'Afrique Occidentale tire la leçon de l'expulsion de l'archévêque de Conakry," Le Monde, October 8, 1961.

consecration at the cathedral and ceremonies in other parts of the city. High government officials, including several members of the President's cabinet and the Political Bureau, were in the cathedral, and the President himself gave a reception for the new Archbishop afterward.

In a speech delivered after the consecration, Touré expressed his satisfaction at seeing a fellow Guinean heading the Catholic Church in his country:

It is particularly agreeable for us at this time to express to the Holy See the gratitude of Guinean Catholics for fulfilling their hopes not only in proceeding to Africanize the Catholic Church in Guinea, but in engaging in a wide Africanization of the upper clergy in Africa.

Africa wishes in the political, economic, cultural and spiritual realms, in exercising freely and conscientiously its historic responsibilities, to rehabilitate itself by proving that its peoples are as capable as other peoples of assuring the universal extension of their technical, intellectual and moral values.

The management of African affairs should revert totally to Africans themselves; such has been, and such remains, one of the principles of our Party. This principle merely expresses the legitimate and unanimous demand of conscientious people of our continent which is engaged in the process of achieving total decolonialization.

Hence our satisfaction at seeing the Guinean Church directed by a son of Africa is founded on the knowledge of the intimate harmony that henceforth will exist between the individual expression of religious faith and the collective exigencies of the revolutionary combat which our people are courageously fighting to acquire the material and moral conditions for their dignity and human liberty, without which there can be no justice, peace, or general happiness.

Today, more than yesterday, we have the profound conviction that the Catholic Church of Guinea will contribute greatly to building up a prosperous and happy nation within which Guineans of all faiths will commune . . .

As the Church, which is the house of the believer, symbolizes the spiritual unity of the faithful, so the nation, which is at once the house of the people and the field of action of the State, symbolizes the political unity of the people and the regime which they have chosen. Thus, as according to the Epistle of St. Paul "priests are the servants of the believer," so ministers of the Guinean state are the faithful servants of the people.

We are thus completely satisfied to see the keys of the house of Christianity in Guinea entrusted to the hands of a son of our people because the unity of Guinean Catholics can only enrich the unity of the nation in consolidating the communal house of the people.[14]

For his part, Archbishop Tchidimbo made it clear that he desired to work for a rapprochement of Church and state in Guinea:

> I hope not only for a normalization of the relations between Church and State, but for a close collaboration progressively beneficial to the future of the Guinean nation. This nation has been called upon not to disappear, but to live, as we had the opportunity of affirming in this cathedral in November 1958 . . .[15]

The appointment of a Guinean Archbishop of Conakry has unquestionably helped to ease tensions between the Catholic Church and the government. Since Tchidimbo's enthronement, few reports have been heard of persecution of Roman Catholic clergy in Guinea.

Yet it would be a mistake to infer from the present *détente* that Church and state have resolved all of their problems. The truth of the matter is that the controversy that once pitted the all-powerful state against a weak mission Church—control of the latter's schools—was resolved unilaterally by the Guinean government. The schools were simply nationalized and the Church, realizing that it could mount no effective opposition, bowed to the inevitable.

The Church in Guinea has survived under Sékou Touré's totalitarian regime by forfeiting its voice, its freedom to form youth groups, to organize labor unions, or to publish newspapers. All of these functions are now under the exclusive control of the Government. African Church leaders are no more willing to speak out against arbitrary acts of the Guinean government than their French predecessors were to criticize similarly high-handed acts of the French colonial regime.

In Guinea, the Catholic Church is now confined to the exercise of a purely spiritual mission, centered largely on the administration of its sacraments. Undoubtedly, it aspires to resume its activity in educational, social, and charitable enterprises, but its leaders are well aware that the Church must lie low for the present. Following this policy, it has been spared the wrath of a government which is merciless toward those who oppose it. At least Catholic leaders can congratulate themselves that the regime has not embarked on a campaign to vilify the Church, stigmatizing it in the minds of the people as a traitorous, counterrevolutionary element. If the tide of opposition now rising

[14] "Declaration de M. Sékou Touré pour le Sacre de Mgr. Tchidimbo," *Afrique Nouvelle*, Dakar, No. 774, June 7–13, 1962.
[15] "Le vrai visage de Mgr. Raymond Tchidimbo, Archévêque de Conakry," *Bingo*, Dakar, October, 1962.

against Sékou Touré should erode the foundations of his power sufficiently to bring down his regime, replacing it with one not committed to suffocating non-government initiative, the Church may then find itself in a position to reassert its independence and amplify its field of action. Its present subservience may be the guarantee of its preservation.

CHURCH AND STATE IN CONGO-BRAZZAVILLE

Equally interesting has been the development of Church-state relations in Congo-Brazzaville (ex-French Congo). This country of 800,000, across the swirling Congo River from the larger, richer, and better known Congo-Kinshasa (ex-Belgian Congo), achieved its independence in 1960.

Congo-Brazzaville had the distinction of being the only state in Africa governed by a priest of the Roman Catholic Church. Its first President was a "non-functioning" priest, Abbé Fulbert Youlou, a member of the Lari tribe, a branch of the Bacongo.[16]

In April, 1963, President Youlou decided that the time had come to strengthen his position by merging the nation's three political parties into one. The leaders of the three parties agreed to his plan and voted for the new measure. August 15, 1963, was set as the target date for effecting the reform.

As that date approached, however, tension mounted in the capital, Brazzaville. Several trade union leaders, fearing that the consolidation of the country's three major parties would be followed by an attempt to force a merger of its three principal labor unions, thereby severely limiting their own freedom of action, spoke out against the plan. The President immediately had them arrested and held in the city's central prison.

This high-handed action sparked widespread disorders throughout Brazzaville. Thousands of unemployed youths surged through the streets brandishing placards denouncing corruption in government and demanding the President's removal. Thoroughly alarmed by this turn of events, Youlou hastily broadcast an indefinite postponement of his plans for a one-party system. He also promised a thorough housecleaning of the government and the institution of widespread social

[16] Youlou's refusal in 1955 to give up a career in politics led to his suspension by the Archbishop of Brazzaville, a Frenchman. His defiance of the Archbishop did not, it appears, jeopardize his relations with the Vatican. He was never excommunicated. On his election to the Presidency in 1959, he even received a congratulatory message from Pope John XXIII. See *Le Monde*, August 13, 1963.

and economic reforms. As a further bit of insurance, he put through an urgent telephone call to General de Gaulle at Colombey-les-Deux-Eglises, pleading with him to order the 3,000 French soldiers stationed in his country to intervene on his behalf. De Gaulle refused, taking the position that, as long as the lives of the 8,000 Europeans in the country were not endangered, Youlou's plight was a purely internal affair to be settled by the Congolese themselves.[17]

Time had run out for Youlou. The frenzied mob tore down the street signs bearing the President's name, stormed the Brazzaville jail, and liberated 400 persons interned there—ordinary criminals as well as political prisoners.

It was soon clear to everyone in Brazzaville, including the President himself, that the people were overwhelmingly against him. Confronted by an excited mob whose fury could be appeased only by his removal from office, Youlou submitted his resignation and was hustled away by soldiers to a nearby military camp which, ironically, bore his name. The army assumed power, pending the organization of a provisional government.

When the composition of that government was announced a few hours later, it included neither the labor union leaders who had sparked the revolution against Youlou, nor the military who had seized control of it. Instead, the government was made up of a group of "technocrats," young civil servants and recent graduates of French universities. Heading the government was Alphonse Massemba-Débat, 42, a former schoolteacher who had given up his career to enter politics and had risen to several important posts, including those of president of the National Assembly and Minister of Development. Massemba-Débat was considered by most people to be a moderate leftist.

After Youlou's overthrow, the provisional government initiated an inquiry into the ex-President's financial affairs. Evidence was uncovered that Youlou had committed malfeasance including the appropriation of government funds for his own use. Among other things, it was alleged that the President had built for his mother a sumptuous commercial hotel at a cost of $625,000 in public funds, had deposited some $120,000 in a personal account abroad, and even had had his cassocks specially fashioned in Paris by Christian Dior.

To discredit the ex-President further, the new regime also directed

---

[17] According to an Associated Press dispatch at the time, Youlou, furious at de Gaulle's refusal to use French troops to rescue him, broke off their conversation. Later, after he had realized that further resistance to the mob would be futile, Youlou is reported to have called de Gaulle a second time on the telephone and to have said to him, "Mon général, I have resigned." *Le Monde*, August 17, 1963.

attention to his unexemplary comportment as a priest. Attention was drawn to the fact that Youlou, ignoring his vow of priestly celibacy, had taken a wife, sired children, and kept a mistress. Some reports had it that he also made a practice of blessing the ball-point pens of school children to assure them high marks on examinations.

Such revelations astounded the country and discredited not only the Abbé but the Roman Catholic Church as well. The Church's good name had been impugned by Youlou's conduct. The masses were largely unwilling to make a distinction between Youlou as head of state and Youlou as a priest. However such was not true of the elite, many of whom were Roman Catholics themselves. The ensuing scandal was kept from assuming greater proportions only by the fact that Congo-Brazzaville's Catholics were understandably reluctant to make a *cause célèbre* of what they preferred to regard as an *affaire de famille*.

The revolution against Youlou had been fought "to overthrow tyranny and restore social justice." Its immediate aim had been to prevent the disappearance of the multi-party system. Those who had represented themselves as supporters of the revolution, and who had taken advantage of the confusion and chaos it engendered to vault themselves into power, were among the first to betray its aims.

Soon after the overthrow of Fulbert Youlou, Massemba-Débat, Provisional President, ordered the dissolution of all existing political parties. All citizens of the republic were to be grouped henceforth into a new political party, the *Mouvement National de la Révolution* (MNR).

Notwithstanding this dramatic reversal of one of the revolution's aims, the first impressions which the MNR made on the outside world were favorable. Its leaders were regarded as moderate leftists who wished only to see social justice for all and an end to corruption in government. The MNR's pledges of honesty, austerity, and reform were accepted as sincere. The fact that an overwhelming majority of the Congolese people seemed to have implicit faith in the new party enhanced its public image.

Very soon, however, cracks began to appear in this image. As the government of Massemba-Débat consolidated its position, it became increasingly totalitarian. In the process of repudiating the preceding regime, the MNR repudiated also the freedoms which Youlou had tolerated. Civil liberties, such as free speech, the right to travel about, and the individual's privilege to decide for himself whether he would participate in political life, disappeared. Under the MNR, criticism of the regime became tantamount to treason. Congolese now had to get permission from local administrative officials in order to move about the country and from the foreign ministry if they wished to travel abroad. No longer were persons allowed to remain aloof from the country's political life if they so wished. Everyone was obliged to join the MNR and to place himself entirely at its disposition. The supremacy of the party over the government was written into law.

With the opposition parties now neutralized, the MNR moved to subdue the one institution that still exercised some influence over the masses—the Roman Catholic Church. The more radical elements in the MNR saw the Church as one of the principal foes of the revolution. The fact that the head of the Church in Congo-Brazzaville was an African, and not a European, made no difference. The Archbishop of Brazzaville was still regarded as an enemy of the regime, an agent of neocolonialism, and an obstacle to the successful fulfillment of the revolution's hopes.

The Church's influence in the Congo emanated in large measure from the labor union and the newspaper it controlled. The union, the *Confédération Africaine des Travailleurs Croyants* (CATC), represented roughly 41 per cent of the nation's work force. Its newspaper, *La Semaine Africaine*, was one of the most respected journals in French-speaking Black Africa. The leaders of the MNR feared that so long as these two existed, they themselves would never have a free rein to do as they wished. They therefore set about to destroy both union and paper.

Under the pretext of instituting "scientific socialism," a vague, catch-all slogan whose meaning Brazzaville's leaders claimed to understand but which they never bothered to define, the MNR proceeded to harass the Church, and especially to intimidate the CATC and *La Semaine Africaine*.

On November 23, 1964, Fulgence Mvila Biyaoula, president of the CATC, was arrested and tortured. To forestall possible criticism in Parliament of Monsieur Biyaoula's arrest and maltreatment, the National Assembly, on the next day (November 24) voted to lift the immunity of certain deputies who had been closely associated with the Catholic labor union, thus leaving them vulnerable to charges of treason should they protest the action.

That same day a gang of hoodlums, members of the youth wing of the MNR, broke into the CATC union headquarters in Pointe Noire, the Congo's second city, and left the place a shambles.

On November 25, 1964, Abbé Louis Badila, the Congolese editor of *La Semaine Africaine*, was arrested. Like Biyaoula, he was also subjected to torture. Abbé Badila was charged with the crime of publishing in his newspaper a letter he had written to President Massemba-Débat criticizing the excesses committed by the MNR youth.

Two days later (November 27), a French priest, Abbé René Larre, was arrested and tortured. On November 29, Larre, another French priest, Abbé Lemaire, and three Frenchwomen active in Catholic welfare work were expelled from the country. On their arrival in Paris, Father Lemaire was quoted as saying that the government of Congo-Brazzaville "more and more is following a communist policy." [18]

On December 21, 1964, the government formally abolished all independent labor unions, including the Catholic CATC. In their place was established a single national labor organization, the *Confédération Syndicale Congolaise* (CSC). The organization of Catholic laymen, *Action Catholique*, was ordered to disband. Henceforward, the only legal youth organizations were the MNR's militant *Jeunesse du Mouvement National de la Révolution* (JMNR), spearheaded by gangs of unemployed, pistol-carrying young thugs, and the *Association des Étudiants Congolais* (AEC), a group of radical high school and university students.

President Massemba-Débat, in an effort to assuage the widespread criticism that followed these actions, issued a statement claiming that his regime was neutral toward the Roman Catholic Church. He denied that the Church or any other religious denomination was being persecuted in the Congo.

But efforts by his government to conceal the persecution of the Roman Catholic clergy were constantly frustrated by the widespread publicity given them by the large number of Catholics who fled Brazzaville shortly after the overthrow of President Fulbert Youlou and who lived in exile across the Congo River in Leopoldville. Through friends and relatives still living on the other side of the river, the exiles were kept informed of the terrorism that was beginning to grip Brazzaville. Through their contacts with influential groups in Leopoldville and pro-Catholic newspapers in that city such as the non-government *Courrier d'Afrique* and *Vérités sur le Congo*, published by the exiles themselves, the outside world learned what was happening. Moishe Tshombe, whom the Brazzaville leaders hated, was at the time Premier of Congo-Leopoldville. Tshombe saw to it that the Brazzaville government's persecution of the Catholics was broadcast to the outside world by Radio Leopoldville. Both the Catholic and non-Catholic press in other parts of Africa and in Europe took up the issue, making certain that the Brazzaville regime's harsh intolerance brought it much discredit.

Despite or perhaps because of Catholic opposition to its policies, the Brazzaville government sought to diminish further the Church's influence on the nation. In August, 1965, it nationalized the Catholic

[18] *Le Monde*, November 30, 1964.

schools and passed a law forbidding the teaching of catechism after October 1st. The law, though not unexpected, provoked the departure of forty of the hundred Roman Catholic missionary teachers, most of whom were nuns. They announced that others would soon follow.

Repeated clashes such as these brought the Roman Catholic Church and the government of the Congo-Brazzaville to logger-heads. The Church, feeling a keen sense of responsibility toward its communicants, refused to bow before the ruthlessness of the new regime. Fearlessly, perhaps imprudently, its leaders spoke out against the numerous injustices perpetrated by party workers in the name of an experiment in "scientific socialism," whose tenets churchmen rejected and whose methods they deplored.

But more than mere outrage against injustice was involved. The Church's leaders resented the government's efforts to circumscribe their influence in the country by forbidding the Church to have youth groups, by disbanding the labor unions it sponsored, and by nationalizing its schools. These leaders showed themselves unwilling or unable to adjust to the demands of the August revolution. By opposing these demands and openly and persistently resisting the adjustments which they implied, churchmen brought down upon themselves the full wrath of the government and seriously endangered their own position.

In opposing the measures enacted by the MNR, Church leaders in Congo-Brazzaville found themselves at odds with Congolese public opinion. Most Congolese were overwhelmingly in favor of the revolution because it held out promise to them: the hope of jobs, an end to governmental corruption, and a regime in tune with their own intense nationalism. By resisting the decisions and methods of the MNR— decisions and methods which the people themselves were willing to accept—the Church leaders in Brazzaville put themselves in the position of seeming to oppose social progress. Rather than bide their time and let others, in a better position than they, oppose the MNR, the Church leaders took this task upon themselves. It was a battle which they could not win but which they nevertheless insisted on fighting.

The curious case of Fulbert Youlou had brought some discredit upon the Roman Catholic Church. But far more important in the eyes of the government was the fact that the pluralism implied by the very existence of the Church appeared to challenge the monolithic state which the MNR sought to build. The Church's schools, labor unions, youth groups, and press had given it an influence over the people far out of proportion to the number of its communicants.

Brazzaville's leaders saw the Church not in its constructive role as teacher and civilizer, but as an agent of foreign interests, insidiously spreading its influence over significant areas of social life. To them the Church was, if not an outright bastion of colonialism, at least an instrument of equally pernicious neocolonialism. The sympathy which its persecution elicited abroad put the Brazzaville government in a bad light. The government was angered by this circumstance and by the Church's scarcely veiled opposition to the growing influence of Communist embassies in Brazzaville, especially the Chinese. The government had quickly established ties with the Communist nations and delighted in charging the Church with interference in affairs of state.

The inability of the clergy to assess correctly, or to be cowed by, the odds against them, their unwillingness to make peace with the civil authorities and adjust to the new revolutionary conditions under which they now had to live, contributed to the dwindling influence of the Roman Catholic Church in Congo-Brazzaville. Certainly unintentionally, perhaps unavoidably, the Church had come to be regarded, rightly or wrongly, as an obstacle to progress and social development. The Congolese Catholic Church will have to struggle against this handicap for years to come.

CHURCH AND STATE IN THE IVORY COAST

Of the Ivory Coast's population of three and a half million, about 325,000 are Christian (250,000 Catholic, 75,000 Protestant), and 750,000 are Muslim, and the remainder are pagan. The President, Félix Houphouet-Boigny, is Catholic, as is a majority of the ruling elite. The Church is headed by an Ivoirien, Monseigneur Bernard Yago, who was enthroned in 1961 as Archbishop of Abidjan.

In the Ivory Coast, the Roman Catholic Church has enjoyed a comparatively trouble-free development. The principal reason for this happy state of affairs is that those who govern the Ivory Coast have not felt themselves personally threatened by the Church. The Church has remained studiously non-political, a policy which has paid rich dividends.

Under Archbishop Yago's forceful leadership, the clergy (who now include fifty-one African priests) have developed into a dynamic and independent body. The liberal disposition of President Houphouet-Boigny and the pluralistic society which he has encouraged have created a climate in the Ivory Coast which is favorable to the Church's growth. The Catholic Church has been allowed to retain control of its schools and its own youth group, privileges it had to forfeit in Guinea and in Congo-Brazzaville.

In Guinea and in the Congo, the Church was unable to take an active, vigorous part in the construction of the nation because its motives were suspect. But in the Ivory Coast the Church enjoys the confidence both of the President and of his government. On many social projects, Catholics, Protestants, Muslims, and pagans alike work hand-in-hand for the common good. This experience in cooperation has contributed enormously to building a sense of fraternity among the country's different religious groups and to enhancing their sense of national consciousness. President Houphouet has encouraged these feelings by arranging periodic meetings of spokesmen for the various religious communities. On important occasions such as official holidays, visits of foreign dignitaries, or moments of national crisis, the President always make it a point to call these leaders together to solicit their counsel, and to ask that they mobilize support for his policies among their correligionists. Thus, in the Ivory Coast, the Church is not regarded as an opponent of the national consensus, but as a part of it.

Working closely with local authorities, the Church has helped the government execute various social programs. It has thrown its weight behind such government-sponsored reforms as a new civil code, the abolition of polygamy and the bride price, the outlawing of scarification practices, the raising of the marriage age, the adoption of dissimilar first names by the citizenry, and the registration of births and deaths. The Church authorities also have helped government officials cope with social problems such as juvenile delinquency, prostitution, dope addiction, and alcoholism. Through the *Institut Africain pour le Développement Economique et Social* (IADES), Jesuit experts in social and economic problems help train civil administrators who desire to specialize in problems of national planning.

The strength of the Christian community in the Ivory Coast today is due in part to the absence of conflict between its own beliefs and those of the regime in power. But it derives also from the strongly bourgeois nature of Ivoirien society itself. The Ivory Coast is one of the few countries in Africa where those who rule have deliberately set out to create a middle-class society patterned after that of Western Europe. Because of the country's great natural wealth and the extraordinarily efficient administration it has had since independence, this attempt to convert a tribal, subsistence-level society into a modern nation of middle-class families has met with some success.

Per capita income in the Ivory Coast in 1966 was $180 (nearly that of Portugal, which is $200).[19] Some 250,000 Ivoirien families enjoyed

[19] These statistics concerning the Ivory Coast were taken from an annual report (unclassified) prepared by Mr. David Gelsenleiter for the U.S. Embassy in Abidjan in June, 1966.

74

a revenue of at least $500 per year. Assuming that the average Ivoirien family has six persons (a conservative estimate), this means that approximately 1,500,000 (or about 40 per cent of the total population) enjoy a substantial revenue. The source of this wealth is mainly coffee and cocoa, the country's two principal exports, 90 per cent of which is produced by Ivoirien planters.[20] The income of Ivoirien families has risen steadily since independence. Continued diversification of agriculture and the establishment of new industries in the years ahead will guarantee the continuation of this upward trend. So wide a distribution of the national wealth is laying the economic basis for the middle-class society which Houphouet wishes to develop in the Ivory Coast.

The Church, meanwhile, is laying the moral basis. By converting more and more persons to Christianity, educating their children in Church schools, enrolling them in Church-sponsored activities, persuading them to change from old ways to a more Christian or *évolué* way of life (in the Ivory Coast the two terms are synonymous), and by steadily supporting the government's reforms, the Church is contributing to the stabilization and Westernization of indigenous society.

There is a substantial measure of agreement between Church and state in the Ivory Coast as to the goals toward which the nation should strive. Thus the Church, far from being an impediment to social change and modernization, is one of its most efficacious agents.

If a serious conflict existed between civil and ecclesiastical authorities like those plaguing Church and state in Guinea or Congo-Brazzaville, the Church in the Ivory Coast could not be of this important assistance in nation-building. But so far such conflicts have been avoided. Civil authorities in the Ivory Coast are aware of the tremendous contribution which the Church is making to national tranquility and development. They have studiously avoided, therefore, putting the Church's leaders in a position where they would have to compromise their principles. No attempt has been made to force the clergy to become party activitists. And the clergy, for its part, conscious of the freedoms it enjoys in the Ivory Coast, has not sought to challenge the ruling party or the government in the exercise of prerogatives which it recognizes as properly theirs.

CONCLUSIONS

As the example of Congo-Brazzaville suggests, African leaders are mistaken if they think that the Africanization of the clergy necessarily

[20] The remaining 10 per cent is produced by French planters in the Ivory Coast.

will render the Church more submissive. Experience has shown that African prelates will consider their first responsibility to be to their Church rather than to the state.

Even if the Church might wish to do so, it would be difficult for it to emulate the state's revolutionary stance. However worthy may be the goals toward which revolutionary regimes strive (social justice, decent living standards and education for all, etc.), the methods which they often employ to achieve them (repression, intimidation, deprivation of civil liberties) are in conflict with fundamental Christian principles.

In neither Guinea nor the Congo-Brazzaville was the Church able to cope with the new problems thrust upon it by the political and social revolution which occurred in those countries. The revolution provided the people of these nations with a vision of a new and better society far more glittering than any which the Church could or dared to offer. It was this ideological promise more than anything else that enabled political revolution to triumph over the Church.

Because the people believed so implicitly the promises of their new revolutionary leaders, that great discipline and self-sacrifice were necessary to achieve the new society, they allowed themselves not only to be deprived of their civil liberties, but to be forced into functional roles different from, and, in some cases, opposed to, those which they had before. One had above all to be a revolutionary. Whereas previously to be a Christian gave one an enviable status in society, to be a practicing Catholic now was no longer an asset but a liability.

Another reason the revolution won out over the Church was that its champions were able to create a rapport with and to activate social elements within that group with which the Church had never been able to establish a meaningful contact: the thousands of jobless and desperate youths for whom life seemed to hold little hope. Not only did the revolution promise these young people a better life in the not-too-distant future but, in the meantime, it gave them a sense of participation in the destiny of their nation by bringing them into the youth wing of the Party, giving them weapons, and investing them with authority to act as social vigilantes and "guardians of the revolution." Thus, for these people—Africa's *descamisados*—the revolution became an intensely personal thing. They were caught up in its fervor; they had faith in its goals; on its outcome their own future seemed to hang. The revolution gave a new meaning, direction, and cohesion to national society which neither the Church nor the previous government had been able to provide. Both Sékou Touré of Guinea and Massemba-Débat of Congo-Brazzaville promised their people innovation. Not the least of the appeals of the brands of "scientific socialism" which they propounded was the promise to bring about the complete transformation and modernization of society, a goal whose realization they accused the Church of impeding.

To bring about this transformation and to hasten the pace of modernization, new social structures have been created, fashioned in keeping with what are felt to be revolutionary requirements. The extension of party dominance over virtually every aspect of social behavior has given to the one-party systems which rule these countries militancy, fervor, and cohesion—the hallmarks of a new faith, and one surpassing by far the appeals of the established churches. The attachment to this militant political faith may prove to be ephemeral, lasting only so long as the regimes which have imposed it. But it is significant that it is this political faith and not the old affiliations to the Christian church that provide the major impetus for social change and modernization in these African societies.

If the conflict between Church and state has been more violent in Congo-Brazzaville than in Guinea, it is in large measure because it has been more difficult in the former country to separate the temporal from the ecclesiastical. The Catholic Church in the Congo, for better or for worse, had over the years extended its influence to areas (education, labor unions, the press) which the state felt should be its own. The state attempted to reclaim these domains because it considered control of them a requisite for its program of social transformation and modernization. When the Church resisted these efforts, conflict was bound to occur.

Both in Guinea and in Congo-Brazzaville, the Catholic Church was scrutinized and judged by the local leaders in terms of how well it fitted into the *revolutionary* scheme of things. In both countries the conclusion was the same: that the Church could not (or would not) adjust to the revolutionary environment pervading the country; moreover, it was felt that the Church would actively seek to oppose it. The inability or the unwillingness of the Church to accept the revolutionary regime doomed it to persecution in both countries.

It is evident that the choices open to the Church under a revolutionary regime in Africa are essentially two. They are illustrated by the examples of Guinea and the Congo-Brazzaville. The Church can work at achieving a sort of *modus vivendi* with civil authorities, confining its activities to purely spiritual functions which do not risk giving offense (the administration of the sacraments); or the Church can resolutely oppose the government, attempting to mobilize the collective force of its communicants. The first choice may seem to involve a compromise of moral principles, but allows survival; the second choice honors principle, but incurs hardship and perhaps risks even death.

77

Yet the conflict between Church and state in Africa does not arise from a disparity of goals. It arises from a conflicting view of how those goals are to be achieved. The essentially hierarchical nature of the Church itself also creates tension; the government looks upon it as threatening to become a state within a state. In tribally fragmented, predominantly pagan, and economically backward countries where such strands of unity as exist are still very fragile, the government fears that the development of a strongly institutionalized Church may jeopardize the still precarious structure of the nation in the making.

The future of the Catholic Church in the recently independent states of Black Africa may well be decided on the issue of how much self-restraint the Church will exercise. Will it refrain from insisting on Catholic-sponsored but non-religious institutions such as labor unions, youth groups, newspapers, etc., whose influence arouses the fears of civil authorities? If it is to survive and prosper, the Church must content itself with being an important, but only one, institution among many in the new society.

The Church in Black Africa, as elsewhere, does not feel that the solution of pressing social problems or the betterment of human living conditions are, or should be, the exclusive concern of government. It conceives that its mission includes a social as well as a spiritual aposto-late. And it is in the exercise of this social apostolate that the Church most often comes into conflict with African civil authorities. Such conflict usually ensues when the Church's conception of its social apostolate is at variance with the Government's idea of the activity proper to the Church. If, however, there is no conflict of views (as is the case in the Ivory Coast), the Church is generally granted freedom of action. But when there is disagreement, it is the state's view, not the Church's, that prevails.

Throughout most of French-influenced Black Africa, the Catholic Church conducts a social apostolate which meets with the approval of government authorities. In large measure this is due to the fact that the men in power still represent the older nationalist generation, and are fairly well disposed toward the Church and its practices. Such sympathy does not, however, characterize the new generation of revolutionary leaders, such as Massemba-Débat, who have come to power in certain states.

The implication for the future, at least in the revolutionary states, is that the Church very probably will be denied the right to exercise any social apostolate whatever. This may be basically because the younger generation of revolutionary leaders tends to think that the myriad activities which have made up the social apostolate are privileges which the Church has received from over-indulgent governments blind to the

78

danger inherent in a small state's toleration of a monolithic institution. If events do so transpire, the Church must be satisfied with performing a purely spiritual function and renounce her charitable and social mission. Whether the Catholic Church will be satisfied with such a role, so different from that which it has played for many centuries, is still a moot question. A revolution, to be successful, may demand the establishment of organizations and patterns of social behavior anti-thetical to the Church and capable of wresting from it social functions which may seem to be more properly the domain of secular rather than ecclesiastical authorities. But the crucial question, as yet un-resolved in French-speaking Black Africa, is whether the process of modernization necessarily requires it.

3.

CATHOLICISM AND DEVELOPMENT:
THE CATHOLIC LEFT IN BRAZIL

BY THOMAS G. SANDERS
Brown University

The most obvious expression of a religious system is as institutional structure. Embodied in persons who serve as authorities, symbols, or representatives, the institution helps maintain order and consistency in the religion. The characteristic marks of religious institutions are that they serve the ends of formalization in place of spontaneity, and as vehicles of continuity for transmitting attitudes and activities to subsequent generations. Religious institutions may be simple and relatively unstructured, as in the case of consisting merely of a recognized group of interpreters of the religious tradition and obligations. On the other hand, they may be highly organized, bureaucratized, and centralized, as in Roman Catholicism. Even in societies where religion has been closely integrated with government, some separate organization always marks the religious dimension of the society.

Despite their drives toward conformity and rigid authority, religious institutions allow or cannot avoid a certain degree of freedom for their members. In the analysis of the relation of a religious group to modernization or any other problem, the position of the institution alone is not sufficient. One must take into consideration the diversities caused by the toleration of individual and group deviation, and recognize that the pressure exercised by the institution is only one of many pressures that the believer experiences. The institution has commitments and responsibilities not only to maintain traditions and sources of income, but to preserve communication with all of its members of whatever political and social beliefs. This institutional tendency is put under greatest

81

strain when it is tested by wide political disagreement among elite members of its own adherents.

The "Catholic Left," with which this paper will deal, was an elitist movement within the divided Brazilian Church that responded in a serious and radical way to pressures within society for economic development and social change. Little known outside Brazil and considered subversive by the present government, it has been treated in a uniformly unsympathetic manner by those who have written about it.[1] The "Catholic Left" should, however, be examined for its positive significance, inasmuch as it constituted an attempt within the framework of a conservative, underdeveloped society and a church closely tied up with dominant elements in that society to become engaged in non-conventional terms with forces like industrialization, modernization, nationalism, and Marxism.

Christian Democracy is usually assumed to be the only Catholic political program of modernization in Latin America, but in Brazil the groups that promoted it elsewhere—intellectuals, students, and younger clergy—gradually came to reject what they understood by Christian Democracy. They formed a vigorous pressure and action group before 1964, and some of their attitudes may suggest an alternative Catholic strategy for countries of Catholic predominance. If at the moment they seem to be a failure, an inescapable judgment in light of the Brazilian political transition of 1964, it can best be ascribed to their desire to change a society more than the power structure was willing to allow. On the other hand, it is most unlikely that eclipse is their final condition. An entire generation of Catholic leadership was trained in the outlook of the "Left," and they may be expected to assert themselves again when times are more propitious.

A few of the assumptions of the "Catholic Left" will indicate their distinctiveness in the Latin American context.

(1) Brazilian Catholics of the Left took very seriously the empirical secularity of their society—that large segments of the population were estranged from the Church, while others, though nominally fulfilling its obligations, were relatively uninfluenced by its teachings. Given this secularism, they came to reject the fundamental temptation of Latin American Catholicism, to assume that it has the answers to the region's underdevelopment in a "Christian" program. Divided and pluralistic in its operative religious and ethical perspectives, Brazil could not pre-

[1] Manoel Cardozo, "The Brazilian Church and the New Left," *Journal of Inter-American Studies,* Vol. VI, July, 1964, pp. 313–21; Leonard D. Therry, "Dominant Power Components in the Brazilian University Student Movement Prior to April, 1964," *Journal of Inter-American Studies,* Vol. VII, January, 1965, pp. 27–48; Eustaquio Gallejones, S. J., *AP: Socialismo Brasileiro,* Rio de Janeiro: Centro de Informação Universitária, 1965.

sume the "Christian" consensus for making such a program work. In fact, the group most perceptive and decisive in interpreting and promoting development is the group most self-consciously removed from the life of the Church—the secular intellectuals critical of the existing situation and committed to secular (nationalist and socialist) solutions.

(2) The Catholic Left concluded that Catholics interested in modernization and the social changes necessary to achieve it should cooperate and participate with other groups interested in the same objectives. There is no such thing as a distinctively Catholic program of modernization. Rather, development is a secular goal that people pursue for different motives. Catholics can participate on a humanist platform with Marxists and other Leftists, because the proper ethical objective for Catholics is not a "new Christendom" but the promotion of human dignity and well-being. In a situation of political polarization such as Brazil underwent between 1960 and 1964, Catholics of the Left found themselves consistently siding out of conviction with nationalists and Marxists, defending governmental planning, an independent foreign policy, changes in the social structure, and a "front" centered on workers and peasants.

(3) They were receptive to ideological movements that emphasized modernization. Against vigorous opposition within the Church, they took a positive attitude initially toward "developmentism" and nationalism, then moved into a socialist and "revolutionary" stage. By 1963 many had subordinated nationalism to a concept of class struggle, because it was felt that nationalism lacked the power to motivate the masses.[2] In short, ideology was recognized as a necessary motivating force, but the relevance of an ideology—its motivating power—depended on the historical situation.

The most significant implication of this assumption, for a Catholic perspective, is the absorption of secular values and the rejection of more ostensibly "religious" answers. The Catholic Left reacted against the defense of "Western and Christian values" and the "Christian position" that is neither socialist nor capitalist associated with Christian Democracy, instead promoting a "new society" whose "subject is man" and whose end is "the community of persons in the transparency and solidarity of an authentically human world." Rather than developing a comprehensive political and social alternative, Catholics were

[2] "The failure of the so-called nationalist struggle and the impossibility of bringing to the masses a struggle which is not directly linked to their situation of class indicate clearly the necessity of a revolutionary strategy based on the concrete conditions of the Brazilian structure." *Ação Popular: Documento Base*, Goiania: Centro Popular de Cultura, 1963, p. 12.

urged to participate in an already unavoidable secular historical process: "Our option is placed and our action is oriented in the direction of the movement that marks the passage of history toward the structures of a socialist civilization." [3]

(4) The concern for modernization was accentuated by a conscious association of Brazil with the "Third World," whose nations shared the common characteristic of underdevelopment. Catholics of the Left supported the "independent" foreign policy of President Jânio Quadros, which was directed toward a position of leadership among the underdeveloped countries. The country's cultural ties with Portugal, traditionally emphasized in Catholic circles, were sharply questioned, the chief interest in Portugal coming to focus on a criticism of its colonialism in Africa. Despite the cultural heritage from Europe, Brazil's economic and social conditions set it off sharply from Europe. Cultural affinities could not obscure a more fundamental worldwide division between prosperous and poor nations in which cultural ties were used to justify a relation of dependence. Only by realizing this locus of Brazil in the world did the Catholic Left feel that the problems of modernization could be seriously analyzed.[4]

Many of the articulators of this position are in exile, though others continue to live in Brazil. They were not eccentrics, but the most able members of the younger generation in the Church. Most of the laity came from Catholic Action, the only genuine lay elite in the country; the clergy who helped promote it were that talented element who had studied in Europe; its hierarchical defenders included such outstanding prelates as Cardinal Motta, now retired but then in São Paulo, and Archbishop Helder Câmara of Recife, at that time secretary general of the Brazilian Conference of Bishops.

The origins of the Catholic Left may be traced to developments in the 1920s and 1930s. In the so-called "Catholic revival" of that period, a lay movement sprang up and expressed itself in liturgical piety, openness to thinkers like Maritain, theological deepening through instruction and discussion, and participation of the laity in social issues through Catholic Action. The concrete expression of the social interests of the Catholic revival ranged from "reactionary," as its leader in the twenties, Jackson de Figueiredo, described himself, to conservatively traditional in his successor, Alceu Amoroso Lima. Operating through the Centro Dom Vital and the journal *A Ordem*, the move-

---

[3] *Ibid.*, p. 8.
[4] An important example of the "Third World" emphasis related to development and nationalism may be found in Cândido Antônio Mendes de Almeida, *Nacionalismo e Desenvolvimento*, Rio de Janeiro: Instituto Brasileiro de Estudos Afro-Asiáticos, 1963, Chs. I–III.

ment prided itself on recapturing for the Church a segment of the intellectual community and promoting a Catholicism that was trying to speak to the problems of the time.

The major political and social activity of the movement was the Catholic Electoral League, a pressure group active especially in 1933 and 1934 and concerned with guaranteeing certain "rights" for the Church, defending "natural" social obligations like the indissolubility of marriage, and a range of economic and social proposals from the encyclicals of Popes Leo XIII and Pius XI. The stunning triumph of the League in having nearly all of its suggestions included in the Constitution of 1934 was to shape the thinking of the older generation of Catholics. Convinced that this type of moralistic program was the proper one for Catholic activity, they were deaf (with the exception of Amoroso Lima and a few others) to a later generation interested in nationalism, nationalization, and development.[5]

In spite of the irrelevance of its program for modernization, the Catholic Electoral League established a tradition in Brazil of opposition to the type of Catholic party common in other Latin countries. Many Catholics did in fact want a party, but Amoroso Lima and the leading prelate, Cardinal Sebastião Leme of Rio, discouraged its formation.

Other Catholics joined the Integralist (Fascist) movement of Plínio Salgado, which tried unsuccessfully for official Church support by adopting the complete program of the Catholic Electoral League. The appeal of Integralism to Brazil's Catholics needs reassessment. Now discredited because of its obvious anti-democratic tendencies and Nazi-like trappings, it nevertheless attracted many Catholics for the same reasons they would turn to Leftist solutions later: its nationalism, its interest in organizing and guaranteeing the rights of workers, its opposition to international capitalism.

The revitalization of Brazilian Catholicism through the Centro Dom Vital took two directions of significance for the future. One was the attraction to religious orders, especially the Dominicans and Benedictines, of mature candidates, usually from universities, whose intellectual qualities helped strengthen these traditionally weak groups. Second, Catholic Action was organized and formalized in 1935 according to the centralized, authoritarian, parish-based, and organic Italian pattern. The early development within this structure of specialized university and workers' elites promoted dissatisfaction, however, with the mediocrity of expectation within an organization embracing large numbers of people. By 1945 there was strong pressure for Catholic

[5] The development and program of the Catholic Electoral League have been described in detail in Alceu Amoroso Lima, *Indicações Políticas*, Rio de Janeiro: Civilização Brasileira, 1936.

Action along the so-called French pattern—specialized elites who would act in a disciplined and sophisticated manner within their occupational contexts. Meanwhile, the Dominicans had assumed a special vocation as advisers to Catholic Action in key parts of the country. French in orientation, the Brazilian Dominicans mediated the progressive "Continental" theology to the Catholic Action groups for which they were responsible.

The 1950s were fateful for Brazilian Catholicism. Its responses are explicable only in relation to what was going on in society, events to which the older Catholic moralistic generation had nothing to say. The more critical members of the younger generation discovered that Brazil was an underdeveloped and economically dependent country. Furthermore, they puzzled over the political events taking place around them: the suicide of Vargas, the pressures against the assumption of power by Kubitschek, and consistent support by middle-class Catholics for conservative candidates and parties whose programs emphasized administrative honesty, control of inflation, and continued illegality for the Communist party. The following developments of the 1950s should be cited.

(1) During World War II Brazilian industrialization, which had undergone earlier periods of selective growth, spurted, and throughout the fifties it had one of the highest growth rates in the world, with chief emphasis on producing goods that had traditionally been imported and paid for by exchange earned from the sale of agricultural products. Brazil changed during this decade from a backward producer of primary goods to a semi-industrialized society. Thoughtful Brazilians, despite the consistent inflation that beset the economy, could foresee for the first time the possibility of Brazil's becoming a developed nation. On the governmental level, exchange rates and inflation were consciously manipulated to channel capital into the hands of industrialists and for governmental investment in infrastructure. In the late fifties that most significant symbol of industrialization, an automobile industry, was firmly rooted.

(2) Nationalistic feeling intensified as a result of two developments. First was the Petrobrás controversy. From 1947 to 1953, Brazil divided over the question of whether oil deposits should be exploited by private or public groups. Nationalists seized on the motto, "The petroleum is ours," in a successful campaign leading to the establishment of a government monopoly on most aspects of oil production. The fact that foreign oil companies actively promoted their own interests tended to give the campaign a tone of conflict between Brazilian nationalism and external, capitalistic pressures. Second, in contrast with earlier periods when Brazilians had urged foreign investment for

development, various groups began to note the problems this mode of development entails: high profits, remission of profits, investment for immediate advantage rather than social utility, foreign control of key sectors of the economy. Brazil, they felt, continued to be dependent, despite its industrialization.

(3) The emergence of the proletariat. The Vargas dictatorship, recognizing the significance of industrial workers, promoted labor organizations—but consistent with its corporative and authoritarian outlook, did so basically to control and use them for its own purposes. With increased industrialization the unions expanded and assumed greater economic and political importance. It has been argued that a major factor in Vargas' downfall in 1945 came when he alienated the middle class (and the Army) by trying to establish his political base more strongly on the workers. In the postwar elections the Communist party emerged as a significant political factor, showing such strength among the industrial proletariat that shortly thereafter it was again outlawed.

Many Brazilians wanted to understand and interpret what was happening. In 1952 an organization was formed that would become an object of controversy in Catholic circles—the Higher Institute of Brazilian Studies (ISEB). At first a broad, diversified discussion group, it early coalesced around the themes of nationalism and development and moved in a steadily leftward direction, losing its more moderate members as it went. When Juscelino Kubitschek was elected on a nationalistic-developmental platform, his government assumed the support of ISEB, making it an official scholarly rationalizer of the government's position. Bolstered financially, ISEB became the center of discussion on economic policy, the relationship of ideology to development, and other themes relevant to the changes taking place in the country. Nationalism and development became common topics of conversation among educated people.

The Catholic response to these events must be understood in terms of several significant developments in the late forties and early fifties.

First, perhaps most important, was recognition by the Vatican of the dismal condition of the Brazilian Church, the world's largest. Motivated chiefly by a desire for pastoral renewal and with Giovanni Montini (now Pope Paul VI) deeply involved, the Vatican strengthened its hierarchy in Brazil, expanding the number of dioceses and putting the most capable people in strategic positions. In 1952 the National Conference of Brazilian Bishops was formed to coordinate planning, with Bishop Helder Câmara as secretary general. An exceptional series of papal nuncios was appointed who were open to discussion of Brazilian problems and wanted the Church to be socially relevant.

Through the nuncios, young and rather liberal men became bishops, and specialized Catholic Action was stimulated. Bishop Câmara himself became national secretary of Catholic Action. His full significance may never be known. Freed from conventional episcopal duties, he moved as an agent behind the scenes, using his ample gifts of persuasion to stimulate renewal. Open to drastic innovation and unafraid of the modern world, this former Integralist who came to call himself a "humanist socialist" did not blanch at and consistently encouraged the struggle for relevance of the younger generation, no matter what turns it took. Sensitive to the misery of his people, he urged governmental planning and appropriate reforms to alleviate it. The great developmental commission in the Northeast of Brazil, SUDENE, was first suggested by a regional bishops' conference organized by Bishop Câmara.

Second, an extremely competent group of young clergy was appointed to positions of guidance in Catholic Action. They came from two types of background: Dominicans, who had studied in France and were familiar with the innovating social ideas of Catholic liberals there; and secular clergy, who had studied at that bulwark of traditionalism, the Gregorian University in Rome. The latter, many of whom came from the backward Northeast, resisted the stolidity of the Gregorian and returning to Brazil, found themselves in the early fifties aware of Brazilian problems and anxious to appropriate the technological and ideological necessities for modernization.

Third, as early as the late forties, some Catholics had wanted to move beyond Maritain. Existentialism being in vogue, they turned to a thinker who had tried to combine Catholic faith with motifs of existentialism, Emmanuel Mounier, the editor of the French journal *Esprit*. The flexibility of Mounier's "personalism" helped dislodge them from the prudential balance of neo-Thomism. While in time Brazilian Catholics would work out their own philosophy, certain themes of Mounier persisted and intensified as time went by: the view of capitalist institutions as "the principal agents of oppression of the human person"; the promotion of the person as the end of ethical activity; the vision of a personalist, communitarian civilization as a historical possibility; the conviction that present history is a revolutionary process leading ultimately to the ascendance of the proletariat; and lastly, openness to Communism, and a realization that anti-Communism is frequently a vehicle used to defend conservative interests. Mounier could say:

> We must recognize that there exists today a political demarcation which is even more profound than a matter of party allegiance. It divides those who, even when fighting them, can only address

Communists as a whole in a fraternal spirit, and those for whom anti-Communism, whether socialistic or reactionary, is the directing political reflex. We are with the first group.[6]

And fourth, in the early fifties a French Dominican economist and sociologist, L.J. Lebret, conducted a number of studies in Brazil. His influence was chiefly felt in São Paulo, where he helped promote a more objective social science that contrasted with the philosophical speculations that passed for sociology in Brazilian Catholic circles.

Lebret and the "Economie et Humanisme" teams he sponsored conveyed the conviction that the solutions to social problems were rooted in the context. Answers relevant in one situation might not apply in others. A deep sense of the distinctiveness of Brazil's problems was the result. Moreover, he seems to have been one of the early critics of the entrenched moralistic way in which Catholics behaved politically. Lebret's books were widely used as a basis for discussion in Catholic Action. Two of them, *Principles for Action* and *Manifesto for a Solidary Civilization*, helped convey a sense of openness, flexibility, and responsible, critical humanism in social action, while his later *Suicide or Survival of the West* describes the desperation of conditions in the underdeveloped world and indicts the indifference of the developed nations.

By the mid-fifties, a growing number of clergy and laity who sympathized with the nationalism and developmentism advocated by ISEB were active in major Brazilian cities. As Christians they were disturbed by the backwardness and suffering of the Brazilian people; they felt that only through governmental planning, public control of key sectors of the economy, and greater domestic industrialization could this condition be overcome. One of the most active of them was a young lawyer and economist, Cândido Mendes de Almeida, the scion of a family noted for its devotion to the Church, who shocked his fellow Catholics by being one of the founders and consistent leaders of ISEB. Others were clergy. The priests who had studied together at the Gregorian University occasionally met in their travels to discuss the problems of Brazilian society. One of their former tutors, Henrique de Lima Vaz, S.J., who at the time was establishing a reputation as an historian of classical philosophy, became interested and began to work on the philosophical and theological bases of modern change, including a careful examination of Marxism. In Belo Horizonte, the bustling capital of the state of Minas Gerais, a group of secondary school students who would become leaders in the Na-

[6] Emmanuel Mounier, "A Dialogue with Communism," *Cross Currents*, Vol. III, Winter, 1953, p. 119.

tional Student Union were undergoing a deepening of their religious understanding as a preliminary to a second conversion to the "Brazilian reality."

It was in JUC, the university branch of Catholic Action, that the most significant early breakthrough came. JUC was affiliated with JEC International, a more radical, elitist-oriented international association of Catholic Action groups than the more inclusive Pax Romana. In 1958 JEC International held a meeting in Dakar, at which Brazilian delegates played a dominant role and problems of underdeveloped areas received extensive attention.[7]

Back in Brazil, the National Student Union was involved in the problem of university reform. The analysis of Brazil's educational situation led to three especially significant discoveries by Catholic youth: (1) Catholic secondary schools, they learned, were a major contributor to the privileged character of university education. Since most Brazilian secondary schools were private and most of those Catholic, the fees they charged automatically excluded the majority of young people. This insight was especially significant as a break with the Catholic past, for it meant that the university branch of Catholic Action ranged itself in favor of public education and against including private schools in public subsidies. They thus clashed with a fundamental assumption of the older generation, that the parental right in education implied public support of private schools. (2) The defects and discrimination in Brazilian universities, they concluded, were only a reflection of far greater problems in society at large. No legitimate university reform was possible until society was changed. (3) In following traditional patterns, Brazilian university education placed inadequate resources and emphasis on the technical and social scientific needs for developing the country.

By 1958 delegates at JUC meetings from Belo Horizonte, São Paulo, and the Northeast were arguing for the interrelationship of university and national problems, as well as the responsibility of Catholics to act upon them.

Within the universities young Catholics encountered a small but active group that had already cogently analyzed the problems of the university—the Communists. Catholics had traditionally supported the conservative side in student elections. By 1959–60, however, a minority of JUCists sympathized so strongly with the more Leftist incumbent position that one of their number, João Manoel Conrado, was elected president of the National Student Union (UNE) with the support of the Communists. UNE had been committed for several years to the prevalent nationalist and developmental ideology. By 1959 both in-

[7] Cf. "Bases Comuns: Carta de Dakar," *Boletim de JUC,* Vol. I, Rio de Janeiro: JUC, 1959.

cumbents and the opposition were nationalist, but the incumbents were more radical and defended the participation of students in all activities they considered important to the public life. The common effort toward university reform with Communists and other Leftists, as well as cooperation in the publication of *O Metropolitano* (Rio) and other student newspapers, convinced the Catholics that they had more in common with the Left than with the Right, and that unity and effectiveness in the student movement demanded a common front of the Left.

This conviction was strengthened by the reaction of the older Catholic generation, who seemed incapable of grasping the students' point of view. Especially during 1960 the debate was carried on in *A Ordem* and various newspapers by the more traditional side, and in *O Metropolitano* by the students. The elders suggested that nationalism was Fascist or Communist, depending on who was writing; and in place of the emphasis on industrialization implied in developmentism and the inflationary policies of the Kubitschek government, they insisted on a slower and "balanced" growth. Against governmental planning, they upheld the "principle of subsidiarity," the prior initiative of some less encompassing group. While the students spotlighted the lack of genuine family life among the lower classes because of economic hardships, their elders piously argued for the preservation of family stability on a moral basis. Against the student participation in UNE and interest in the general problems of the country, they recalled the liturgical and theological traditions of Catholic Action in an earlier day. The students pointed to Brazil's underdevelopment as part of the Third World; their parents insisted on Brazil's ties with Europe and the maintenance of the values of Western civilization. And so forth on a whole range of issues.

The climax of this conflict came with the Cardonnel incident. A French Dominican, Thomas Cardonnel, visited Brazil in 1960, making a stunning impact on student groups. Young Catholics, who had been on the defensive because of the conservative attitude of leading Catholic spokesmen, discovered a vivid symbol of the relevance of the Church. Cardonnel's themes included a strong existentialist note, a criticism of the "hypocrisy" in the Brazilian Church, a denunciation of injustices, an openness to the culture (he spoke warmly of movies that many Catholics considered immoral), and a questioning of anti-Communism as a legitimate attitude. Moreover, he depicted a brighter future for Brazil.

> After eight months in Brazil, I think that the first and most urgent problem is the fight against misery, against the brutal fact that the majority of men do not have an elementary possibility of living like men.

To contest the legitimacy of this fight for men . . . and in the name of a Communist danger, seems to be the worst of impostures. . . . In Brazil we have the elements—workers, peasants, students—who ought to plan in common the form of a new society. To awaken the Brazilian people to its soul, to the originality of its common life, is the work for us to realize today.[8]

Cardonnel's comments horrified conventional Catholics, and he was publicly and bitterly criticized by Gustavo Corção, considered a major spokesman of the Centro Dom Vital and the "advanced" Catholics of an earlier era. Moreover, this criticism and pressure led the Dominicans to consider it prudent to send Cardonnel out of the country. From that point on communication between the generations broke down, for as one student put it: "The Dominican friar inaugurates in Brazil a new stage in Christian social-philosophical thought: this stage in which the Christian encounters history and adheres to its factuality through incarnation itself." [9]

Meanwhile priests active in Catholic Action had been working out a perspective for engagement in history, one which did not try to adjust Brazilian society to preconceived norms, but was directed toward a structure in which the Brazilian man might gain fulfillment. It was also designed to provide an alternative analysis of man and history to that offered by the Marxists. In its earlier stages the Catholic Action "ideology" was called the "historical ideal," [10] but in its more developed form as elaborated by the scholarly Father Vaz, it became a highly sophisticated philosophy of "historical consciousness." [11] It sought to provide a transition between the theological and social teachings of the Church, on the one hand, and the practical necessities of Brazilian history, on the other. It emphasized man's ability to shape history and envisioned a utopian, humane and harmonious "new world." Modern history Father Vaz saw as "anthropological" in spirit, "an essentially open conception of history, in which human subjectivity appears as the matrix of the 'projects' that give the direction and rhythm of the historical process." The "essence of Christianity" is likewise historical

[8] Thomas Cardonnel, "Deus não é mentiroso como certa paz social," in Luiz Alberto Gomez de Souza (ed.), *Cristianismo Hoje*, Rio de Janeiro: Editôra Universitária, 1962, p. 23.
[9] Carlos Diegues, "A Missão de Cardonnel." *O Metropolitano*, December 18, 1960, p. 3.
[10] Cf. Luiz de Gonzaga Sena *et al.*, "Ideal Histórico," *Boletim de JUC*, Vol. IV, Rio de Janeiro: JUC, n.d.
[11] The bibliography of Henrique de Lima Vaz, S. J. is very extensive. The quotations below are taken from: "Cristianismo e consciência histórica (II)," *Síntese*, Vol. III, No. 9, jan.-março, 1961, pp. 36, 48, 61, 64-5; and "O cristianismo na direção axial da história do pequeno mundo antigo á aventura cósmica," in Luiz Alberto Gomez de Souza (ed.), *op. cit.*, p. 86.

and consists in "an existence and an action, the Existence and Action of Christ, which is located and exercized in the very heart of history." In fact, "the dynamic premises from which the modern world evolved were given in the Christian vision of history and already in the deeply original 'historical humanism' of the biblical people."

How are the modern historical consciousness and the Christian consciousness united? "The person encounters, in the participation in an absolutely personal and concretely universal Center of history, the basis of his historical action: he cooperates then in a real process of *personalization* of the universe. . . . The problem of the *sense of history* is placed for him on the absolute level of an option which decides finally the destiny and *being* itself of the man who *makes* history. . . ."

> I believe that only with difficulty can one formulate a more rigorous demand of historical responsibility than in this conception in which history is not the development of an ideal totality . . . but is the drama of freedoms struggling in the conquest of a full realization of the historical task of instituting a world of man on which the divine peace finally can descend. . . . The Christian conscience conducts the Christian to the most advanced frontier of the historical struggles in which man is engaged in the conquest of a more human world, of the universe of real freedoms. Thus, the great sin of the Christian will be today the sin of historical omission.

Catholic involvement in the social order was envisioned as open to the future rather than nostalgic toward the past, emphasizing a historical process directed toward human possibilities and fulfillment into which the Christian conscience inserts itself.

Although the new directions in Catholic thought and action first appeared in JUC, many other Catholics followed suit, especially from other branches of Catholic Action. Various schools of thought began to emerge. Tension between these points of view was to intensify in the next few years. On one end was a small group that was extremely Marxist in thought and language;[12] on the other end an attempt at a more Centrist position, Solidarism, gained some support.[13] However, most of the Catholic Left was in between.[14]

---

[12] A widely publicized, but relatively uninfluential, example was Aloísio Guerra, *A Igreja, Está com o povo?*, Rio de Janeiro: Civilização Brasileira, 1963.

[13] Brazilian Solidarism is especially associated with Fernando Bastos de Ávila, S. J. Cf. *Neo-capitalismo, Socialismo, solidarismo*, Rio de Janeiro: Agir, 1963; *Solidarismo*, Rio de Janeiro: Agir, 1965.

[14] From March 17, 1963 to March 28, 1964, 55 issues of *Brasil, Urgente*, a weekly newspaper designed to popularize the Catholic Leftist position, appeared. Overlooking the somewhat inflammatory headlines, one may discover in *Brasil, Urgente* the positions of major figures in the movement and their response to the fateful issues leading to the military intervention of April 1, 1964.

The year 1961 was important in the crystallization of the Left. Early in the summer a controversial manifesto from the student leadership of the Catholic University in Rio expressed the commitment of the more articulate students to the necessity of social change.[15] About the same time Aldo Arantes, a product of the new Catholic views, was elected president of UNE in a conscious coalition with Communists and others of the Left. The same united "front" and the same Catholic point of view were defended by Arantes' successors, Vinícius Caldeira Brandt and José Serra,[16] up until the Revolution of 1964, despite increased criticism even from moderate Catholics. In August President Jânio Quadros, who had excited this group by his moves toward leadership of Latin America and independence from the United States, resigned, allegedly under Rightist and military pressure. The attempt by the military to prevent his legal successor, João Goulart, from assuming office and the subsequent diminution of presidential power indicated the essentially undemocratic character of political processes in the country. Members of Catholic Action, criticized for their political interests by members of the hierarchy, began to plan a political group that would reflect the philosophy of "historical consciousness" but would include non-Catholics and be independent of the Church.

Most significant, however, was a broadening of the issues of interest and a radicalization of the positions taken. The easy stage of economic development was now over, with imports substituted by Brazilian industries, and a new range of problems appeared: the archaic and inefficient agrarian structure, the backwardness of many regions, the continued remission of profits, lack of education and technical skills for development, absence of civic organizations and politization among most of the population, and the economic degradation of salaried workers in the lower categories who had carried the heaviest burden of the inflation. Nationalism and development began to be replaced by class struggle and socialism in the thinking of many Catholics and others. They questioned whether the "industrial bourgeoisie," who had been the chief agents of development in the fifties, could carry through the changes now necessary. Was not their nationalism and "anti-imperialism" simply a matter of self-interest? In order to counter

[15] "Manifesto do Diretório Central do [sic] Estudantes da Pontifícia Universidade Católica," in Luiz Alberto Gomez de Souza (ed.), *op. cit.*, pp. 89–98.
[16] "We do not intend to deny the presence of Communists in UNE. But neither do we believe in excluding any student from the common work because of his ideological or confessional positions. The construction of the common good is not a task only of Christians, but of all men . . . who agree to work together against injustices and in favor of the liberation of the Brazilian man." Vinícius Caldeira Brandt, "Presidente da UNE e Cristo: Finalização das Estruturas humanas," *Painel Brasileiro*, Vol. IV, No. 41, 1962, p. 16.

94

that interest, were not new vehicles necessary, such as a front limited to workers, peasants, and their sympathizers?

Young Catholics wanted to participate in projects that would contribute to development. A number of the most involved recent graduates associated themselves with the Movement of Base Education (MEB), an already existing adult literacy program sponsored by the bishops but chiefly financed by the government. The adhesion of many of the younger Leftists shifted the focus of MEB. While literacy training remained a fundamental objective, it was seen as an instrument for *conscientização*, an awakening of consciousness on the part of the inert and illiterate masses to themselves, their problems, and the options possible for solving them. As a consequence of the entry afforded by a literacy program, MEB soon found itself intimately involved in promoting community development, health and sanitation training, popular art and culture, and labor unions.

The involvement with labor unions was a key issue in distinguishing the secular implications of the "humanist" perspective of the Catholic Left from the more conventional and better-known activities of Father Paulo Crespo in the state of Pernambuco. The labor organizers in MEB disagreed with four assumptions that they felt oriented the *clericais* (clericals): (1) that the fundamental responsibility for solving the rural problem lay with the *Church*, especially through stimulating unions under Christian inspiration and leadership; (2) that priests (rather than laymen) should symbolize and lead Christian activity in the labor movement; (3) that Christians should promote labor unions to counteract Francisco Julião's "Ligas Camponesas" and other Leftist groups (those in MEB were less disturbed about Leftist labor activities than they were about the status quo or the aspirations toward a "new Christendom" among some Catholics); and (4) that unions are essentially for economic ends. (For MEB, unions were instruments for *conscientização*, which entailed not only economic betterment, but politization.) Correctly or not, they thought they discerned in Father Crespo and his associates the mentality of a "new Christendom."

The tension between the two Catholic groups came to a climax when, in December, 1963, unions that had been stimulated by personnel from MEB entered a coalition with unions assumed to be under Communist influence to elect officers for the National Confederation of Agricultural Workers. The major group left out were the unions of the *clericais*, which were rigidly opposed to cooperation with Communists under any circumstances.

The Catholic Left culminated in Popular Action (AP), a "political-ideological," "non-confessional" organization founded in 1962 and set on its way by a "Base Document" early in 1963. Popular Action stemmed directly from a recognition that Catholic Action, as a group under the direction of the episcopacy, could not participate in the political processes taking place in Brazil. AP's lay character is indicated by the fact that no priests belonged to it, though many served in advisory roles and it was expected that they would eventually join as "citizens." In early 1964, AP had about 3,000 members composed of recent graduates, some students, and other interested persons. It included one prominent government official in Paulo de Tarso, minister of education for several months in 1963.

Any attempt to discuss AP's perspective distorts it, but we will sketch a few themes. AP represented the "option" of a generation in response to the challenge of social forces exploiting and mutilating man.

> Our single commitment, then, is with man. With the Brazilian man, above all. He who is born with the shadow of premature death extending itself over his cradle. Who lives with the spectre of hunger inhabiting his miserable roof, accompanying inseparably his uncertain steps, the steps of one who journeys through life without hope and without aim. Who grows up brutalized and illiterate, exiled from the benefits of culture, from creative possibilities, from the authentically human ways of real liberty. Who dies an animal and anonymous death, stretched out on the hard floor of his misery.[17]

Rejecting capitalism and colonialism, but also criticizing the loss of the humanist impulse in socialism in its Communist forms, the Base Document envisions the historic movement as one in which the underdeveloped world has a revolutionary function to further international socialism in the interests of humanity.

In contrast with certain interpretations of Marxism, AP views man as a free, transcendent being, "the norm and end of history." The contemporary actualization of "historical consciousness" occurs in a given context, namely, a system of capitalist domination over underdeveloped areas which has marginalized the masses from possibilities of socialization and the demands of the present. "Historical consciousness" implies an option to participate in the development of a socialist civilization through the revolutionary process taking place in Brazil.

Socialism offers no single pattern, but rather a diversified and changing reality presently moving away from rigid orthodoxy. Though the document does not indicate the exact form in which the revolutionary process will move, it refers to a "practical reformulation" of the ownership of the means of production and the use of state power to represent the interests of the majority against the minority of exploitative property owners.

[17] *Ação Popular: Documento Base*, p. 1.

96

According to the authors, history indicates that structures do not change without violence generated by the resistance of those structures to the changes. In the revolutionary moment the "popular" forces must unite, into a single party if necessary, in order to articulate the needs and achieve the aspirations of the people. In the pre-revolutionary period the people are mute because of lack of representation in the political structures, the dependence of labor unions on the government, and the oppressive consequences of the agrarian system. The present task is to mobilize the people through a "policy of revolutionary preparation," entailing *conscientização* and the formation of organizations for a struggle against feudalism and national and international capitalism. Radicalizing pressure against the existent structures is suggested, as is permanent dialogue with other anti-imperialist and revolutionary sectors. The vanguard of the revolution is to be composed of workers, peasants, and students.

Members of AP acted out their convictions in two directions, reflecting a certain ambivalence in the Base Document. One focused on immediate participation in political power. While the last months of the Goulart regime are still somewhat clouded, a few key members of AP are believed to have supported Jango's continuistic ambitions in hopes of sharing in the government. The bulk of the members, however, engaged in activities promoting *conscientização* and social changes through MEB, the National Plan of Alphabetization, the Superintendency of Agrarian Reform, Popular Culture Movements, and the reformist state governments in Pernambuco and Goias.

Active for only a year before the military takeover of 1964 and now subversive (though continuing in control of the officially abolished but still very active National Student Movement), Popular Action did not have time or opportunity to serve as a test of Catholic strategy. Nor did the rapidly deteriorating situation of the country under Goulart provide an adequate context. Catholics of this persuasion basically opposed Goulart, not because of his supposed "Leftist" inclinations, but because he was not a Leftist. Rather Goulart was a temporizer and opportunist without policy or pattern who moved across the spectrum in a desperate search for a political base.

Since Christian Democracy has gained strong support from younger and more critical Catholics elsewhere, something should be said about the lackluster character of the Christian Democratic party in Brazil. This party began in the late 1940s with a notably moralist and traditional program, under the leadership of Msgr. Arruda Câmara, a priest-legislator who had written extensively on the legal prerequisites for maintaining "family integrity." By the 1950s the party's political base had shifted to dynamic São Paulo, where with Antônio Queiroz Filho

97

and André Franco Montoro as symbols, it presented to the public a mildly progressive wing. Unfortunately the Centrist strategy of the party, which claimed to be neither capitalist nor socialist, did not appeal to Catholic intellectuals who wanted a clear option in a time of political polarization. In the last years of pre-Revolutionary Brazil, a more radical wing developed, exemplified by Paulo de Tarso and Plinio Sampaio, who sympathized with socialism, Popular Action, and the Left, but affiliated with the Christian Democratic party because they had to run under some party label. This group, though in a sense it represented the party's most successful politicians, never deluded itself into thinking that it represented a majority. In fact, it really wanted to transform the party into a "humanist socialist" body.

The Catholic Left and AP were not without their deficiencies. Their thought was notably utopian in its view of history and quite innocent of the real power structure in Brazil. There is evidence that many assumed that tension would increase to the breaking point and the government would simply fall into their hands. They underestimated the *golpista* mentality of the military which had repeatedly asserted itself on other occasions, the ongoing influence of the rural aristocracy which finally acted when Goulart planned a minimal expropriation of land, and the anxious insecurity of the middle classes before what they interpreted as a "proletarianization" of Brazilian society.[18] For a group that hoped in time to come to power, their economic and political plans for the future were underdeveloped. Apologists today, undoubtedly correctly, insist however that the ideas and people were there, but time was too short to work them out. To argue that they were "dupes" of international Communism, the standard American reaction, is to overlook the basic conservatism of Brazilian Communism. Participants in the "united front" found that on specific policies the Communists were cautious, comprehensive, and reformist, while the Catholics were the wing more vigorously pressing for immediate changes.

The development of this unusual manifestation of religious thought and action suggests the possibilities of response within Catholicism to problems of development. I do not care to argue that nationalism and socialism are necessarily the options a movement must take in order to promote development. I have instead pointed to the capacity for innovation, break with tradition, and radicalism of persons and groups

---

[18] Not everyone was so unaware of the underlying forces in the country. Cf. the remarkably prophetic book by Wanderley Guilherme, *Quem dará o golpe no Brasil? (Who Will Carry Out the Coup in Brazil?)*, Rio de Janeiro: Civilização Brasileira, 1962.

within an authoritarian, conservative religious system deeply rooted in the status quo.

While Catholicism is assuredly an authoritarian church, it nevertheless maintains sufficient freedom for members of the hierarchy, clergy, and laity to set out in new directions, though not without difficulty and struggle. An elite, derived overwhelmingly from the middle class, in Brazil appropriated and interpreted Christian ethics in such a way as to appreciate essentially non-religious aspirations and ideologies concerned with advancing development and changing the structures of society. The fluid and diversified nature of Catholic thought (or its vagueness) enabled them to find theoretical support from theologians and popes (especially John XXIII). They benefited from the contributions of thinkers in developed and secularized countries, who had no illusions about the return of "Christian civilization" and regarded politics as a secular phenomenon whose end is the well-being of citizens. The appropriation of forms of existentialist thinking freed them from the persistent inclination of Catholics to apply to all situations universal patterns whose universality is questionable. Particularly in Latin America, with its long tradition of absolutist ethics grounded in religion, secularity and ethical contextualism entailing pragmatism and experimentation may be the vehicles by which Catholics can deal positively with political processes leading to development.

4.

THE RETREAT FROM JOSEPHINISM:
AUSTRIAN CATHOLICISM RESPONDS
TO THE TWENTIETH CENTURY

BY DENNISON I. RUSINOW
American Universities Field Staff

The special relationship between Catholic Church and state which evolved in Austria during the last centuries of Habsburg rule bequeathed to the Church in the Monarchy's successor states a set of attitudes and traditional roles which have made it particularly difficult for the Church to accept, participate in, or exploit most of the social and political changes that have overtaken these societies since 1918. The primary exceptions in the years before 1950 appeared to prove the rule: most of the Austrian hierarchy and clergy welcomed, and frequently sponsored, the 1934–38 effort to establish a "Christian corporative state" in Austria, an experiment to which most historians would be willing to apply the word "reactionary." In neighboring Croatia (and under rather more complex local post-Habsburg conditions, to be sure) the same groups, hierarchy and clergy, gravely compromised the Church's reputation by association and often participation in the 1941–45 attempt to build a Catholic-fascist state on the basis of the most brutal use of force and the assumption that all non-Catholics (except, paradoxically, Muslims) were enemies of the state.

In recent years, however, a growing number of churchmen, both clerical and lay and including some of the top hierarchy, have been attempting in some of the successor states to effect a basic change in the Church's attitude and relationship to the secularization of public life and the problems of an industrial society, two of the most fundamental aspects of what is usually called "modernization." The purpose of this analysis is to suggest some of the factors favoring this development and some opposing it in one of the ex-Habsburg territories, the Republic of Austria. In the other successor states, which are today under Communist regimes, a different and fundamentally hostile political environment has invoked a partly different response by the religious institution to "modernizing" social change. While the nature varies from one Communist-ruled former Habsburg province to another, recent developments in some of them (for example, in Croatia and Slovenia) bear a partial but striking and significant resemblance to what has been taking place in the Austrian Republic.

HERITAGE OF THE COUNTER REFORMATION AND JOSEPHINISM

By 1570 Austria was almost entirely Protestant, reflecting the strength of Protestant nobles contesting the power of the Catholic Habsburgs and assisted by the pro-Reformist sympathies of one of the latter, Maximilian II (1564–76). The reconversion of the country after 1590 was the work of Maximilian's successors, less tolerant religiously and more determined to establish authority over the nobility, and was carried out by the army assisted by the Jesuits. The Catholic Church in Austria overcame its Reformation crisis, therefore, only through the agency of Habsburg swords. A special link was then forged between Church and Dynasty, in which the former was dependent on the latter, which in turn considered itself the divinely ordained guardian of the faith. The armies of Austria in later years marched to battle against Turk, Protestant, or fellow Catholic under the banner of the Mother of God, special protectress of the House of Austria, the *Magna Mater Austriae*—but it was the Habsburgs who remained the true protectors of the Church.

Austrian Catholicism became a *Reichskirche*, a state church, to an extent perhaps unequaled in other Catholic lands, although there are abundant parallels in the Orthodox world. However often the Habsburgs might come into political conflict with the Roman Curia, the Dynasty and its Church seemed inseparably one:

> The welcoming imperial double eagle and the coats of arms of Habsburg lands that appeared on the Baroque facades superimposed on old Gothic churches, and the pillars of the Holy Trinity or of Mary that shot up in the markets and city squares of the Bohemian-

Austrian territories, were triumphal emblems for the Catholic Church and also for the ruling dynasty; the great pilgrimages and processions—like the Corpus Christi procession, in which, from the time of Ferdinand II, the Emperor himself and the members of the imperial family expressed the special Habsburg veneration for the Eucharist by walking behind the Holy of Holies—were festive parades of the dynasty as well as the Church.[1]

The introduction into the Habsburg Empire of the modern European theory of the secular state, separate from if not entirely detached from its religious foundations, was therefore peculiarly retarded. The multi-national nature of the Empire also played a role: where other Western European rulers found in the concept of the nation a substitute for religion as a legitimation of their authority, this course was not open to the Habsburgs, who clung perforce to medieval conceptions of the foundations of political power. One consequence was that the 18th-century Enlightenment assumed a special form in Austria, one which "modernized" state-Church relations without separating the two, i.e., without secularization. The set of policies and ideas which accomplished this transformation are known to history as *Josephinismus*, a label applied to ecclesiastical-political reforms actually initiated under Maria Theresa and merely extended and codified by her son, Joseph II, but often used to characterize an entire century in Habsburg history, from 1750 to 1850. The reforms abolished many religious orders and monasteries, placed some aspects of monastic life under state control (for example, minimum ages for taking vows), abolished the clergy's exemption from taxes, expelled the Jesuits, instituted state seminaries, prohibited visitations by papal legates, and controlled the traffic of Austrian bishops to Rome. While many of these restrictions appeared superficially to be in accord with the secularizing spirit of the Western Enlightenment, in the Austrian context they assumed a different meaning. The state's control over the Church was reinforced, but at the same time the state's role as protector of the Church was reaffirmed because the Church's function was redefined: for the Josephinian Enlightenment the religious institution appeared as a singularly useful adjunct to bureaucracy and police, both in controlling the people and providing for their welfare.

One contemporary Austrian Catholic sociologist defines this set of concepts as "a typical made-in-Austria branch of the European Enlightenment, a first modern attempt to establish a Catholic state church in the service of the absolutist welfare state, but without

---

[1] Adam Wandruszka, *The House of Habsburg*, New York: Anchor Books, 1965, p. 107.

divorcing it from Rome." [2] A second Austrian Catholic writer describes the system as "a state-church-regime [*Staatskirchentum*], with the state as reformer and regulator of a Church battered by malpractices and evil circumstances, and the Church for its part as an auxiliary of the state in the fulfillment of its worldly tasks." "Since the Baroque age," the same author also comments, " 'Catholic' was a kind of imperial religion, strong as an emotion and a style of living, weaker in intellect and totally weak as a non-conforming power derived from faith. It was in no way a religiosity that calls forth saints, or that is marked by significant theology or mysticism, but rather a servant of the state and the military." [3]

The result, a leading historian of the Church under the Habsburgs has noted, was that "a fatal dependence on the state remained the hallmark of Austrian Catholicism, a dependence which was all the more harmful for the development of the Church because the majority of the clergy as well as the people became accustomed to viewing state and church as a unity, to making an immutable and self-evident principle of the position of the Church, which was really only an historical consequence of the Counter Reformation and Josephinism." [4]

The pattern was shaken after 1850 by a sequence of developments which marked the belated arrival in Austria-Hungary of the industrial revolution and its political consequences. Constitutional experiments, although destined to prove abortive, brought with them liberal governments with a dedication to capitalism and secularism. A Concordat with the Vatican concluded in 1855 under neo-absolutism was denounced in 1870 by liberal ministers of the Emperor. Meanwhile, an anti-liberal reaction—which was in reality a reaction against the physical and spiritual sufferings accompanying the transition to the modern, industrial society and class structure that liberalism represented—led to the appearance of the Empire's first modern, mass-movement political parties. The process is significant. From an originally unified movement of protest in the 1870s there emerged three parties based on divergent and mutually antagonistic ideological solutions to the problems of modern times: the first, Christian-social, the second, Marxian socialist, and the third, nationalist. The feud among them, dangerously serious because it was ideological as well as political, was to dominate Austrian public life in the 20th century, discrediting

[2] Erich Bodzenta, *Die Katholiken in Oesterreich, Ein religions-soziologischer Ueberblick*, Vienna: Herder, 1962, p. 21.
[3] Otto Schulmeister, *Der Wandel von der Reichsreligion zür freien Kirche im freien Staat*, unpublished ms., p. 2.
[4] Taras von Borodajkewycz, "Die Kirche in Oesterreich," in Nadler-Srbik (eds.), *Oesterreich, Erbe und Sendung in deutschen Raum*, Vienna: 1963, p. 306.

parliamentary institutions under the First Republic, and leading to civil war and to totalitarian experiments by two of the parties.

The Christian-social party was initially a clericalist political movement based on mass support and socially reformist in philosophy and program, a party formed in the spirit of Pope Leo XIII's encyclical *De Rerum Novarum*, which was Catholicism's first progressive attempt to answer what was then called "the social question." With the Christian-socials a new factor had been inserted into the Austrian religious equation, one which did not fit into the old pattern of a medieval-cum-Enlightenment state-Church establishment. Religion was joined with protest instead of with authority for the first time since the Counter Reformation. The initial reaction of both Dynasty and episcopacy was symbolized by Francis Joseph's thrice-repeated refusal to recognize the new party's electorally triumphant leader, Karl Lueger, as mayor of Vienna.

The conflict was short-lived. Regime and episcopacy quickly discovered that by accepting the new movement and by identifying social reform with the devil of atheistic Marxian socialism, they could tame the Christian-socials. And with their taming, the clericalist party gained the conservative Catholic countryside as an electoral bastion and lost industrial Vienna, which in 1910 gave the Socialists an absolute majority that was to endure (in free elections) until 1966. The Christian-socials became a black-yellow *Reichspartei*, another arm of the state-Church establishment. The social protest current in the movement never quite vanished, but became the preserve of a few Catholic "outsiders," important to the historian interested in tracing a continuity from the radical origins of the party through the social romanticism of the inter-war years to the resurgence of Christian reformism in the Second Republic after 1945.[5]

For a Church with this kind of history, the initial reaction to the disappearance of the Habsburgs in 1918 was, perhaps inevitably, an urgent search for a new patron capable of preserving Austria's presumed character as a "Christian" state. The obvious candidate was the Christian-social party, emerging as the largest in the Republic. "In place of the identification of Church and state, there now entered an identification of Church and party . . . The Church had authorized the Christian-social party as the Catholics' political representation."[6] The symbols of the new establishment were the person of the party's leader and outstanding Federal Chancellor of the 1920s, Monsignor

---

[5] See Gerhard Silberbauer, *Oesterreichs Katholiken und die Arbeiterfrage*, Graz: Verlag Styria, 1966, parts IV and V.
[6] Schulmeister, *op. cit.*, p. 7.

Ignaz Seipel, and the traditional Corpus Christi procession, with Christian-social ministers now marching behind the Eucharist in place of the vanished Imperial Family. The socially conservative inclination of both Church and party was reinforced by two additional factors. First, the principal enemy, elevated in Catholic minds into an atheistic and quasi-Bolshevik bogey, became the Socialist party. And second, during the constitutional period of the First Republic, the need for a parliamentary majority forced the Christian-socials into a "bourgeois bloc" with the national-liberals, whose own traditional anti-clericalism also bowed before the need for a common anti-socialist front but who demanded liberal economic policies as the price of cooperation. *"Modo capitalistico vivit Ecclesia catholica,"* Msgr. Seipel is supposed to have said.

Identified with the party, the Church was also identified with its policies, including the violent suppression of Austrian socialism in 1934. In this mutual dependence, ideological and political, both found themselves willing sponsors of the Dollfuss-Schuschnigg experiment in establishing a "Christian corporative state" (1934–38), a self-conscious attempt to build a social order on the basis of Pope Pius XI's Encyclical *Quadregesimo anno,* which had also condemned any attempt at an understanding with socialism or the development of a Christian socialism ("Religious socialism and Christian socialism are contradictions in terms"). "The attempt at a corporative state," a contemporary Catholic writer has noted, "represented a last flicker of the Catholic state-forming will and its pretensions to a monopoly position," and made of "Austria the only country, except Salazar's Portugal, in which the Papal Encyclical was invoked as the principle on which the ordering of public life should be based." [7]

POST-1945: FACTORS INDUCING CHANGE

This historical summary, inevitably distorted by brevity, is a prerequisite to an understanding of the social and political position of the Austrian Catholic Church in the Second Republic and the quality of its response to its changed situation, including the beginnings of a new orientation to contemporary problems, a belated acceptance of the secular state, and the equally belated recognition that an industrial, urban society demands of the Church new techniques and a new style.

Austrian Catholicism is today in a transitional period involving ferment and strife and (in the opinion of some of those involved) a

[7] *Ibid.*, p. 13.

risk of schism. The shape of the outcome is still in many ways unclear, for the relative strengths of the factors involved have yet to be tested. These factors are, however, the subject of the remaining pages of this brief study.

The principle which underlies present developments was described to this writer by three of the participants (one a Catholic politician, the others churchmen) in almost identical terms: "The Austrian Church is still what Joseph II made of it. What is happening today represents the beginning of an undoing of Josephinism." The editor of a serious Catholic weekly calls it, more apocalyptically and perhaps more ethnocentrically, "the end of the Constantinian Era in Christian history."

The sources of this alleged change are various and complex, sociological and political, domestic and international, and causally related. They include the following:

1. The experience of both the Church and the Christian-socials with National Socialism after the *Anschluss* and during the war. This was the Austrian Church's first real experience with an unfriendly regime. Many of the hierarchy had initially thought, and been encouraged to think, that they could reach an amicable *modus vivendi* with the new secular authorities, who would recognize a special Catholic status for their Ostmark. The early and still controversial obeisances made to Nazism and to Hitler personally by the Archbishop of Vienna, Cardinal Innitzer, did much to discredit the Church among most anti-Nazis. Austrian Catholicism was soon subjected, however, to the same *Gleichschaltung* that the Church in Germany had already suffered, and many priests, like their Christian-social patrons, found themselves sharing persecution and concentration camps with their former enemies, the Austrian socialists. Today liberal and conservative Austrian Catholics are unanimous in citing this sobering experience as the beginning of the Church's political re-education.

2. The similarly shared experience of twenty postwar years of permanent coalition between the clericalist People's Party (successors to the Christian-social party) and the Austrian Socialist party in ruling the Second Republic. The Church withdrew officially from direct involvement in republican politics, reaffirming a 1933 decision of the episcopate forbidding priests to hold political office, though still (until 1959) offering election-year advice to parishioners to vote for the People's Party. The party, too, seeking to present itself as the representative of all non-socialist voters, disengaged from the Church, declaring itself to be a Christian but not specifically Catholic party and disavowing the strictly clerical philosophy which had led to the experiment with a "Christian corporative state." In effect, both party and

Church recognized, for the first time in Austrian history, the secular nature of the state. At the same time the People's Party-Socialist partnership in governing the state and a deliberate "deideologification" of politics, both aspects of the reaction by the two parties against the bitter partisan strife which had led to the civil war of 1934 and to dictatorship, encouraged the beginnings of a dialogue between a more tolerant Catholicism and a reformed Marxian socialism. It also made possible an opening to the left within the People's Party: Christian Socialist and socialist Christian both became tolerated categories and the strictures of *Quadregesimo anno* were gradually forgotten. The socially reformist and sometimes anti-capitalist tradition in Austrian Catholicism, maintained by groups marginal to the main stream since the beginning of the century, was again acceptable as a left wing to the still predominantly conservative party.

3. The role of personalities. The most significant personnel change affecting the response of Austrian Catholicism to social change was the almost simultaneous appearance of a reforming Cardinal-Archbishop in Vienna (Franz König, succeeding Innitzer in 1956), and a reforming Pope in Rome (John XXIII, succeeding Pius XII in 1959), both deeply concerned with furthering pastoral activity in urban industrial centers and with ecumenism. Cardinal König had the additional advantage, rare in the Austrian hierarchy, of cosmopolitanism: his prewar travels and studies abroad and his foreign academic degrees are cited with significant insistence by his disciples today in explanation of his "progressive" attitudes toward urban pastoral work, separation of Church and state, and ecumenism. The effect of the new atmosphere thus created at the "summit" both nationally and internationally was then further enhanced by the influence of John XXIII's social encyclicals, *Mater et Magistra* and *Pacem in Terris*. Their role was similar to that of Leo XIII's *De Rerum Novarum* in sanctioning Lueger's Christian-social party and winning dynastic and episcopal approval for it, or of Pius XI's *Quadregesimo anno* in sanctioning the clerical corporativism of the 1930s: valuable Papal blessing had been conferred at the strategic moment.

4. The psychological impact of Austria's geopolitical position. Most of the country, including six of its eight dioceses, is surrounded on three sides by the Communist-ruled states of Eastern Europe, and most of the Archdiocese of Vienna was for ten years under Soviet occupation. Austrian Catholics are therefore particularly conscious of the status of religious institutions under Communist regimes. One may speculate freely about the nature of the conclusions both the faithful and their clergy draw from their observation of the East and its "silent church," but some liberal Catholic leaders insist that, like the Nazi

experience, a close look at Eastern Europe has made Austrian Catholics more conscious of the risks inherent in a struggle for political monopoly waged between ideologically based parties, and therefore more convinced believers in the value of a democratic and secular state as a neutral political marketplace and sponsor of a pluralistic and open society.

5. Demographic and associated political change. The transformation of Austria into an urban, industrial society accelerated after the Second World War. Where 31 per cent of the population had been dependent on agriculture or forestry for its livelihood in 1910, and 27 per cent in 1934, this figure had sunk to 16 per cent by 1961; the percentage dependent on industry had meanwhile risen from 32 per cent in 1910 and 33 per cent in 1934 to 40 per cent in 1961. The population of the mountain valleys was declining, that of the cities (except Vienna) growing. A Catholic Church that Cardinal König himself calls "traditionally and still a country church" was increasingly inappropriate or at least inadequate in such a society. "It is increasingly imperative," the Cardinal notes, "for the Church to reach out to the urban population, including the working class, in an idiom they understand." [8]

With similar logic the People's Party has been reaching out for a share in the working-class vote, and its recent partial success in nibbling at the fringe of the traditional socialist electorate has strengthened the bargaining position of the party's organized left wing (the Austrian Workers' and Employees' League, OeAAB) within the party federation. The growing relative importance of the urban and industrial element in Austrian society has thus induced both Church and clericalist party to give more serious attention to effective pastoral or electoral cultivation of sectors they had traditionally tended to ignore; as a consequence, both institutions have been forced to consider more attentively the views and policies of those within their ranks who claim to speak for these sectors and who have developed "progressive" views about their handling.

6. The development of a Catholic intelligentsia. In the view of Cardinal König this is a factor of considerable importance. The Josephinian Church was traditionally "weak in intellect," as has been noted. The intellectuals of the Empire in its last century tended to be liberal-nationalists or socialists, "freethinkers" or Jews. The University of Vienna in its better days was the disputed citadel of these two groups, both of them by nature and interest anti-clerical. The physical liquidation of the Jews and the discrediting of their "free-thinking" nationalist adversaries, both consequences of Nazism, left an intellectual vacuum in Austria within which Austrian higher education came

[8] In an interview with the author, June, 1966.

to be dominated by Catholics for the first time in contemporary history. The intellectual elite of the Second Republic is to a slowly increasing extent composed of the products of this changed intellectual environment. There are few socialist university students and, with the nationalist party a marginal force in national politics, even the nationalist student organizations are being gradually overshadowed by growing numbers of the prudently "Black." The Austrian intelligentsia of the Second Republic may be second-class intellectually, but it is—for the first time—Catholic and inclined to be liberal Catholic.

None of these factors can be taken in isolation without risk of distortion. It is not true, for example, that the Church and the Christian-social movement had always ignored the "social question." The latter, as already noted, had its origins in an attempt to deal with the problems of an urban, industrial, "modern" society, and a thin red line of continuity can be traced in the form of a few individual names and movements operating on the fringe of both institutions, from Vogelsang, Lueger, and *De Rerum Novarum* to the OeAAB, Cardinal König, and the encyclicals of John XXIII. The dominant policies of both institutions remained traditional and conservative until World War II, however, and their most serious and official combined effort to engage the allegiance and energies of the classes and forces generated by and suffering under modern social conditions was the "Christian corporative state," pathetically medieval (in the strictest historical sense of the word) and inappropriate in the 20th century.

A conjunction of all the factors enumerated here was therefore necessary to effect the beginnings of a change in the attitude of the Church. The symbol of the conjunction has been the Cardinal-Archbishop of Vienna, who had studied sociology and labor relations at the University of Lille and in the factories of northern France, who lectured at Vienna University, when receiving an honorary doctorate, on "The Social Function of the Church in the Democratic State," [9] and who told a Catholic Action assembly in a speech of May, 1964:

> The mandate which the Church received from the Lord is not that of achieving or defending certain forms of society or even certain forms of economy . . . The Church in its earthly form lives in time. Thus it will always live within the forms of a given time, but it will not and must not be absorbed by these forms . . . Primarily, it is not the task of the Church to achieve changes in society. Nor is it the task of the Church to oppose such changes. During feudalism the Church lived in a feudalistic manner; in the

[9] Cardinal Dr. Franz König, *Worte zur Zeit, Der Erzbischof von Wien zu aktuellen Fragen in Kirche, Staat, und Gesellschaft,* Vienna: Kathpress-Dokumentation, Heft 3, 1963, p. 85.

period of capitalism it lived in a capitalistic manner; in the age of
the industrial mass society it lives in forms complying with current
sociological patterns; and in periods to come it will live in forms
which dominate these periods.[10]

Weighing against these factors tending to produce a revised relationship between the Church and urban, industrial society, and hence a
new role for the Church in that society, there remains the powerful
residue of history and tradition. Clerical and lay Catholic subscribers
to Cardinal König's "progressive" social, liturgical, and ecumenical
views appear to the superficial researcher to be a vocal but small
minority in Austrian Catholicism, largely confined in the Archdiocese
of Vienna to the Archbishop's entourage, some senior prelates, the
Catholic Press Agency, influential but small-circulation Catholic periodicals (notably *Die Furche* of Vienna, considered by many conservative Catholics to be "crypto-socialist"), at least one seminary, and a
handful of parish priests.

On the other side there is the continuing social and religious
conservatism of the majority of active Catholics, including those on
whom the Church is most dependent financially, who are reportedly
not shy about threatening a withdrawal of support if policies and
attitudes they dislike are not abandoned. There is also the resentment
felt by activists in the People's Party, including many of the national
and provincial leaders, who cannot forgive the Church for its party-
political neutrality at elections since 1959, or for König's accommodation with the Socialist party in 1958 which led to that neutrality. They
yearn instead for a return to the good old days of identification of
Church and "its" party, and of support from the pulpit against the
"Belial" of socialism.

A follower of the Cardinal can emphasize happily, "Now it would
be impossible, or at least very difficult, for the Socialists ever again to
make anti-Catholic propaganda in Vienna." But for a senior People's
Party official, the Cardinal is "the red König," who is held responsible
for the party's failure to gain even more votes in the 1966 parliamentary elections (when in fact the People's Party gained four seats and an
absolute majority in Parliment for the first time since 1945, partly
with the help of traditionally Socialist votes in Vienna).

The conservatism of most of the rank-and-file clergy is also an
important factor, and is related to the serious lack of younger priests
and a consequent dependence on poorly trained, badly educated older
men raised in a Church whose primary task was ministering to peasants

[10] Cited in Richard Barta, *Francis Cardinal Koenig*, Notre Dame, Ind.: University
of Notre Dame Press, "Men Who Make the Council" series, 1964, p. 21.

and helping the state to keep them well behaved. (In Austria in 1956 there was one parish priest for each 1500 Catholics; in Europe only Portugal had a worse ratio. Thirty per cent of Austrian priests were over sixty years old, and only 12 per cent were under thirty-five.[11]) A non-Austrian priest, long resident in the country, describes the result as "a rural Church, with little grasp of the problems of industrial, urban society, even in Vienna, despite the work of the Cardinal here."

Most important, perhaps, is what one progressive priest in the Cardinal's circle calls "the Austrian religious attitude," which he considers primarily a consequence of Josephinism. The Austrian's Christianity is "either primitive pagan or for convenience only: religion is good for the children, it makes them behave; for the wife, it makes her faithful; for culture, because so many cultural monuments are religious. The Church is still what Joseph II made it: a service institution of the state, helping preserve the social order, peace and stability. Priests become nervous only at election time, only then do they seem to feel that something is at stake."

FIRST FRUITS OF "PROGRESSIVE" CATHOLICISM

In the present transitional period of hesitant and half-hearted retreat from Josephinism, "progressive" Austrian Catholics can be roughly and rather obviously divided into two overlapping but not coeval groups. The first consists of persons whose primary concern is for the Church's pastoral mission in a secularized state and society and among an urban proletariat that lives almost entirely without the Church. They are in effect neo-traditionalists, for their concern is to find new strategies appropriate to a rapidly changing social and political environment that will preserve and further the traditional function of the Church in Austria: the care of souls (*Seelsorge*), conceived as an exclusively other-worldly function, and so justifying an attitude of conformism toward and support for any social and political order that offers the Church untrammeled freedom in this one field. (Cardinal König himself would appear to belong to this group, if the quotation from his speech cited above is fairly representative of his thinking.) The second group consists of those persons who, in addition to sharing these pastoral concerns, also believe that a Christian Church has a positive duty actively to promote social reforms designed to ameliorate the condition of man in contemporary society. Only the latter group can be expected to play a consciously active and positive role in the kind of

[11] Bodzenta, *op. cit.*, p. 26.

"modernization" implying self-sustaining change and the pragmatic attitudes which make it possible.

The catalog of Austrian Catholicism's post-1945 institutional (as distinct from individual) involvement in social reform is modest and occasionally ambivalent, as is its record in such fields as political parties and urban missionary work. Many of the details can be found in Gerhard Silberbauer's recent study, *Oesterreichs Katholiken und die Arbeiterfrage*.[12] Only a summary of some of them can be offered here for purposes of illustration.

The Austrian Workers' and Employees' League (OeAAB) was founded as a "political movement for Christian social reform" on April 14, 1945, by veterans of the Christian trade union movement, banned by the Nazis in 1938. Three days later the new organization joined with two revived pre-*Anschluss* Christian-social interest groups, the Farmers' League (*Bauernbund*) and the Economic League (*Wirtschaftsbund*, an entrepreneurs association). They founded the Austrian People's Party, organized—in contrast with the monolithic Christian-social party—as a federation of the three leagues, representing divergent interests but bound together by their common "fundamental Christian orientation." "In the following years," Silberbauer comments, "the OeAAB proved to be the strongest non-Marxist force dedicated to social progress, along with the Christian trade union fraction which represented the program of the OeAAB, based on Christian social traditions and Christian social teachings, in the Austrian trade union federation."[13] By the 1960s the OeAAB had also become the most important of the three interest groups joined in the People's party, because it was the only one in a position to add significantly to party voting strength by courting marginal but previously Socialist voters. Its strength, however, continued to be based primarily on employees rather than workers, who in most areas remained true to the Socialist party, and its initial program, drawn up in 1946, was conservative enough to appear outdated and therefore to require revision after the social encyclicals of Pope John XXIII had surpassed it in social radicalism.

One aspect of the OeAAB's program is of particular interest for the insight it offers into the continuing influence of traditional Austrian Catholic social thought on contemporary social reformers. The program is based ideologically on a denial of class warfare and consequently on a belief in the "partnership principle" as a positive alternative to either pure capitalism or Marxian socialism as organizing principles for economic life. While this line of thought has its

[12] Silberbauer, *op. cit.*, pp. 353–97.
[13] *Ibid.*, p. 355.

counterparts, for example, in West Germany or France, OeAAB efforts to elaborate the principle into organizational forms are also reminiscent of "Christian corporative state" experiments under the First Republic, of *Quadregesimo anno*, and of the medieval craft-guild nostalgia common to many European Catholic traditionalists. Also characteristically, the one early and important statutory expression of this plank in the OeAAB program, the *Werksgenossenschaftsgesetz* passed by Parliment in 1946, remained a dead letter, its application obstructed by both entrepreneurs and social trade unionists.

Perhaps the most radical expression of a new approach to contemporary problems has come from the highest level, in the form of an open pastoral letter "to the Catholics of Austria," issued by a conference of all Austrian bishops and archbishops at the end of 1956 (the year that Cardinal König became Archbishop of Vienna), and published in January, 1957, with a lengthy commentary by Bishop Paul Rusch.[14] A Christian social organization, the letter notes, should be based on three principles: the responsibility principle, the social principle, and the principle of humanization of the economy. The first is directed to the individual, who has the duty to work and a consequent right to just wages for his work. The second principle concerns society as a whole: "The economy is to be organized in such a manner that all have an adequate income [defined by Rusch's commentary as a 'family income adequate to meet the needs of a six-member family'] and lasting security. This principle also includes the right to work, the right to capital accumulation through thrift, the right to security against old age." The "humanization principle" is concerned with the primacy of man over machine: "Industry exists to do man's will, the entire economy exists to do man's will. Therefore when human and economic values come into conflict, the human value must be favored."

The bishops' letter specifically identified a Christian social system with a "social partnership system," which Silberbauer describes as "presented here in an essentially more modern form than in the Church's social proclamations of the 1930s, which were overladen with occupational-guild *(berufsständischen)* modes of thought."[15] The goal is to be achieved through company constitutions, guaranteeing the workers a voice in management through joint commissions. (There is also a vague statement to the effect that this form of "partnership principle" should be implemented at "higher social levels" as well, an idea reminiscent of the Yugoslav quasi-corporativist concept of govern-

---

[14] *Der Sozialhirtenbrief der österreichischen Bischöfe*, Innsbruck: Tyrolia-verlag, 1957.
[15] Silberbauer, *op. cit.*, p. 361.

ment by a "pyramid of supreme workers' councils.") Finally, the letter specifically approves the "welfare state," but disapproves the "provider state (*Versorgungsstaat*)," characterizing the latter as a paternalistic do-everything state condemned because it restricts individual freedom unnecessarily and is consequently destructive of individual responsibility and initiative.

The bishops' letter was followed several months later by two events of significance of which it may have been a partial cause. The first was an agreement of March, 1957, between the Socialist-dominated trade union federation and the federal chamber of economy and agriculture calling for the establishment of a federal "paritetic" commission representing workers and management to advise the government on wages and price policies. The second was the informal *modus vivendi* (already referred to in this chapter) reached by the new Archbishop of Vienna and a new leadership in the Austrian Socialist party, ending seventy years of *Kulturkampf* between Church and socialism; its first tangible fruits included Church neutrality in the 1959 federal election campaign, following Socialist agreement in 1957 to recognize the validity of a Concordat with the Vatican signed by the Dollfuss government in 1933.

Thus the process of formal disengagement of the Church from partisan politics was completed, a process which had its public origin in the "Mariazell Manifesto" issued after the first postwar national Catholic conference, which had declared in favor of:

> No return to the state-church regime of past centuries, which degraded religion to a kind of ideological super-structure adorning a citizenly attitude, and which educated generations of priests into passive state bureaucrats. No return to a union of throne and altar, which lulled the consciences of the faithful to sleep and blinded them to the dangers of outer forms devoid of inner meaning. No return to the protectorate of one political party over the church, which may have been necessary under certain circumstances, but which caused tens of thousands to leave the Church. No return to those efforts to realize Christian principles on a purely organizational and legal basis and through force.[16]

With formal disengagement, political clericalism did not disappear. It has been replaced by what one reforming priest calls, disapprovingly, "anonymous clericalism": informal pressure to get the "right man" into a job, the "wrong man" out. In a society as thoroughly "politicized" as Austria's in the era of the Grand Coalition, such anonymous clericalism can play an important role. The demands, one is told, come more frequently from lay Catholics than from the clergy,

[16] Quoted in *ibid.*, p. 372.

and take the form: "X must be dismissed from the faculty (or ministry), he is an atheist," or, "We must have Y as professor of child psychology, he is a good Catholic."

Meanwhile the renewed "social wave" in Austrian Catholicism has produced a flowering of institutes, schools, organizations, and missionary efforts in factories and working-class homes. In some, like the Institute for Social Policy and Social Reform (founded in 1953 under co-sponsorship of a survivor of the interwar Christian-social effort to establish contact with the working class), the tendency was again evident to think in corporativist terms—in terms of what Silberbauer calls "the social pathos of the Vogelsang school, with its ideas of distributed ownership, co-ownership, social contract, etc." [17] The rest, with the exception of a Catholic Social Academy engaged in sociological research as well as education and propaganda for the working class, have been concerned primarily with mission work among the proletariat and only secondarily, if at all, with social problems and social reform. Their combined influence has remained marginal, if Silberbauer's conclusions are correct. They are caught between two fires: on the one hand the passivity or active obstruction of parish priests, for whom the "care of souls is often a superficial and bureaucratic administration of souls," while "church life even in a metropolis is still largely dominated by rural cultural forms"; on the other hand the attitude of most (especially older) workers who "still equate Church and political party" and for whom the "parish house even today appears to be a military bastion supporting an anti-working-class policy." [18]

CONCLUSIONS

"The Church is still what Joseph II made it." That frequently repeated statement, although historically inaccurate in loading the full responsibility for a more complex evolution on one Habsburg, is still the first step toward an interpretation of the attitude of the Austrian Catholic Church to the problems of a changing society. It is fundamentally a self-contented religion, one which sanctifies the existing social order, not one which seeks to reform that order. It asks only that those in charge should accept its role and its place. "Priests become nervous only at election time, only then do they seem to feel that something is at stake."

An American sociologist of religion has spoken of "changes obscured by the continuity of symbols" as a frequent phenomenon in a religious evolution. In Austria today the symbols appear to have

[17] *Ibid.*, p. 368.
[18] *Ibid.*, pp. 377–86.

changed more than the religion. After Vatican II, a visiting Protestant clergyman notes, "the disciplined Austrian clergy introduced nave altars, the westward orientation of the mass, German liturgy, and the rest, but this means little in terms of understanding or approval. The problem of communicating the meaning of Vatican II, even to the parish clergy, is with some notable exceptions acute. 'With it' priests are not uncommon, but they are not common either." On the other hand, the same priest found the "spirit of ecumenism" more widely accepted by Austrian Catholic officials than by English. In Austria it is the Protestants who are reserved and suspicious. The obvious explanation is the apparently secure majority position held by Catholicism in Austria and the insecure status of a tiny Protestant minority—89.1 per cent of the population declared itself Catholic in 1951, 6.2 per cent were members of Lutheran or Calvinistic congregations, and 0.7 per cent belonged to other Christian denominations. Ironically, however, Austria is the only European country in which Protestantism has actually been gaining ground in this century: 93.7 per cent of the population was formally Catholic in 1910, with only 3.3 per cent registered in other Christian churches.[19]

Protest in the social sense is consequently an almost exclusively secular phenomenon in Austria, the preserve of non-Catholics, either socialists or nationalist-liberals. In a random survey the writer of these pages posed to a series of Catholic priests and laymen the question, "Does the Church have a social as well as a pastoral function?" The almost universal answer, from Cardinal to editor and parish priest, can be rendered as follows: in principle, yes, but in Austria today, unlike many other Western societies, there are no grave social problems requiring such an engagement of Church energies. Three of those interviewed, including Cardinal König, volunteered as evidence for this conclusion the non-existence of organized gangs of young delinquents in Austrian cities.

The Church is in movement, however, led by the top of the hierarchy supported by some lay Catholic intellectuals and some younger clergy. In the past twenty-five years these men, followed reluctantly if at all by the parish priesthood and engaged laymen, have (1) accepted the secular state, (2) made formal peace with traditionally anti-clerical Austrian socialism and entered gingerly into a "dialogue with Marxism,"[20] (3) sought to withdraw from unqualified identification with any regime, political party, or economic system, and (4) attempted to

---

[19] Bodzenta, *op. cit.*, p. 18.
[20] Several examples can be found in the Viennese *Neues Forum*, edited by a Catholic Socialist intellectual, Günther Nenning (e.g., a report on the Paulus Society dialogue at Herrenchiemsee, in Heft 150–151, June–July, 1966). The Socialist party's theoretical weekly, *Die Zukunft*, carried a two-part dialogue in June, 1966 (Heft 11–12).

find a strategy that will give the Church access to social classes in which past disinterest or political mistakes have left it largely unrepresented.

Finally, this brief survey of a clinical history and some contemporary symptoms suggests another question, or set of questions, of relevance to the theme of this volume. Is the failure of the religious institution to play a more active and "engaged" role in dealing with problems of modern society a reflection of a genuine secularization of Austrian life underlying a superficial religiosity? Is this not the real "change obscured by a continuity of symbols?" Do the Austrians not have the religious institutions most of them want, concerned with "caring for souls" but not with caring for man in society, because the latter function has been taken over by other, secular institutions? (The head of Austrian *Caritas*, a well-known liberal priest close to the Cardinal, told this writer that he would like to see the scope of *Caritas* activities reduced, with the state taking over kindergartens, much of the charitable work, and the provision of student hostels, but that there is strong lay Catholic opposition to such a development.) Is the religious Austrian so notoriously "comfortable" about his religion (and the non-religious Austrian so comfortable about his lack of it) because they do not ask more of it than security for the after-life and a little help in making the children behave and the wife faithful?

If all of the above is indeed the case, or becoming so, then is the Austrian Church as a social institution once again merely the occasionally useful handmaiden of the state—but this time the almost superfluous religious handmaiden of a secular, modern, and "modernizing" state? If so, it is again, rather than still, "what Joseph II made it": a passive auxiliary, neither conservative nor progressive. Under such definitions Cardinal König is in fact not "undoing Josephinism" but proving a perfect Josephinian prelate when he declares, "The Church in its earthly form lives in time . . . within the forms of a given time. . . . It is not the task of the Church to achieve changes in society. Nor is it the task of the Church to oppose such changes."

III ISLAM

It is not easy for authentic religions of faith to generate anti-traditionalist, rational trends of the patterning of life. In the nature of the case these religions lack any drive toward the rational control and transformation of the world.

Max Weber
The Sociology of Religion

5.

REBELLION, REVOLUTION, AND
RELIGIOUS INTERMEDIARIES
IN SOME NINETEENTH-CENTURY
ISLAMIC STATES

BY STUART SCHAAR

University of Wisconsin

In the Ottoman (Turkish), Sharifian (Moroccan), and Qajar (Persian) states at the beginning of the nineteenth century the palace, governmental, and bureaucratic elites, which collectively could be called the political elite, formed only one of several competing forces.[1] By no means was it preponderant. Rather, power fluctuated depending on the relative strength of tribal units,[2] villages, urban centers, religious com-

---

[1] The author is in the process of investigating how the Mughal (Indian) and Fulani (Central Sudanese) states fit into or diverge from the patterns explained below. His conclusions are still too tentative to include in this paper. He is indebted to Mohammed Guessous at the Center for International Studies, Princeton University, for suggestions after he read an earlier draft of this paper.

[2] Tribal structure in Islam can be summarized most conveniently by an idealized construction of the reference groups closest to the individual as follows:

   a. Tent: 1 family
   b. Extended family: 2–3 tents or a home.
   c. Hamlet or small town: 2–3 extended families.
   d. Subfraction or clan: 3–4 hamlets.
   e. Fraction or canton: either 3–5 clans, about 15 hamlets, 2 large villages, or

munities, occupational groups, monarchs, royal troops, and the political elite. These forces crystallized sets of interests and values that clashed, competed, and at times coincided. Politics worked and the systems held together because these forces conflicted yet cooperated when Islamic societies faced internal and external threats that menaced elite positions. Tensions became institutional in such a way that enemies could not easily destroy one another without seriously weakening or ruining themselves.

Several major sets of competitors vied for power, authority, and influence in these states. First, the political elite included the relatives, courtiers, and personal slaves of sultans and shahs who often played their roles behind the scenes. These actors sometimes remained apart from the rest of the elite and formed numerous cliques. The elite also encompassed government personnel who worked near their sovereigns, and the higher stratum of the provincial military and civil administrators, who often spent a part of each year at court. The most influential within this elite tended to be those who came in frequent contact with their monarchs. Access to the source of power and authority therefore determined elite position in this type of system.*

Pitted against the political elite, and divided themselves, were urban and rural local elites, composed of secular and religious notables from tribes, villages, and cities. Independent rulers ably used all elites (by allying segments of one with others) in order to dominate the political scene. Royal princes, rebellious governors, and powerful military chiefs sometimes fluctuated between these elites. Religious judges (*qadi*-s) and the *'ulama* ** in general, though nominally independent of politics, nevertheless ended up collaborating with government officials.

At the opening of the nineteenth century the political elite maintained only a slight edge over its competitors. This domination always remained precarious, however, and did not lead to constant or total submission of other elites.

200–300 tents. Its size was limited by the maximum distance notables could easily travel to reach a central meeting place.

   f. Tribe: several fractions which coalesced and operated only on grave occasions among sedentary people and more frequently among nomads.

   g. Confederation: several tribes of about 8–10,000 tents which, in most cases, coalesced in times of extreme stress and extended warfare.

* By system we simply mean patterns of authority.

** Transliteration: In this and the succeeding chapter the Arabic letters "hamza" and "ayn" are both represented by the symbol '. Long vowels are omitted except in citations when they have appeared in the original (editor).

ELITES AND MASSES

Politics in these societies at the opening of the nineteenth century may be viewed in terms of their elites. Rulers depended on the grand chiefs of their realms to govern. They, and not the masses, were the ones who counted.

The political elite remained cushioned from most mass reactions. Governors had few links with the bulk of the population. Fundamentally they were manipulative rulers. They had few duties and the masses expected little from them. Nevertheless, governors and administrators were necessary, since they aided monarchs to defend their states against outside encroachment and the faith of Islam against external threats or internal sectional strife. Rulers had great leeway in interpreting the law as long as they maintained the political independence of their states and convinced the righteous that they followed prescribed rules of Islamic ritual and custom.

Central administrations in these states catered to the will of the sovereigns and served as extensions of their divine persons.[3] Bureaucracy centered about them and acted as their private secretariats. Personal influence in decision-making depended on direct contact with rulers and their entourages. Bureaucrats were chosen either for their kinship ties, alliances, or personal loyalty to the throne. Fools and philosophers alike who gained favor were rewarded with high office. Yet power, position, and riches were sometimes ephemeral possessions, easily removed by changes in royal whim, by confiscation, natural disasters, or warfare.

Political institutions were of course not meant to provide the services and welfare benefits which 20th-century Muslims now expect from their governments. Bureaucratic structures remained simple and undifferentiated for the most part, and lacked divisions of function or power. Secular, religious, and moral lines of authority overlapped. Monarchs could intervene in government wherever and whenever they pleased. Tribal chiefs, local landed lords, or even slaves served both as army officers and as the highest state functionaries. The judiciary,

[3] Although Islamic rulers were not divine monarchs, in the way that Egyptian Pharaohs were, Muslims viewed them as earthly representatives of divinity. Legitimate rulers held the highest position in a world which Allah arranged and ordered. See Niyazi Berkes, *The Development of Secularism in Turkey*, Montreal: McGill University Press, 1964, pp. 10 and 13; Ann K. S. Lambton, "Quis Custodiet Custodes: Some Reflections on the Persian Theory of Government," *Studia Islamica*, Vol. V (1956), 125–48 and Vol. VI, (1956), 125–46; and Ed. Michaux-Bellaire, "L'Organisme Marocain," *Revue du Monde Musulman*, Vol. IX, (1909), pp. 1–2.

though theoretically independent, had become a tool of power throughout most of the Islamic world.

Political organization was inefficient. Ministries were organized haphazardly. Officials were constantly shifted from one position to another with little regard for talent or experience. Provincial boundaries varied periodically, depending on the exigences of changing royal strategies in dividing and ruling over tribes, cities, and villages.[4]

LAISSEZ-FAIRE PRACTICES

The basic position of government within Islamic society in the early nineteenth century was similar to the liberal theoretician's view of the *laissez-faire* state. Under this conception the government was supposed to defend the community from outside threats, maintain a minimum of law and security, and engage in token public works which were too expensive to construct with local resources. Politics was an unimportant factor in the lives of most Muslims. Economic decisions had little relation to peasant needs. Religious institutions and local notables, not government, supported welfare organizations and most schools.[5]

The effect of governments on the lives of the Islamic communities

[4] For 19th-century Moroccan government structure see Léon Eugène Aubin, *Le Maroc d'Aujourd'hui*, Paris: Colin, 1904, Chs. X–XII and Henri Terrasse, *Histoire du Maroc*, Casablanca: Éditions Altantides, 1950, Vol. II, Ch. VI. For the Ottoman Empire see H. A. R. Gibb and H. Bowen, *Islamic Society and the West*, London: Oxford University Press, 1950, Vol. I, Part I, Chs. I–II, amended by Norman Itzkowitz, "Eighteenth Century Ottoman Realities," *Studia Islamiac*, Vol. XVI (1962), pp. 73–94, and Bernard Lewis, *The Emergence of Modern Turkey*, London: Oxford University Press, 1961, pp. 356–94 *passim*. See also Robert Mantran, "L'Évolution des Relations entre la Tunisie et l'Empire Ottoman du XVIᵉ au XIXᵉ Siècle," *Cahiers de Tunisie*, Vol. 7 (1959), 319–33; Jean Ganiage, *Les Origines du Protectorate Français en Tunisie (1861–1881)*, Paris: Presses Universitaires de France, 1959, Chs. II and III; Y. Lacoste, A. Nouschi, and A. Prenant, *L'Algérie Passé et Présent*, Paris: Éditions Sociales, 1960, pp. 143–55 and 193–99, and P. Boyer, *L'Évolution de l'Algérie Médiane*, Paris: Adrien-Maisonneuve, 1960, pp. 9–77. For Persia see John Malcolm, *The History of Persia*, London: J. Murray, revised ed., 1829, Vol. II, Ch. XXI, 411–14, and Ann K. S. Lambton, "Quis Custodiet Custodes," *Studia Islamica*, Vol. VI (1956), 142–5.

[5] For the view of the state as a "necessary evil," see Jacques Weulersse, *Paysans de Syrie et du Proche-Orient*, Paris: Gallimard, 1946, 6th ed., pp. 83–5 and Peter Avery, *Modern Iran*, New York: F. A. Praeger, 1965, pp. 93–4. See also Lucien Raynaud, *Étude sur l'Hygiène et la Médecine au Maroc*, Algiers: Léon, 1902, pp. 53–4. For two views of the traditional welfare system in North African tribes see G. Hanotaux and A. Letourneaux, *La Kabylie et les coutumes Kabyle*, Paris: Challamel 1893, 2nd ed., pp. 55–60; and Robert Montagne, *Les Berbères et le Makhzen dans le Sud du Maroc*, Paris: F. Alcan, 1930, Ch. V. For a more generalized view of this system see R. Montagne, *La Civilisation du Desert: Nomads du Orient et d'Afrique*, Paris: Librairie Hachette, 1947, pp. 86–9.

they ruled remained superficial. So long as the people paid their taxes, supplied corvée labor, and refrained from rebellion, central governmental officials rarely penetrated into villages.[6] When they did, their audiences consisted of local notables.

These members of the local elites gained their positions by birth, wealth, and social standing. They served as the prime intermediaries between subjects and officials and acted as mass mobilizers when called on. In this way they controlled rural and urban influence, supplied soldiers, and drained resources from their dependents. In turn, they received privileges and honors. As long as they remained satisfied, the government could ignore mass interests.

Even if rulers wished to intervene in local affairs on a large scale, they lacked the means to do so. Their actions were limited by rudimentary bureaucracies, shortages of skilled personnel, insufficient resources, and poor communications. At best their informants could keep them aware of local problems which they watched develop from a distance. Only when it seemed certain that they would benefit from intervention did rulers become involved in local matters.

The government was rarely aware of the grievances or the needs of the broad masses who were loosely organized. Mass grievances were not channeled through regular institutions to the rulers. The population controlled no elected officials whom they could hold responsible. They depended on rather fickle spokesmen, their community secular and religious notables who tended to ally themselves with the political elite as often as they did with the peasants, and who could not always be trusted.

---

[6] Tax burdens became so heavy in the 18th and the 19th centuries, that peasants, unable to pay their debts and fearful of tax-collecting armies that roved through their midsts, left their land and migrated elsewhere. In Egypt, for example, conditions were so bad that mass escapes became commonplace. In 1831, 6,000 men fled toward Syria to escape Muhammad 'Ali corvée conscriptors and tax collectors. Z. Y. Hershlag, *Introduction to the Modern Economic History of the Middle East*, Leiden: E. J. Brill, 1964, p. 91. See also A. Reifenberg, *The Struggle Between the Desert and the Sown: Rise and Fall of Agriculture in the Levant*, Jerusalem: Publishing Dept. of the Jewish Agency, 1955, pp. 105–107; Gibb and Bowen, *op. cit.*, Vol. I, Part I, pp. 256-8; Norman N. Lewis, "The Frontier of Settlement in Syria 1800–1950," *International Affairs*, XXXI (1955), 48–52; A. H. Hourani, "The Fertile Crescent in the Eighteenth Century," *A Vision of History*, Beirut: Khayats, 1961, pp. 40–42; Gavin Hambly, "An Introduction to the Economic Organization of Early Qajar Iran," *Iran, Journal of the British Institute of Persian Studies*, Vol. II (1964), 70–71; and Ann K. S. Lambton, *Landlord and Peasant in Persia*, London: Oxford University Press, 1953, pp. 162-3 and pp. 169 and 172 where Miss Lambton points out that by 1890 Persian peasants were tied to the soil and could not migrate without a permit. Tax burdens on Moroccan peasants became unbearable only after 1878. Jean-Louis Miège, *Le Maroc et l'Europe (1830-1894)*, Paris: Presses Universitaires de France, 1962, Vol. III, 375-439.

In theory anyone could approach a ruler through his courtiers. Alternatively, subjects might queue up patiently at the gates of royal palaces, hoping that luck would bring them face to face with an official in favor, or the ruler himself. By thrusting petitions on the sultan or shah, a poor Muslim might gain immediate attention. Those who succeeded in doing so, however, remained rare.

CITIES AS CENTERS OF ROYAL CONTROL

Islamic cities, more than tribes or villages, formed the focal points of central control. A provincial capital served as a zone of contact between ruler and notables. There a governor and perhaps a score of minor officials, supported by a garrison, established their regional offices. Traditionally in Islam cities acted as strategic foci of Muslim civilization and secular power. Islam took root in cities. Army garrisons stationed apart, but nearby, maintained the peace. Moreover, urban centers produced the most articulate members of Islamic society. In them important religious leaders flourished and trade and industry attracted merchants and artisans.

Urban notables who acted as community leaders developed subtle political wisdom and acumen which rulers occasionally exploited. Their sophistication sometimes earned their cities semi-autonomy. Periodically, however, when rulers refused to grant these notables special privileges, or when governors demanded too much tribute, after protracted negotiations had failed, the notables proceeded to transform their cities into centers of dissidence. Most often they would begin spreading anti-government propaganda by merely using the natural channels of communication, such as extended families, mosques, religious schools, dervish brotherhoods, guilds, pilgrimage sites, markets, and even public baths. When they did not actually organize resistance, these notables—as traditional opinion leaders—could easily plant embarrassing and unfounded rumors here and there and thus sow the seeds of dissent.[7]

[7] If we use Moroccan cities as indicators, during the 18th century major revolts against central authority took place in Fez in 1727–28, 1734–38, and 1747–48. On the first and last occasions the city's population supported rivals to the throne. During the 19th century they revolted in 1820 and 1874. On the earlier date they were joined by the inhabitants of Tetuan, to whom many notables of Fez were related. On the second they refused to recognize the authority of the new Sultan Mawlay al-Hasan I. Marrakesh revolted in 1867 and again in 1873, and Rabat in 1845 and 1866. Abou 'l-Kasem b. Ahmed ez-Zayyani, *Ettordjeman elmo'arib 'an douel elmachricq ou' lmaghrib* [Abū al-Qāsim ibn Aḥmad al-Zayyānī, *al-Turjimān al-Maghrib 'an Duwal al-Mashriq wa al-Maghrib*], text published and translated by O. V. Houdas, *Le Maroc de 1631 à 1812*, Paris: E. Leroux, 1886, pp. 30–34, 41–

Political legitimacy in Islam was based only partly on the secular criterion of performance. Just as important were appeals to religious or superstitious symbols and rituals. Because legitimacy was based primarily on divine right and abstract ideals, sovereigns could rarely establish their authority and power on firm foundations. Anyone who claimed better descent from the divine source, or greater religious grace than a ruler, could challenge legitimacy.[8]

By merely initiating subversion, the notables of major cities could therefore exact concessions from monarchs or their governors. Urban religious figures—the intellectual leaders of Muslim states and major political forces—could always refuse their allegiance to new and old rulers and thereby intensify political crises. Often enough the countryside surrounding the major cities sheltered potentially dissident tribes, whose presence could be exploited by rebellious urbanites through their rural dependents. Since all cities maintained contacts with rural regions both near and far, urban revolt could easily spill over into rural dependencies.

It was not uncommon for urbanites to instigate sedition in remote mountain and desert regions. Such activity could spawn revolt simultaneously in divergent rural localities without implicating the instigators directly. The best-placed Muslims for stirring rural rebellion included dervishes who had their lodges in both rural and urban areas, or whose *baraka* ("gift of grace") was renowned over great distances; *talib*-s who filled the roles of public scribe, notary, and professional student in cities and villages; itinerant traders who entered principal tribal markets where they exchanged local agrarian produce for manufactured goods; and absentee landlords.

NATURE OF ISLAMIC REBELLION

Continually throughout the century, local elites in Turkey, Morocco, and Persia tried to disturb the position of government representatives in their provinces. Some aided royal pretenders, where they existed,[9]

2, 60–62, and 64 (Arabic text), or 57–63, 75–6, 110–115, and 117 (French tr.), Aḥmad ibn Khālid al-Nāṣirī, *al-Istiqṣā' li-Akhbar Duwal al-Maghrib al-Aqṣā*, eds. Ja'far al-Nāṣirī and Muhammad al-Nāṣirī Casablanca; 1954–59, Vol. VIII, 141–59 and Vol. IX, 137–9 (Arabic text) or French translation from the 1312 A.H. (1895) manuscript by E. Fumey, "Chronique de la dynastie alaouite du Maroc," *Archives Marocaines*, Vol. X (1907), 62–86 and 291–2.

[8] See Robert Montagne, "Réflexions sur la violence en pays d'Islam," *Preuves*, Vol. IV (1954), 9–17, esp. p. 10.

[9] By the middle of the 19th century it became uncommon for royal pretenders to threaten the stability of Muslim states. Great Britain especially had become the major arbiter of thrones in the Middle East and Morocco. Apparent heirs

while others organized regional rebellions or supported *Jacqueries*. Periodic rebellions had the salutary effect of keeping rulers in check. When viewed over the long run, they nevertheless did little to change the nature of society.

Revolts had to be framed in millennial terms to succeed. Rebels either looked forward to a heavenly paradise, or promised return to an idealized Islamic past which had little relation to 19th-century reality. The present was invariably painted in the blackest terms. Secular ideology played no role in such rebellions. It was not needed to mobilize a following. The combination of religious appeal and local discontent sufficed to draw adherents into opposition movements.[10]

Most rebellions tended to be limited in size and scope. Actual fighting, when it occurred, was of short duration and of mild intensity. Once victory was decided, the rebels returned to their plows, their shops, or their flocks, some with booty and others without. The real victors were those who gained power. Once in office, however, they ruled as did their predecessors.

Peasant rebellions usually had little impact on political stability. They were mainly short-lived and aimed at correcting local abuses. The fellah submitted to the vexations of his landlord or shaykh as long as he stayed within the customary bounds of exactions. When they had complaints, peasants registered them with local religious leaders who sometimes transmitted them to the landlords or to the local *qadi* who on occasion appealed to a higher authority. When these attempts

commanded predominant military strength. Islamic elites fearful of European penetration by mid-century feared the unstable effects of succession crises. When the powers were divided on which prince should rule, however, such as in Morocco at the opening of the 20th century, succession crises renewed and intensified. For Persia see Joseph M. Upton, *The History of Modern Iran*, Cambridge: Harvard University Press, 1960, pp. 3–11. For Morocco see al-Nāṣirī, *Al-Istiqṣā'* cited in note 7. For the Ottoman Empire see Carl Brockelman, *History of the Islamic Peoples*, trans. from the German by J. Carmichael and M. Perlmann, New York: G. P. Putnam's Sons, 1947, Ch. 4.

[10] The Babi revolt in Persia beginning in 1844 has recently been interpreted as a protest movement of southern mercantile, educated, and youthful elements against political domination and centralization of power in the North at the Qajar capital, Teheran. It also involved reactions against conservative religious leaders subject to distant governmental direction, and against European encroachment into the country. Like other rebellions that preceded it, the Babi revolt took the form of a messianic movement. See P. Avery, *op. cit.*, p. 52 seq. and A. Bausani, "Bab," *Encyclopaedia of Islam*, 2nd ed., Leiden: E. J. Brill, 1960, Vol. I, 833–5. The other great 18th and 19th-century religious rebellion which shook Islam to it roots was Arabian Wahhabism which postulated its millennialism in the form of a return to classical Islam. See Wilfred C. Smith, *Islam in Modern History*, New York: Mentor, 1957, pp. 48–51 and R. Bayly Winder, *Saudi Arabia in the Nineteenth Century*, New York: St. Martin's Press, 1965. Both movements were "traditional" in the sense that neither tried to institutionalize change nor desacralize politics.

failed, as they often did, peasants refused to work, destroyed irrigation networks where they existed, or exploded into violence by killing or beating up the landlord, his agents, or government officials.[11] Alternatively, when there was little other choice, peasants withdrew from their communities and fled to cities or to distant vacant lands.[12]

Most tribesmen and villagers were ignorant of their potential power through unity. Of great advantage to all elites was the fear and trepidation with which individuals approached most contacts with the world outside of their hamlets. Usually a peasant expended his energy, wealth, and ambitions on local bickerings. Outside his village, clan, or hamlet, custom and tradition varied. That other broader world was subject to abrupt changes dictated by forces beyond his control. There momentary allies intrigued, carried on conversations behind his back, and used him as a mere tool for their own ends. Only the very rich and the notables, who could easily absorb losses, and who had numerous clients to aid them beyond local precincts, could venture into the

---

[11] See Stanford Shaw, *The Financial and Administrative Organization and Development of Ottoman Egypt 1517–1798*, Princeton: Princeton University Press, 1962, pp. 75–6. In Egypt in 1825 about 350,000 men (amounting to about one-third of the country's labor force) engaged in corvée labor, on irrigation canals primarily, during four months of the year. Z. Y. Hershlag, *op. cit.*, p. 90. In 1823 the Egyptian peasants in al-Minufiyah province rebelled, only to be suppressed by palace guards using cannons. In 1824 revolts spread from Isna to Aswan. These were crushed by troops aided by irregulars. In 1826 Muhammad 'Ali refused to accept his own promissory notes, issued to the fallahin, as tax payments. Six villages rebelled but their insurrection was easily suppressed by a royal regiment. In 1838 another uprising occurred in Manfalut province. Again they refused to support the corvée, but were put down by the Inspector General of Upper Egypt. See Helen Ann B. Rivlin, *The Agricultural Policy of Muḥammad 'Alī in Egypt*, Cambridge: Harvard University Press, 1961, pp. 113–21, 201–202, and 207; and L. Bréhier, *L'Egypt de 1798 à 1900*, Paris: Combet, no date, pp. 149 seq. Also Jacques Berque, "Dans le Delta du Nil: Le Village et l'Histoire," *Studia Islamica*, Vol. IV (1955), 104–105. Alternatively, downtrodden peasants gained satisfaction by beating up their village shaykhs, who cushioned the government against mass upheaval. James Augustus St. John, *Egypt and Mohammed Ali*, London, Longman, Rees, etc., 1834, Vol. II, 460–61; and Edward W. Lane, *The Manners and Customs of the Modern Egyptians*, London: J. M. Dent and Sons, 1908, p. 132. The village shaykh nevertheless maintained a dominant position over Egyptian rural life throughout the century. See Gabriel Baer, "The Village Shaykh in Modern Egypt (1800–1950)," *Scripta Hierosolymitana*, Vol. IX (1961), 121–53. For comparisons elsewhere in the three states see Ernest Gellner, "Patterns of Rural Rebellion in Morocco: Tribes as Minorities," *Archives Européenes de Sociologie*, Vol. III (1962), 297–311; Y. Lacoste, *et al.*, *op. cit.*, pp. 193–4 and 271–343; J. Ganiage, *op. cit.*, Ch. V; Z. Y. Hershlag, *op. cit.*, pp. 28–9; Wayne S. Vucinich, *The Ottoman Empire: Its Record and Legacy*, Princeton: Van Nostrand, 1965, pp. 82–3 and 154–6; Bernard Lewis, *op. cit.*, pp. 444–5; J. Malcolm, *op. cit.*, II, 307, 331, 334–5; P. Avery, *op. cit.*, pp. 49–50.

[12] See note 6 above. Withdrawal may be viewed as an alternative to rebellion and submission. It represents a protest against unsatisfactory conditions, but like rebellion it does not necessarily challenge the goals of society and it does not help to define new social purposes.

larger realm of politics across village and factional lines. Consequently, except on rare and defined occasions, the ordinary man avoided the perils of proceeding beyond the limits of his local community.

No Islamic rebels until the end of the century challenged the institutional bases of divine kingship, and there were few drives for complete independence led by Muslims within the three states. The major liberation movements came primarily from Christian subjects in the Ottoman Empire.[13] The autonomous zones under nominal Turkish rule, such as Algeria (to 1830), Tunisia (to 1881), Egypt (to 1882), and Lebanon (under Amir Bashir II and the Egyptians), gained their status due to their distance from the Porte and the weakness of the central government, rather than through armed rebellion. They continued to recognize the moral authority of the sultan, and the most rebellious of them, Egypt, continued to pay tribute to Istanbul. Muhammad 'Ali rebelled late in his life, but even he, when success seemed just around the corner, never contemplated becoming sultan over the Ottomans. Rather he thought in terms of assuming the regency of the Empire. Likewise, in Persia and Morocco, tribal dissidents rarely broke completely with the crown, even when they lived in inaccessible mountainous regions.[14] Only gradually, beginning in the last quarter of the century, did a small group of Muslim thinkers emerge who envisaged changing the nature of the Islamic political system.[15] Until the 20th century, however, most Muslims could not conceive of their states devoid of religious legitimist supports.

[13] For these see Albert Hourani, "Race, Religion and Nation-State in the Near East," in *op. cit.*, pp. 80–83; Traian Stoianovich, "Factors in the Decline of Ottoman Society in the Balkans," *Slavic Review*, Vol. 21 (1962), esp. pp. 628–32; Roderic Davison, *Reform in the Ottoman Empire 1856–1876*, Princeton: Princeton University Press, 1963, Ch. IV; B. Lewis, *op. cit.*, Ch. X, *passim*. For Christian and Druze Revolts in 19th-century Lebanon see Kamal S. Salibi, *The Modern History of Lebanon*, London: Weidenfeld and Nicolson, 1965, Part I, *passim;* William R. Polk, *The Opening of South Lebanon 1788–1840*, Cambridge: Harvard University Press, 1963, Chs. VIII and XII, and Malcolm H. Kerr, *Lebanon in the Last Years of Feudalism 1840–1868*, Beirut: American University of Beirut, Faculty of Arts and Sciences, 1959. For a general review of minorities see Albert Hourani, *Minorities in the Arab World*, London: Oxford University Press, 1947, pp. 23–32.
[14] In Morocco, even in those parts which were not subject to the sultan's worldly rule, the population thought that the welfare of the empire depended on the prince's *baraka*, his holiness or gift of grace. When it was strong and unpolluted, life was bountiful and harvests flourished. Women begat healthy children and the country prospered. Edward Westermark, "The Moorish Conception of Holiness (BARÁKA)," *Finska Vetenskaps—Societens Fördhandlingar*, LVIII (1915–16), pp. 9–10. When Moroccans became convinced that their sultans had lost their baraka, however, tribal notables could easily spark revolts to challenge his right to rule. For Persia see John Malcolm, *op. cit.*, II, 214, 307, 331, 334–5; and Sir Harford Jones Brydges, *Dynasty of the Kajars* (tr. from the original Persian manuscript), London: J. Bohn, 1833, pp. 29 seq., 46–9, 51, 55 seq. and 133–44.
[15] The intellectual currents behind 19th-century social changes, as interesting and important as they are for understanding the entire movement, do not concern

Elite composition changed constantly in the three states during the first half of the nineteenth century, yet political systems varied little. These societies remained relatively stable—except for Egypt under Muhammad 'Ali—despite continual elite fluctuations. The divorce between rulers and ruled was so great that abortive palace coups or intensive elite competition at the apex of the political systems scarcely provoked any reaction among the masses. The peasants, absorbed by their local problems, paid little heed to these fluctuations. Though the masses participated in messianic rebellions and *Jacqueries*, no revolutions took place which redefined institutions and established new social purposes. Elites fought each other in a game reminiscent of musical chairs, with sultans and shahs acting as the umpires.

World transformations beyond the control of Muslims, European penetration into parts of the Islamic world, and internal changes upset the traditional forces in Islam and redefined global power relations. By the middle of the nineteenth century, if not earlier, Muslims throughout the world acknowledged that they had become second-class citizens of a new world Eucumene dominated by the West.[16]

WORLD TRANSFORMATIONS

By the sixteenth century Islam was completely surrounded by (1) Portuguese who rounded the Cape of Good Hope at the end of the 15th century and controlled the Straits of Malacca, near modern Singapore, by 1511; (2) Cossacks to the north whose movements culminated in the Russian drive to the Pacific through northern Siberia by 1638; (3) Lama missionaries in the eastern half of Asia; and (4) eastern European armies who began to coalesce into formidable opponents

us in this paper. Instead its prime purpose is to elucidate how social and economic changes affected politics. A number of excellent studies exist dealing with intellectual changes in the Middle East and North Africa during the 19th century. See E. E. Ramsauer, *The Young Turks*, Princeton: Princeton University Press, 1957; Sherif Mardin, "The Mind of the Turkish Reformer 1700–1900," *Western Humanities Review* (Autumn, 1960), 413–36; Serif Mardin, *The Genesis of Young Ottoman Thought*, Princeton: Princeton University Press, 1962; Albert Hourani, *Arabic Thought in the Liberal Age 1798–1939*, Oxford: Oxford University Press, 1962; W. C. Smith, *op. cit.*, Ch. II; Nadav Safran, *Egypt in Search of Political Community*, Cambridge: Harvard University Press, 1961, pp. 38–50 and 62–75; Elie Kedourie, *Afghani and Abduh: An Essay on Religious Unbelief and Political Activism in Modern Islam*, London: F. Cass, 1966; Nicola A. Ziadeh, "Cultural Trends in North Africa," *Journal of World History*, Vol. VIII (1962), esp. 122 seq.; and Khaldun S. al-Husry, *Three Reformers: A Study in Modern Arab Political Thought*, Beirut: Khayats, 1966.

[16] For a succinct general interpretation of these transformations see William H. McNeill, *The Rise of the West*, Chicago: University of Chicago Press, 1963, Part III.

after Ottoman troops failed to take Vienna in 1529. Islam reached her Eurasian limits by the 17th century. Only Africa thereafter remained as an open area for large-scale new conversions.

Much of the vitality and renewal of Islamic dynasties in the past had come either through the integration of captured slaves into military and administrative posts or from the conversion of march warriors stationed on Islam's frontiers into rulers. Periodically these groups had overthrown effete monarchs and reaffirmed Islam's dynamism. As sources of fresh manpower dried up, and as march warriors continually met defeat after the 17th century, Islam was forced to turn inward and devise new means to generate its vitality. To a great degree, crises in Islam from the 17th century onward involved quests for new forms of internally generated dynamism.

As the centuries passed, the shift of commerce from the Mediterranean Sea and overland caravan routes to Atlantic-Indian Ocean direct routes created gradual but mounting economic and social problems for Muslims. By the 18th century, Dutch and British monopolies of Indian Ocean trade deprived Turks, Arabs, and Persians of rich commercial resources. This turn of events corresponded with Western penetration into relatively virgin territories of the Americas and Asia, where they discovered new resources at the moment that those of the Muslim world began to show signs of depletion. The year 1580 marks the beginning of a continuous flow of New-World precious metals into the Near East and North Africa.

INTERNAL TRANSFORMATIONS

As a result of changing commercial routes, the influx of Peruvian and then later Mexican silver into the Mediterranean, and the steady depletion of resources, 18th-century Muslims lived through a period marked by general financial crisis and social dislocation. Europe demanded raw materials in exchange for her precious metals, so that the supply of goods within Islam grew scarce. Prices spiralled. Inflation depressed the value of tax revenues, military pay, and pensions, creating unprecedented tax burdens on Muslim peasants. Military and peasant rebellions therefore became endemic in the deteriorating situation of the 18th century.

At the moment that governments needed increased tax revenues, landowners transferred their property titles to religious foundations. Once converted into *waqf,* lands escaped periodic tax reassessments and general governmental control. Landowners under this sytem paid insignificant rents to pious foundations whose administrators held the land for them in trust. As prices and taxes rose, this practice became widespread.

By the 18th century, decentralized political power became the general rule in the three states. Local lords, independent of central controls, provided needed revenues to rulers in return for autonomy. Intensification of tax collections forced peasants into debt, and ultimately the rural population began migrating into towns in order to seek out an existence as porters and servants. Crop yields generally declined and tax revenues likewise fell off. Nomads infiltrated into depopulated zones of Syria, Iraq, Iran, and the southern oases of North Africa. The Qajar Dynasty in the last decades of the 18th century developed as a tribal power in the north and won control of Persia from southern commercial interests temporarily ruined by the decline of Persian Gulf trade and Afghan invasions.

In the cities, artisans and their trade guilds, threatened by economic dislocation, developed into major barriers to innovation and later failed to compete with new European manufactured goods which began to enter Islamic markets on a large scale in the 19th century. The rich continued to derive their fortunes from fiscal and political manipulation and refused to invest their surplus capital in productive ventures. Most industry where it existed remained in the hands of non-Muslims and therefore lay outside of the Islamic community.[17]

EUROPEAN PENETRATION

Outright conquests, growing internal nationalism (in part inspired by European models), and Western diplomatic domination forced Islam to confront Europe directly in the 19th century. Gradually the Islamic world had become integrated as agricultural and raw material units of European-dominated politico-economic systems. Although several Muslim states managed to retain their political independence either completely or at least until the 20th century, Europe nevertheless controlled their development.

The three states under review all succumbed to Western influence.

[17] For the above two sections see B. Lewis, *op. cit.*, pp. 21–72; Hershlag, *op. cit.*, pp. 7–26; A. Hourani, "The Fertile Cresent" in *A Vision of History*, pp. 35–70; W. H. McNeill, *Europe's Steppe Frontier 1500–1800*, Chicago: University of Chicago Press, 1964; Gibb and Bowen, *op. cit., passim;* Norman N. Lewis, *Int. Affairs*, Vol. XXXI (1955), 48–60; Gavin Hambly, *Iran*, II (1964), pp. 69–81; *ibid.*, "Aqa Mohammad Khan and the Establishment of the Qajar Dynasty," *Royal Central Asian Society Journal*, Vol. 50 (Apr. 1963), 161–74; A. Lambton, *Landlord and Peasant*, Ch. VI; J. Poncet, "Aux Sources de l'Histoire Nord-Africaine: Prosperité et Décadence Ifriqiyennes," *Cahiers de Tunisie*, Vol. IX (1961), pp. 240–43.

The Ottoman Empire had already suffered a series of costly defeats in warfare from the 17th century onward which depleted its treasury reserves, weakened traditional military forces, and undermined popular morale. It took Napoleon's invasion of Egypt, however, to shatter Islamic smugness and demonstrate concretely that the West by 1798 had gained the decisive upper hand over Muslims. The event has rightly been interpreted as a watershed in modern Islamic history.[18]

The transformation of European powers into Near Eastern over-lords had its immediate repercussions. Morocco at the end of the 18th and the beginning of the 19th centuries turned inward and adopted a policy of isolation in order to reduce the strength and appeals of the southern rebels backed by Spanish money and arms.[19] The Qajars found their newly established state seriously threatened by involvement in Napoleonic power politics between France, Great Britain, and Russia. Henceforth, until the end of the century, Europeans, not Persians, dominated the crucial decisions of Iranian politics. Internal transformations of the Ottoman Empire partly impelled the Serbs, Greeks, and Rumanians to revolt between 1804 and 1830. These were no mere traditional rebellions, but rather independence struggles which based their mass appeals on nationalist symbols and the growing conviction among Balkan Christians that they were superior to their overlords. The French conquest of Algeria beginning in 1830 illustrated Islam's incapacity to repel invasion once a European power was determined to annex and hold Muslim territory.

It was Muhammad 'Ali's assertion of Islamic dynamism that provided a new pattern for change and reform within Islam. His conquest of Syria accomplished for this area what Napoleon had done for Egypt a generation earlier: old political and economic systems crumbled and European influences spread. Muhammad 'Ali's decisiveness and success had threatened Ottoman dynasts (but not divine kingship). European intervention ended the Albanian's imperial dreams at the same time that it forced Ottoman elites to reform or be conquered. The reformers ultimately won. In Morocco, isolation ended with her defeat by France in 1844 and again by Spain in 1860. After this date it became impossible for the Sharifian Empire to remain aloof from European influences.

[18] Nadav Safran, op. cit., p. 26; J.J. Saunders, "The Problem of Islamic Decadence," Journal of World History, Vol. VII (1963), 702; P. Avery, op. cit., p. 35. Bonaparte's Egyptian proclamation was distributed in Arabic throughout Morocco. R. Thomassy, Le Maroc et ses Caravanes, Paris: F. Didot frères 1845, 2nd ed., pp. 357–8.
[19] The role of Spain in forcing the Moroccans to adopt a policy of isolation has not yet been clarified in the literature. See F.O. 52/11 Public Records Office, London, Correspondence 1795–1801.

EUROPEAN ECONOMIC DOMINATION

In the same period that Europe pressed its political domination on Islam, the Muslims fell under the economic sphere of Western capitalist influences. The open-door principle took root in the Ottoman Empire through the Convention of Balta Liman in 1838. Persia likewise submitted by granting a series of capitulation treaties which insured European powers preferential and low tariffs for their imports into Iran. Morocco agreed under duress to Great Britain's pressure for similar rights by 1856. As a result of this movement of "commercial liberalism," the flow of Middle Eastern and North African raw materials to Europe increased significantly, while Muslims absorbed Western surplus manufactured goods and colonial products such as cotton cloth, sugar, tea, and coffee in growing quantities.

The new commercial treaties abolished state monopolies, eradicated commercial inequalities between regions which rulers sometimes manipulated to political advantage, and generally restricted the right of Muslims to raise or lower tariffs as international trade fluctuated. Egypt initially became one of Britain's granaries, then her supply center for cotton. Lebanon filled Lyon's silk needs. Algeria never turned out to be the tropical paradise that Paris hoped to find in North Africa, but it nevertheless absorbed France's unemployed workers and frustrated revolutionaries. The Islamic states were integrated into world-wide trade networks to the point that economic and financial crises in any part of the world affected their internal stability.

During the last quarter of the century, the increased demand for European products created major commercial imbalances in Europe's favor. This, combined with mounting European reclamations and indemnities, drained Islam of its resources, absorbed rural reserves (making famines more severe as the century progressed), and fostered new monetary crises. Changed styles and tastes contributed to the growth of new moral problems and widened the distance between the Islamic vision of what was good and the reality of everyday existence.[20]

[20] For a convenient summary of Turkish, Persian, and Egyptian economic transformations based on European sources see Hershlag, *op. cit.*, Book I. For Morocco, Jean-Louis Miège, *op. cit.*, Vols. II–IV. Egypt's trade balance remained favorable due to high exports, but "there was a deficit on current account due to the heavy burden of the services, interest charges, and expenses payable to creditors abroad." Hershlag, *op. cit.*, p. 106.

REDEFINITION OF INTERNAL FORCES

These transformations upset the traditional forces in Islam and brought about their redefinition. Two trends emerged which foreshadowed a new direction for political development. On the one hand, the three governments assumed direct authority over some formerly autonomous zones and increasingly intervened in rural life. On the other, landlords and tribal chiefs consolidated their control over small-holders or newly settled nomads and either dispossessed them from their lands, illegally claiming title to their property, or integrated them into large-scale commercial enterprises.

Governments increased their interventionist roles in rural communities by several means. The creation of new infantry forces necessitated the mobilization of Muslims from all parts of each state, and also provided the rationale for augmenting taxes. As trade with Europe expanded, and before the capitulation treaties went into effect, Muslim rulers increased their commercial regulatory powers. They established controls on imports and exports, manipulated custom tariffs, created monopolies over industry and trade, and engaged in large-scale buying and selling to raise revenues. Improved communications—telegraphs, steamships, and railways—gave monarchs rapid access to rebellious regions and the means to exploit empty lands or formerly inaccessible resources.

To meet new demands on government, bureaucracies expanded and became somewhat more rational as the century evolved. The complexity and growing quantification of problems forced rulers to turn over decisions to more competent hands—mainly secular trained technicians—who were integrated into the political elite. Bureaucrats gained greater autonomy and security, and provided continuity for regimes. The functions of administrative operations received greater definition. There was less overlapping of duties and more division of labor. The personnel slowly developed which permitted rulers to expand the scope of their operations.

Control of modern armaments supplied sultans and shahs with the requisite strength needed to break the power of local lords in accessible areas such as Anatolia, the triangular coastal region of western Morocco, and the central zone of Persia surrounding Teheran. Normally sovereigns could obtain resources, foreign technical personnel, and large quantities of surplus European armaments to maintain their military predominance in these regions. The use of cannon also raised the number of casualties in warfare and increased the restraint of rebels when dealing with the central government.[21]

RURAL CONCENTRATION OF POWER

Muslim grandees who benefited from hereditary land rights, European commercial ties, or consular protection by mid-century formed a class of large landowners. Many of these persons originally were taxfarmers, usurers and/or speculators, who either dispossessed debtors from their holdings or successfully organized new large units of rural production and foreign distribution.

The inroads of a money economy and European commercial penetration into Islam disrupted old patterns. All three regimes faced costly wars, rising service charges on foreign debts, and growing European reclamations. Bureaucracies grew and all states introduced ambitious and expensive reform programs. Governments increasingly demanded tax revenues in cash instead of kind. Simultaneously foreign manufactured goods and tropical products were shipped into Muslim markets at prices peasants could afford. Landlords and sometimes governors engaged peasants to produce raw materials, foodstuffs, and, at the end of the century, traditional handicrafts in cottage industries, which they marketed in South Asia, Europe, and America. Regions specialized in such cash crops as cotton, tobacco, nuts, rice, opium, wheat, barley, silk, and wool. Initially all seemed to gain by this new system, but gradually peasants accumulated more debts than money. Creditors foreclosed many mortgages and absorbed these properties into larger units.

By various means landlords had become magnates and no longer were the patriarchical figures of old. Many of them even represented their governments in some localities. The distance between them and their villagers grew. They ceased protecting their peasants and no longer arbitrated their disputes.

During the last decades of the century, growing numbers of rich landed families migrated to the cities. The overseers and middlemen that they left behind cared little about insuring the welfare of the peasantry. They worried primarily about meeting quotas and export

---

[21] See B. Lewis, *op. cit.*, Chs. IV and VI; R. Davison, *op. cit.*, Niyazi Berkes, *op. cit.*, pp. 272–3; P. Avery, *op. cit.*, Chs. V and VI; A. Lambton, *Landlord and Peasant*, Chs. VI and VII, *passim;* the author's unpublished doctoral dissertation for Princeton University (1966), "Conflict and Change in Nineteenth-Century Morocco," Ch. IV; Charles Issawi, *Egypt in Revolution*, London: Oxford University Press, 1963, p. 19.

requirements. Absentee landlordism tended to convert the Muslim peasantry in Persia, the Fertile Crescent, and Morocco into slave-clients of regional grandees, while the profits of rural labor increasingly accrued to the cities.

The dominance which towns once enjoyed in the old system returned as new wealth concentrated in urban villas. Gaps widened between rural and urban elements. The rich became ostentatious and the ranks of the poor swelled. Class differentiation developed as a prelude to the class conflicts that emerged in the 20th century.[22]

In the traditionally more autonomous zones tribal chiefs, with the aid of artillery, consolidated their power to an unprecedented degree. They often won appointments as hereditary governors after consolidating their holdings. In this way large communities were converted into nominal tributaries of central governments. Some chiefs amassed great fortunes by having slaves work land expropriated from defeated enemies or ruined peasants, by collecting road tolls, taxes and protection fees; by buying unripened crops cheaply and selling them later at large profits; and by organizing fairs or by establishing monopolies for the sale of goods on their territories.

As the grand chiefs expanded their regulatory powers and intervened in private life, subjects began to assume that only their overlords could solve communal problems. When they consolidated their power, chiefs often destroyed the more important fortresses which also functioned as communal storehouses where families set aside surpluses needed in times of famine. Community chests—which supplied charity and hospitality for the poor and strangers—were emptied and confiscated on the grounds that the Grand Seignor assumed responsibility for the welfare of his subjects. Regional corvées of mutual assistance were converted into levies of forced labor which the lord exploited.

The intermediaries of these societies, who had previously lent politics a rudimentary pluralism, were weakened. Holy men, though

---

[22] By the end of the 19th century small-holders in Anatolia benefited from land reforms introduced under Mahmud II and maintained their ownership thereafter. Large commercial agents organized the marketing of their produce. In Egypt land tenure was polarized: half was controlled by large owners, a majority of whom were members of the Khedive's family, while the other half remained divided into very small parcels. Large owners dominated in the Fertile Crescent and Persia. When Mahmud tried to abolish feudal fiefs in 1831, Arab Pashas in Syria and Palestine rebelled and he had to return the fiefs to their former owners. All later attempts to break them up failed in the 19th century. In Morocco commercialization and absentee land ownership developed most intensely in areas surrounding cities. Strongmen throughout the country centralized their power. Hershlag, *op. cit.*, pp. 15–17, 28–31, 33–4, 38–41, 57, and 68–70; A. Lambton, *Landlord and Peasant*, Ch. VII; J.-L. Miège, *op. cit.*, Vol. IV, 397 seq.; J. Berque, "Médinas, villeneuves, et bidonvilles," *Cahiers de Tunisie*, Vol. VI (1958), p. 10; P. Avery, *op. cit.*, p. 76 seq.

abounding, were forbidden to intervene between ruler and ruled. Local notables could no longer meet in village councils which the chiefs disbanded. Without the backing of a community forum and deprived of allies, local notables could no longer check the power of their chiefs as they had in the past. The powerful were either bought off, were defeated, or rallied to the new local lords. Advancement in such societies demanded submission. Prisons henceforth guarded recalcitrants for periods much longer than a customary few days.

The success of these chiefs thus led to the destruction of local structures, traditions, and customs. In building their dominions they wiped out cantonal boundaries fixed by custom and united groups with long histories of hostility. Local feuds came to an end or were limited. New outlets for tensions developed when these chiefs mounted external wars of conquest and battles for supremacy. In the processes of this disintegration the trappings of urban Islam entered into the chief's territory. *Qadi*-s were chosen to insure justice favorable to the interests of these local magnates.[23]

QADIS

At an earlier time in Islamic history, *qadi*-s, or religious judges, had effectively channeled mass grievances to officials. There are many cases recorded of judges bringing peasant claims before rulers. By the 19th century, however, they could rarely afford to represent anyone other than themselves. Furthermore, the increased application of customary (*'urf*) and civil (*qanun*) law in cases handled directly by centralizing powers tended to narrow the scope of religious law (*shari'ah*), which the *qadi*-s dispensed.

Moreover, the venality of the Islamic bureaucracies created a situation in which judges, like other officials, had to purchase their posts. Many of them enjoyed the fruits of corruption and gained fortunes by selling degrees, favors, and influence, or by engaging in tax farming and land speculation. Some became rich landowners. Instead of the wisest or the most upright men being chosen for the religious judiciary, the richest or the most corrupt filled vacancies. There were exceptions, of course, but they only highlighted the rule that rendering justice was the means to acquire wealth.

In those cases where *qadi*-s might still have attempted to represent mass grievances and plead the cause of peasants, they had become

---

[23] A. Hourani, "The Fertile Cresent," in *op. cit.*, p. 46; R. Montagne, *Les Berberes et le Makhzen*, p. 269 seq.; *ibid.*, *La civilisation du desert*, Ch. VII; Ann Lambton, *Landlord and Peasant*, Ch. VII, *passim*.

compromised by their position between large landowners or powerful governors and depressed peasants. Judges who remained in rural areas attempted to convince peasants that their lot was not as bad as they imagined, while they simultaneously convinced the overlords of the same villagers that their dependents did not really mind tyranny at all.

These judges were caught between Scylla and Charybdis, for if they channeled mass grievances to the secular powers effectively, they faced the danger of having their grain rations and pensions reduced, or cut off entirely. If, on the other hand, they sided openly with the overlords, they faced the danger of being lynched by the peasantry. Most *qadi*-s in the Ottoman Empire and in Morocco therefore adopted the middle ground of consoling both masses and elites, and thereby reinforced the status quo.[24]

THE DEVELOPMENT OF A MASS

By the middle of the 19th century a very precarious intermediary structure separated the masses from the dominant power. Traditional forms of social integration, welfare establishments, and community chests began to disappear. By the end of the century large segments of the peasantry had become a mass: growing numbers of individuals confronted power directly without being cushioned by traditional buffers or intermediaries. These peasants henceforth had to refer directly to the dominant power for their welfare, for their very survival.

Formerly peasants had been isolationists. Their welfare had been insured by extra-governmental institutions. Rebellions had represented protest against government interference in local affairs. But by the end of the century peasants in growing numbers became interventionists and demanded more government interference to insure their well-being. Complaints grew that government was not doing enough. At that point modern revolution became conceivable.

That is not to say that Ottoman, Moroccan, or Persian peasants developed into rural Jacobins. Nevertheless, an available mass gradually emerged which could have been organized into a potent force for change. The leaders who met the challenge in the 19th century, however, were holy men, not revolutionaries.

[24] Niyazi Berkes, *op. cit.*, pp. 43, 61–2, 165–9; H. Efendī, *Ottoman Egypt in the Age of the French Revolution*, trans. from the Arabic by S. Shaw, Cambridge: Harvard University Press, 1964, pp. 95–9.

MUSLIM HOLY MEN

Popular living saints, *mullah*-s, *talib*-s, *sharif*-s, leaders of dervish orders, and other holy personalities long have performed the function of intermediary throughout the Islamic world. These local religious personalities often lived in separate communities, villages, or if they belonged to dervish orders, in lodges near their patron saint's tomb surrounded by family and disciples. They were generally respected through their possession of the holy baraka commensurate with their descent from the prophet, or their frequentation of holy personalities, and their store of local influence and religious knowledge. They formed a natural aristocracy whose normal job (aside from performing rituals and teaching) was to arbitrate disputes. Peasants preferred to have holy men settle their disputes rather than submit them to authoritarian landlords, corrupted officials, or agrarian overseers. In this way, religious figures extended their influence over many localities throughout the Islamic world.

In order to fulfill their role as intermediaries and pacifiers, holy men had to know the slightest nuances of regional alliances, family ties, and enmities. Their holiness and their knowledge gave them the means by which they gained their livelihood, so that they could be free of government interference or pressures from regional lords if they so desired.

In those regions where monarchs, landlords, or tribal chiefs were powerful, and when holy men were too weak to establish independent zones of influence, or too numerous to benefit from charity or arbitration fees distributed by fellow believers, they offered their services to these rulers. They then supported official policies of divide and rule in order to profit from their role as arbiters. Some *sharif*-s in Morocco (often but not always the less fortunate relatives of regional magnates) guaranteed support to the sultans in almost every locality. Certain of them even received tax exemptions, a yearly income, and periodic bonuses in return for their services and loyalty. Through the intermediary efforts of such personalities, rulers might control populations that normally would have escaped their jurisdiction.

The large supply of holy men in Islam meant that these religious figures could be found in every camp. They were in great demand as protectors and spokesmen for peasants and artisans. Rulers used them as spies or to centralize control in inaccessible regions. Landlords employed some to prod the peasantry forward for greater agrarian production. By patronizing holy men and supporting Islamic learning, tribal chiefs legitimized their rule.

Periods of crisis increased the ascendancy of the holy men over the masses. Often without power, and at times insensible to the appeals which power offered, some of them could afford to criticize power-holders freely without offering viable solutions to 19th-century dilemmas. They were often alienated from the upper echelons of the Islamic hierarchy, the more important urban *'ulama*, who tended to ally themselves with rulers and supported their reforms. The lower levels of religious leadership remained closed to the masses and mixed freely with peasants and artisans. More than any other articulate group in Islamic society they understood mass grievances. Sometimes sincerely, but nevertheless ably, they exploited xenophobic feelings latent in their Muslim followers and capitalized on European domination over Islam and the seeming incapability of rulers to defeat or reject Christians. In the Ottoman Empire they roused communal conflicts between the millets, aided in defeating the British tobacco monopoly in Persia, and fomented anti-Jewish riots in Morocco. In their interaction with secular elites, it became clear that holy men were being used for non-religious ends. On the mass level, however, some of them fulfilled meaningful, if at times destructive, functions as intermediaries between a dominant power and a crisis-ridden population.[25]

CONCLUSIONS

As a result of the evolution we have outlined above, governments were forced to confront the unenviable task of having to provide for the well-being of their subjects in many scattered areas simultaneously. This tendency has accelerated in the 20th century as most governments have destroyed or reduced the power of landlords and tribal chiefs remaining in the Middle East and North Africa. The effects of this centralization of power by government which is rooted in the 18th and 19th centuries are revolutionary. Henceforth, only those governments which are able to meet popular demands for more food, more employment, and more schools may hope to salvage their hold on

[25] R. Brunel, *Le Monachisme Errant dans l'Islam*, Paris: Librairie La Rose, 1955; Emile Demeghen, *Le Culte des Saints dans l'Islam Maghrébin*, Paris, Gallimard 1954; Niyazi Berkes, *op cit.*, pp. 18, 43–5, 61, 82, 90, 258–9; P. Avery, *op. cit.*, Chs. VII and VIII; Herbert L. Bodman, Jr., *Political Factions in Aleppo, 1760– 1826*, Chapel Hill: University of North Carolina Press, 1963, Ch. IV; Uriel Heyd, "The Ottoman 'Ulemā and Westernization in the Time of Selīm III and Mahmūd II," *Scripta Hierosolymitana*, Vol. IX (1961), 63–96; Serif Mardin, *The Genesis of Young Ottoman Thought*, pp. 140 seq.

power over the long run. This implies that those regimes which wish to maintain their positions must modernize—i.e., institutionalize change, in order to fulfill the expectations of those over whom they rule. Yet, the staying power of conservative regimes—those who refuse to institutionalize change, or who do so too slowly—has been notorious in the area under review, not, if our analysis is correct, because the masses are reticent in expressing their grievances, but rather because few revolutionary competitors of these governments have been allowed free access to the masses. Likewise, even when military regimes have assumed power through coups and have proclaimed their revolutionary intentions, the fear of allowing Pandora out of her box by organizing, *ex post facto*, a demanding peasantry which wants reforms simultaneously in all sectors, has prevented these regimes from using the full revolutionary potential of their masses.

The revolutionary impact of the peasantry has therefore been more indirect than direct in the Middle East and North Africa. Their pressures and demands have been made felt more by the weight of their sheer numbers than through revolutionary movements. By their mere presence they have had and will continue to have a dynamic impact on Muslim regimes. The day is yet to come, however, when the revolutionary force of Muslim peasants will be harnessed directly and channeled into movements to modernize their societies. Meanwhile, if secular leaders fail to improve the living conditions of Muslims, religious leaders still abound and will exploit mass discontent for their own ends. Let us remember that an available mass may be mobilized both by revolutionaries and reactionaries.

6.

LOCAL THEOCRACY AND NATIONAL SECULARISM: THE MALAY-MUSLIM STATE OF KELANTAN

BY WILLARD A. HANNA

American Universities Field Staff

Of all the parts of peninsular Malaysia, the northeastern coastal states of Kelantan and Trengganu are the least developed and the most backward. By ordinary Southeast Asian standards, it should immediately be added, all of the eleven states of the former Federation of Malaya, those of the east coast included, have achieved remarkable progress. Kelantan and Trengganu, however, have not in the past kept pace with the rest, and Kelantan in particular now suffers a severe handicap. Besides being one of the two most retarded—or, to put it more delicately—the least advanced of the Malayan States, Kelantan is the one which is most meagerly endowed with natural resources and the most subject to population pressures. In colonial days it was the most remote from the main centers of British interest, investment, and authority, and the least exposed to modern education or other improvements. In post-independence days it has been estranged from the national government and subject to serious disability with regard to participation in development programs. Together with Trengganu, it constitutes the region of Malaysia in which the concentration of ethnic Malays is highest (92 per cent in Kelantan, 95 per cent in Trengganu) and the Malay cultural and Muslim religious influences are greatest. In Kelantan, to an even greater extent than in Trengganu, the Malay-Muslim system is deeply traditionalistic and thus resistant to modern change, not merely in political, economic, and social affairs, but also in strictly religious matters.

The State of Kelantan (area 5,570 square miles; population 650,000) affords opportunity for a neatly capsulized case study for any researcher interested in determining the relationship between religion and development, particularly for anyone prejudiced by belief that the two are to some significant degree incompatible. In the commonly accepted description of Kelantan as a retarded state in which Malay-Muslim influence is stronger than anywhere else in Malaya, the implication is obvious that Malay-Muslim predominance has not served to drive the society vigorously toward development. Race and religion, nevertheless, are by no means the only factors which must be considered in explanation of Kelantan's relative backwardness. Resources, education, planning, and politics are also of major importance—the last three are also related directly to race and religion, of course. Yet if the Malay-Muslim influence has not and does not now make for swift progress, it does provide a highly significant safety factor. By reason both of racial disposition and religious training, the Kelantan Malay-Muslim has been inclined contentedly to accept relative deprivation with regard to the amenities of modern life. He does so even when he observes others, including west coast Malay coreligionaries, already enjoying a far greater share of them.

HISTORY

The State of Kelantan has never been well integrated into the rest of the nation, and has been far removed from the main stream of Southeast Asian civilization. It is geographically isolated by almost impenetrable mountain jungle. It lacks a seaport or even, although it occupies the rice-growing valley of the Trengganu River, any very busy or prosperous river port. During its obscure early history Kelantan experienced the usual regional procession of Khmer, Hindu, Siamese, Malay, Indonesian, and Chinese travelers, traders, warriors, priests, pirates, and fugitives. But it created no particularly advanced or distinctive society of its own and achieved no great measure of power, emerging into recorded history in the 17th century as a group of feuding little rajadoms, dependent generally upon the nearby Malay-Muslim state of Pattani (now part of southern Thailand). Pattani itself was intermittently subject to the Siamese Buddhist kings whose capital was at Ayuthia and later Bangkok. At the turn of the 20th century, Kelantan featured conspicuously in an Anglo-Siamese contest for control over what is now northern Malaya. In 1902 the British placed a Resident Commissioner in Kelantan, and in 1909 they gained Siamese acquiescence to inclusion of the state within the British sphere of influence. They treated it thereafter as a "protected" but "non-federated" state of the British Malayan colonial system. Between Kota Bharu (present population: 50,000), the capital of Kelantan, and the Malay-Muslim population centers of peninsular Thailand to the north, the ties of race and religion remained strong, as did—and does— sentiment for political reunification.

Shortly before its formal entry into the British system, Kelantan became burdened by a handicap such as no other state of Malaya ever knew. In about the year 1900 the Sultan was constrained to award to a British adventurer by the name of Duff a vast concession of territory, originally at least half of the state. Mr. Duff, who in effect had gained sovereign rights to this vast tract of jungle in the interior of Kelantan, thereupon raised private capital in London to float rather a leaky concern known as the Duff Development Company. For the first several decades the Company itself did little development, seeking rather to enrich itself by claiming compensation from those who did, first the government builders of the state railway, which had to cross company land. The Duff Development Company and the Kelantan government kept making demands upon each other and entering into prolonged and costly lawsuits. By 1930 the company had mined its bonanza for something on the order of £900,000 in compensation and damages, while still retaining title to some thousands of acres of land some of which by then it had taken the trouble to plant in valuable rubber. In the years prior to World War II the Kelantan State Government never collected more than about M$2,500,000 (£170,000) at most in revenue, so its payments to the Company saddled it with quite disproportionate debts.

Kelantan's experience with the Duff Development Company, which remains today the largest foreign concern in the state but one which operates on much reduced holdings and on a much more enlightened basis than before, did not make for cordial reception of non-indigenous enterprise. Other British operators, as well as Chinese, did enter the state, especially to plant rubber, but not quite with the confidence or enthusiasm they exhibited elsewhere. The British administrators of the state, who deplored Mr. Duff and all his deeds, shared with the Malay population a desire to maintain Kelantan's relative isolation. In 1930 they passed the state's Malay Reservation Enactment, a piece of legislation similar to others being enacted elsewhere in Malaya but much more sweeping in scope. By the terms of the Kelantan Act almost the whole of the State of Kelantan was constituted a single large Malay Reservation except for two enclaves in the interior and parts of the towns of Kota Bharu, Tumpat, and Pasir Mas. On a Malay Reservation, according to the law, only an ethnic Malay was permitted to own property although, with special consent of the government, certain lands could be leased to non-natives for the purpose, say, of planting a rubber estate. In Kelantan the terms of the Malay Reservation Enactment were so strictly interpreted as severely to limit British and more especially Chinese entry and investment.

Under benevolent British protection the Kelantan Malay population multiplied rapidly and enjoyed the opportunity to satisfy the characteristic Malay-Muslim ambition. This meant to acquire land, plant rice, and lead the traditionally serene life on the kampong, with simple but adequate food, clothing, and shelter, and sufficient surplus to provide for the mosque and the palace. In addition to or instead of planting rice, many of the Malays also planted copra and rubber and engaged in river or coastal fishing. Some practiced the traditional arts and crafts of carpentry, metal working, basketry and batik making. Others devoted themselves to music, the dance, and the puppet theatre.

The State of Kelantan became, in short, an attractive museum of traditional Malay-Muslim life and custom. Its mosques and its *suraus* (small kampong mosques) flourished and proliferated. Its feudal court, which centered upon the Sultan and his family living in the royal palace in Kota Bharu, retained most of the trappings of feudalism, but the British saw to it that the oldtime feudal abuses were abolished. They also made certain that the drains flowed and the taxes were efficiently and honestly collected and spent. The British established a few schools (only one at the secondary level, however, an English language school in Kota Bharu), a hospital, and some clinics. They built roads, a railroad, a minute port, public utilities, and made various other modern improvements. But the British did not thrust broad social change upon the Malays, nor did the Malays themselves demand it. The Chinese, being a mere 5 per cent element in the population (as compared with 50 per cent in Selangor), supplied no very noteworthy pressure or example.

THE CONTEMPORARY PERIOD

Kelantan thus drifted placidly into the mid-20th century. Then suddenly, after World War II, as Malayan independence neared, Kelantan began to recognize the disparity between itself and its neighbors. In

148

the new Federation of Malaya, Kelantan had the lowest per capita income of all the member states. (It is still only about M$750 per year, as compared with M$1,200 for Malaya as a whole.) In a basically agricultural society at least half of the population owned no land, and of those who did, a good half owned less than the minimum economic holding of three acres. Rapid growth of population and the Malay-Muslim system of inheritance—equal shares for all sons—meant that fragmentation of holdings was proceeding at an extremely dangerous rate. Besides being the poorest of the Malays, the Kelantan people were also the worst educated. Far less than half the children of primary school age were actually registered in school, and most of them in schools of distinctly inferior standard; very few persons had achieved the secondary, let alone university level. The state had virtually no manufacturing industry, its communications system was rudimentary and its towns and cities were soporific. Furthermore, although this factor was not openly acknowledged, Kelantan was saddled with onerous obligations to the traditional authorities of both church and state. And it was beginning to steer what might prove to be a collision course with the federal government.

To a greater degree than any other state of the nation, Kelantan retains today the distinctive features of the traditional Malay-Muslim Sultanate, albeit in its leisurely decadence rather than in its vigorous prime. It is much preoccupied with the affairs of the palace and of the mosque, and seeks in the tranquility of the kampong to escape from the perplexities of the modern world. The Sultan has long since relinquished his civil authority, but the feudal hierarchy nevertheless remains extremely powerful in local politics and administration. The Sultan has delegated his ecclesiastical authority principally to the Majlis (Religious Council) and the Mufti, but the official church bodies and their leaders remain far more powerful than in any other state. The popularly elected State Assembly, the Council of Ministers, and the career civil service (which has declined to merge with the federal civil service) are all heavily freighted with feudal scions, *ulamas*, *imams*, and *hajis*.* The state government, thus, for all its veneer of modern form, seems to other state governments, and more especially to the federal government, to be something of an anachronism. State-to-state and state-to-federal governmental relations are thus complicated by mutual misunderstanding.

His Highness, Tuanku Yahya Petra, Ibni Sultan Ibrahim, D.K., S.P.M.K., S.J.M.K., D.M.N., S.M.N., is "Sultan and Ruler of the State of Kelantan and its Dependencies" (the latter undefined). Born in

---

* Transliteration in this chapter corresponds to prevailing usage in Malaysia (editor).

Kota Bharu in the year 1917, educated in Kota Bharu, Penang, and later, for five years, in England (although not at a university), Sultan Yahya Petra ascended the throne on the death of his father, the late Sultan Ibrahim, in 1960. According to local official report, the Sultan takes his duties quite seriously. It seems that he does not take them so very seriously, however, as to keep himself *au courant* with the latest political, economic, and social developments, or to compose his own "speeches from the throne" (the annual reviews and forecasts which mark the opening of the State Assembly), or to show up very frequently at school commencements, athletic meets, development project inaugurations, or other routine affairs. His appearances on state occasions, however, are marked by much ceremony as, for instance, at the beginning or the end of Ramadan (the Muslim fasting month), or the Prophet's birthday, or on his own birthday, or at the opening of the State Assembly. His Highness' state function, in other words, is mainly ceremonial.

The Sultan's official wife is his first cousin, Tengku Zainab, by whom he has four daughters and one son. The son, Tengku Ismail Petra, age about twelve in 1966, and studying with a private British tutor in the palace, is the heir apparent. His Highness has at least one other wife, but only the Sultanah enjoys any official position. His hobby is motor cars—an old Rolls Royce, a new Cadillac (purchased by the state in 1966 for M$33,000), and a small fleet of Jaguars and other racy models, which he himself propels sedately about the town and along the state highways.

The Sultan and his family occupy the new royal palace—in fact the former British Residency, an imposing mansion set in well-gardened grounds within the city limits on the bank of the Kelantan River. The old royal palace, a rambling, rickety frame structure built around the turn of the century, stands in a high walled compound in the center of the town and is now reserved for state occasions and royal houshold functions. There the privileged visitor may view the royal thrones, the river barges, the drums, the lances, the royal regalia—including a magic jeweled *kris*, an elaborately worked silver betel box, and the crown jewels.

It is a revealing aside upon the finances of a Malay-Muslim state that the Sultan draws an annual tax-free stipend of M$180,000, the Sultanah M$45,000, the Heir Apparent M$18,000, some thirty-one other members of the royal family a total of approximately M$52,000, and various other royal pensioners a total of about M$30,000. To approximately M$370,000 in stipends and pensions must be added another M$244,085 in 1966 for maintenance of the royal palace and household. This figure includes the wages of five cooks, five gardeners, one religious teacher, and one *bomah* (soothsayer), out of a grand total of fifty-three persons. The direct costs for the upkeep of the royal family, thus, come to approximately M$615,000 per annum. This represents 10 per cent of the 1966 total (M$6,725,198) which accrues to the government from state (as contrasted with federal) sources of revenue. It represents only about 2 per cent, however, of the total state expenditure (the federal government makes up the difference between state revenue and state expenditure). The expenses of the Kelantan Sultanate, it should be noted, are not out of line with those of the other states. So long as the traditional ruler retains, as he still does, the loyalty of his Malay subjects, it is possibly a cheap price even for a poor state like Kelantan to pay for the luxury of peace and order.

The chief religious body of Kelantan is the *Majlis Ugama dan Adat Istiadat Melayu* (Council of Religion and Malay Custom), a body of fifteen *ulamas* (distinguished religious leaders) appointed by the Sultan. The most important members of the Majlis are the President (appointed for three years), at the present time a distinguished ex-civil servant, Dato Mohammad Yusuf bin Hassan, and the Mufti Kerajaan (Grand Mufti, also appointed for three years), at the present time Haji Mohammad Mahir. In Kelantan the Majlis is an autonomous body operating independently by authority of the Sultan; in the other Malay states, it is subject to the control of the State Department of Religious Affairs. It exercises direct control over all of the mosques and suraus, appoints the imams, operates the religious schools, supervises the religious examinations, and collects the *zakat* (compulsory tax on agricultural products) and the *fitrah* (compulsory contribution at the end of the fasting month). It controls and administers all church property, including money, lands, and buildings which have been bequeathed to the religious establishment and constitute a charitable trust. It also distributes charity to the poor and provides for the sustenance of converts during their period of probation.

A new state enactment (May 30, 1966) carefully redefines the powers and responsibilities of the Majlis, seeming, somewhat surprisingly from the outsider's point of view at least, rather to strengthen than to weaken its authority. The new enactment, for instance, not only stipulates the exact amount of the zakat and fitrah but provides stiffer penalties than before for failure to pay. The old act, say the sponsors of the new, was too loose in its terms and the prescribed penalties had long since ceased to correspond to the increased cost of living.

The prescribed zakat for the Muslim padi farmer in Kelantan today is 10 per cent of his crop in kind or cash, if he produces not less than 375 *gantungs* of rice per year (the average yield of one acre of rice land). In terms of cash, this means M$20 on 375 gantungs of rice worth M$200 at present market prices, multiplied, of course, by the number of acres the farmer harvests. On cattle the zakat is one calf for the first 30–39 head, more for a larger herd; on sheep it is one young sheep for a flock of 40-120. On gold, silver, and merchandise, it is 2½ per cent of value; on any "found treasure" it is 20 per cent. Zakat is collected only from the relatively prosperous, but fitrah is an obligation upon all except outright paupers. The prescribed fitrah today is two gantungs of rice or the equivalent in cash for every three members of a family, or approximately M$0.33 per person. Of the zakat, one-fifth goes to the imam of the local mosque and the remainder to the Majlis. Of the fitrah, three-fifths goes to the Majlis and the remaining two-fifths, at the contributor's pleasure, to the imam, to the poor, or to some charitable cause. In addition to his share of the zakat and the fitrah, the imam may receive other gifts. Only the imam of the Kota Bharu mosque receives any fixed salary (approximately M$100 per month). The imam also receives half the fee (M$12) for a marriage or a divorce.

By all reports, the collection of zakat and fitrah in Kelantan is extremely efficient. The imam prepares and maintains a careful record of all persons for whom he is responsible, and his records are regularly inspected. The individual tithe payer, incidentally, is qualified to claim his zakat and fitrah payments as exemptions on his federal income-tax returns. The minority of the population who pay income tax thus gain some relief. The majority who pay no income tax are systematically tapped by the religious establishment.

The income of the Majlis, according to informed report, comes to about M$1,000,000 per year, inclusive of zakat, fitrah, legacies, and revenue from charitable trusts. The state government makes an official grant, furthermore, of M$41,000 for the Majlis' administrative expenses and pays the salaries of the president and several other officials. The state government also makes available directly or indirectly to the Majlis an additional M$1,000,000, approximately, for purposes of propagating the faith by engaging teachers for work in the religious schools and in the kampongs. The Majlis thus dispenses annually something on the order of M$2,000,000—as compared with the State Government's total budget of M$30,000,000 for administration and development.

Of at least equal importance to the Majlis is the statewide system of Shar'iyah Courts. The new enactment of May 30, 1966, redefines and clarifies the entire Shar'iyah system of church discipline and justice. The Grand Mufti (salary: M$12,364 per annum) combines with his function as chief religious leader of the state the supervision of the Shar'iyah. The Grand Mufti is chairman of a body of three ulamas who sit as magistrates in a supreme court of appeals. The Kadhi Besar and thirteen other Kadhis (salaries: M$280 to M$711 per month) preside over eight Kadhi courts, one each for the eight *mukims* into which the state is divided. The state government appropriates approximately M$400,000 per year for salaries and other expenses of the Shar'iyah system.

In Kelantan the Shar'iyah courts are co-equal with the civil courts; the more serious offenses against religious law are just as rigorously prosecuted as offenses against civil law, and sentences of fine and imprisonment are as strictly enforced. The Shar'iyah courts deal with both civil and criminal offenses of Malay Muslims against the Shar'iyah laws. Civil cases involve such matters as marriage, divorce, inheritance, custody of dependents, and so forth. Criminal offenses relate, for instance, to ill-treatment of a wife, disobedience to a husband, *khalwat* or "suspicious proximity" (intent to commit adultery), incest, falsification of records, irregularities with regard to payment or collection of zakat or fitrah. Except for very special cases and very special offenses, the maximum penalties which the courts can impose are fines of M$300, imprisonment of three months, or both.

As illustrations of the scope and scale of the Shar'iyah proceedings, it is worth itemizing a few offenses and the maximum penalties prescribed:

> Failure without adequate explanation of any male Muslim, age 15 or over, to attend Friday prayers: M$25 fine or one week's imprisonment or both for first offense; M$100 fine or three months' imprisonment for subsequent offenses.

> Consumption, or purchase or sale for immediate consumption by a Muslim during daylight hours of Ramadan of any food, drink, or tobacco: M$50 fine or two weeks' imprisonment for first offense; M$150 fine or one month's imprisonment or both for subsequent offenses.

> Purchase, sale, or consumption of intoxicating liquor: M$100 fine or one month's imprisonment or both for first offense; M$300 fine or three months' imprisonment or both for subsequent offenses.

> Building a mosque or *surau* without the consent of the Majlis: fine of M$1,000 or imprisonment of six months.

> Preaching the Islamic religion outside the home without a license from the Majlis: M$250 fine or one month's imprisonment or both.

> Performance of marriage or divorce in contravention of the provisions of the law: fine of M$200 or two months' imprisonment.

> Failure to pay assessed zakat or fitrah: M$300 fine or one month imprisonment.

Ill-treatment of a wife: M$100 fine or one month imprisonment.

Disobedience to a husband: M$25 fine for first offense; M$100 fine or one month's imprisonment for subsequent offenses.

"Suspicious proximity": M$100 fine or one month's imprisonment for first offense; M$300 fine or three months' imprisonment for subsequent offenses.

The great bulk of the business of the Shar'iyah courts relates to its civil cases, and of all cases, those involving divorce are the most common. The Malay-Muslim divorce rate is extremely high, the prevailing attitude toward marriage being that it is a relationship that may be either contracted or terminated at will, particularly by the male. The new Kelantan enactment includes safeguards for the rights of the wife. Nevertheless, the husband can still divorce the wife merely by pronouncing one, two, or three *talak* (the command "to go," the first two being revokable) whereas the wife must seek out the court. In the past, the husband could pronounce or revoke the talak without necessarily notifying his wife in person or even informing the imam. Such laxity of practice now costs M$200 or two months in jail.

It remains to be seen whether a more stringent regulation of marriage and divorce will result in any marked change in social attitude toward it. The disposition of the Kelantan Malay—like that of the Malay elsewhere—is to regard marriage as experimental and to break off the experiment abruptly if it seems to fail. Any litigation with regard to the divorce itself is likely to be much less prolonged or complicated than that with regard to property settlement, including the disposition of the dowry. According to the latest available statistics, in Kelantan in the year 1965 there were 8,266 marriages, 5,124 divorces, and 530 reconciliations. Comparative figures for the year 1963 were 7,987 marriages, 5,270 divorces, and 517 reconciliations. No statistics are available with regard to multiple marriage, but the Kelantan Malay-Muslim male is entitled by law to have four wives simultaneously, provided only that he "treat them equally," a technicality about which the wives sometimes grow disputatious. The practice of polygamy is now dying out, mainly because it is a luxury which only the more affluent can now afford.

Besides prosecuting in the Shar'iyah courts the less faithful of those whom it leads in worship in the mosques and taxes through the agency of the mosque staff, the Majlis also maintains a complex system of religious schools. Possibly the most important elements of the system today are seven Arabic-language primary and secondary schools and a newly established Pusat Pengajian Islam, or Center of Islamic Studies.

Here the religious-minded student will soon be able to complete his education without being obliged, as before, to journey to Cairo or Mecca for the final stages. In the primary and secondary schools as well as the Center, the language of instruction is Arabic and the most important subject of instruction is the Koran, but other subjects— Malay and English, for instance, as well as mathematics, history, and so forth—are also taught. Enrollment now totals approximately 5,000, including 1,000 inscribed in one large secondary school in Kota Bharu town and about forty in the new Center.

The Pusat Pengajian Islam, the special project of the Chief Minister and leader of the Pan-Malayan Islamic Party, Dato Mohammad Asri binti Hadji Muda, is a matter of pride for the entire religious community. According to present plans the Center will soon surpass all other religious schools in Malaya in academic importance, not even excepting the long-established Islamic College at Klang (Selangor). In early 1966, when instruction first started, the Center enrolled a total of forty students in its first-year class, including at least one student from each of the other states of Malaya. In the next three years it will build up to a three-year course of instruction, and in the near future it will expand its curriculum and offer degrees equivalent to those conferred by Cairo's Alazar University. Such, at least, is the announced intent of the sponsors, although even within the Kelantan religious community itself a few skeptical voices have made themselves heard. The state government has provided temporary quarters for the Center in a former royal palace located about six miles outside the town of Kota Bharu and has appropriated M$72,000 for 1966 operating expenses, inclusive both of teachers' salaries and student scholarships. The government proposes in the near future to provide the Center with an endowment, probably in the form of a new Government Rest House to be built on the site of a derelict colonial relic in downtown Kota Bharu and turned over to the Center to operate or, as seems more probable, to lease out to a Chinese to operate.

The traditional Malay-Muslim system of education centered on the *madrassah* and the *pondok*, both of which continue to function in Kelantan, although the latter is now rapidly losing ground to the Arabic school system. The madrassah is attached to the mosque or the *surau;* the children attend, frequently, after the regular school day in government schools, for instruction in the Koran. Since government primary schools offer Muslim students a few hours instruction per week in *Jawi* (Malay language in Arabic script) and also in the Koran, the parallel system of the madrassahs is now beginning to seem redundant.

The pondok is a school for young men where a religious acolyte in effect apprentices himself to a religious teacher for a period which may last from a few months to a few years. The youth takes up his residence in a little shack built by his family on the premises of a surau. He becomes the personal disciple and in fact the personal servant as well of some learned ulama. He remains in residence either until he completes formal examinations (administered through the Majlis) for his own accreditation as a religious leader or until he decides for one reason or another to return to lay life. Although the popularity of the pondok has declined, the pondok and the ulama who operates it remain potent factors of religious—and educational—conservatism or, as many of the Malay Muslims themselves concede, sometimes of reaction and fanaticism.

In order to encourage and indeed to intensify religious instruction, the Kelantan government now provides an annual subsidy of approximately M$750,000 (increased about 10 per cent over the 1965 figure) for employment of some 415 religious teachers. These teachers are assigned to the various schools supported by the church. They also engage in a general program of propagation of the faith, including the making of converts, particularly from among the Chinese and Thai minorities and occasionally from the Western community.

Their great preoccupation with religious matters means that the people of Kelantan are intensely aware of their membership in the world-wide Islamic community. The Malay-Muslims themselves belong to the Shafi'e sect, but they regard other major sects with brotherly tolerance—not, however, the splinter Kodiana sect which is proselytizing at present among the local Pakistanis. The local Muslim leaders themselves are divided, as they have been for years, between those known as the *kaum tua* (the old ones) and the *kaum muda* (the young ones). The former are disposed to concentrate largely upon doctrinal matters, the latter to enlarge the scope of religion to include much else. Both are increasingly disposed to regard religion as inseparable from politics, which means an exclusive sort of Malay-Muslim nationalism.

The kaum tua in Kelantan look to Mecca for their inspiration, the kaum muda more to Cairo and increasingly to Pakistan and to Indonesia as well. For the past three years all have felt very seriously the effects of the Kuala Lumpur-Djakarta political breach of which the major manifestation has been Indonesian "confrontation." From Kelantan state leaders, accordingly, have come repeated demands that Kuala Lumpur reconcile its differences with Djakarta. These demands have been so insistent as to lead Kuala Lumpur to suspect that Kelantan did not fully support the government's policy of resistance to Indonesian aggression. While repeatedly affirming their loyalty to Malaya and Malaysia, the Kelantan leaders have reaffirmed at least as strongly their solidarity with the Islamic world. They have made specific reference, furthermore, to Afro-Asian states (Pakistan, for instance) which, from Kuala Lumpur's point of view, have seemed tepid if not in fact quite cool in their reactions to Malaysian protests regarding Indonesian confrontation. Thus, to Kuala Lumpur, Kota Bharu's sense of Islamic brotherhood frequently seems to be stronger than its sense of Malaysian membership. The sense of kinship is kept refreshed, furthermore, by constant traffic to and from the Middle East. Of Malaya's total of some 4,000 pilgrims to Mecca last year, Kelantan accounted for approximately 500 (at a cost of M$1,500 for a third-class sea passage and considerably more for first-class or air). Of these at least a hundred remained in the Middle East for prolonged periods of religious study from which they seem likely to return, as have their predecessors in Kelantan, with a rather more fundamentalist outlook than their fellow students from other parts of Malaya seem to acquire.

PARTY, CHURCH AND STATE

In Kelantan the marriage of religion and politics has resulted in the rise to state political paramountcy of the Pan-Malayan Islamic Party (PMIP). A party based on race and religion, the PMIP is dedicated to the creation of a nation in which the rights of the indigenous Malays will be vigilantly protected against alien (i.e. Chinese, Indian, British, and other) encroachment and the political system will be soundly founded upon the teaching of the Koran. The PMIP (or PAS, as it is called in Kelantan, where people prefer to use an acronym based upon the Malay name of the party, one which is not so vulnerable as is PMIP to typographical transposition) is the creation of a politician of Indonesian parentage named Burhanuddin Al-Helmy. Educated in Malay, Arabic, and English-language schools in Malaya and subsequently in New Delhi and Palestine, Burhanuddin has been a teacher, a merchant, a journalist, a theosophist, a herbalist, and a revolutionary who was jailed by the British for his role in the Singapore race riots of 1950. Recently imprisoned by the federal government on charges of pro-Indonesian conspiracy, but now released on condition that he forego political activity, he remains a popular hero of Kelantan.

The PMIP now constitutes the most formidable national opposition to the ruling Alliance Party, of which the United Malay National Organization (UMNO) is the leading component. PMIP-UMNO rivalry for the support of the Malay community throughout the nation constitutes one of the most significant manifestations of current national politics. UMNO adheres, although not without serious dispute within its own ranks, to the view that the Malays must cooperate with and adjust to the other racial communities while at the same time asserting Malay indigenous rights. It deplores the "communalism" (racialism), religious "fanaticism," and social and economic "reactionism" of the PMIP and accuses PMIP leaders of being dupes of the Communists and the Indonesians and of seeking to create an anachronistic theocratic state. The PMIP, in turn, deplores the "betrayal" by UMNO of Malay interests, the "worldliness"—in fact, the "sinfulness"—of the conduct of UMNO leaders, and the "alienation" of Muslim co-religionists. The PMIP savagely refutes the charge that it is "communal." It is "communal," runs the PMIP thesis, to discriminate against the Malay Muslim elements in the nation, as the Alliance itself does by catering to the Chinese; it is not "communal" vigorously to champion the rights of the Malays as the "true sons of the soil" as the PMIP does. "Communalism" is the most deadly political charge which any Malaysian political faction can level against any other, the pragmatic consensus within the nation being that the races must co-exist or perish. The dialectic of "communalist" charges becomes correspondingly involved and incendiary, the fine line between Malay communalism and Malaysian patriotism being extremely difficult to define.

In Kelantan, where religious influence and the religious establishment are all-pervasive and Malay-Muslim traditionalism and conservatism (reaction and fanaticism, say the critics) prevail, the PMIP appeal is ready-made for the ulama, the imam, and the great majority of the common people. The PMIP calls for a nation firmly based upon the Koran, for national leaders who are devout Muslims scrupulously adhering in politics as in other matters to the teachings of the Koran —for "genuine democracy" as the Prophet himself, if properly interpreted, defined it. It attacks the UMNO leaders and the government for seeking profane rather than sacred inspiration and for violating the Koranic principles in their day-to-day conduct of government.

On the basis of this appeal, and with many embellishments regarding specific personalities and policies, the PMIP managed, much to the surprise and dismay of the Alliance, to score a landslide victory in the Kelantan state and federal elections of 1959. It then proceeded to form a state government strongly opposed to Alliance national policies. In the 1964 elections, for reasons which will presently become clear, the PMIP scored a less complete victory but managed nevertheless easily to retain control of the state government. In 1959 Kelantan was one of two states (the other was Trengganu) in which the PMIP made an extremely strong showing. In 1964 it was the only state. The following table shows the comparative results of the 1959 and 1964 Kelantan state and federal elections. On a nation-wide basis, the PMIP won 21.2 per cent of the vote in the 1959 (Malayan) federal elections and 13 out of 104 seats in the Parliament. The Alliance in those elections won 51.5 per cent of the votes and 74 seats. In the 1964 (Malaysian) federal elections, the PMIP won 17 per cent (355,000) of the votes and 9 out of 159 seats. The Alliance took 57 per cent of the vote and 125 seats.

ELECTION RETURNS, KELANTAN STATE, 1959 AND 1964

	State		Federal	
	PMIP	*Alliance*	*PMIP*	*Alliance*
1959	114,858	48,509	116,087	53,382
1964	108,578	89,398	129,429	100,705

The PMIP today holds twenty of the thirty seats in the Kelantan State Assembly. The Alliance holds nine, and a former PMIP member who has now left the party occupies the other. The PMIP thus controls the state government, but not so firmly as in 1959 when it held twenty-eight of the Assembly seats. Political animosities between the PMIP and UMNO have resulted in suspicion and non-cooperation between Kota Bharu and Kuala Lumpur. Between 1959 and 1964 the state and federal governments were hardly on speaking terms. Distinguished visitors from Kuala Lumpur, ministers of state included, were subject to slight if not to outright rebuff when they visited Kelantan. Officials from Kota Bharu found their own welcome in Kuala Lampur correspondingly chilly. It has not helped to bridge the gap that Kota Bharu observes a Saturday through Thursday morning working week (Friday is the Muslim holiday), whereas Kuala Lumpur observes a Monday through Saturday morning schedule. Thus, for a good half of the seven-day week, the two sets of officials are virtually incommunicado.

The decline of PMIP strength in the Assembly, certain changes in party leadership, and two-way effort on the part of state and federal officials to achieve a measure of rapport have served of late noticeably to improve PMIP-UMNO communications. Tun Abdul Razak, Deputy Prime Minister and Minister of National Development, paid a goodwill visit to Kelantan in late 1964 in order to negotiate an informal moratorium on open political feuding and a beginning of cooperation on special development projects. The results are now beginning to show. Political antipathies remain potentially explosive, nevertheless, and in Kota Bharu today it takes little more than a casual reference to federal-state relations to precipitate a political tirade.

ECONOMIC DEVELOPMENT

PMIP-UMNO rivalry in Kelantan is perhaps best interpreted in the light of the Kelantan reading of recent events in neighboring Trengganu. There, the PMIP in 1959 was almost equally strong, but in 1961 the State Assembly swung over to UMNO and in 1964 the voters did too. The UMNO achieved its gains in Trengganu, say informants in Kota Bharu, by bluntly stating that development programs would be carried out only on UMNO terms and then pressuring—and bribing— PMIP and other political leaders to jump aboard the UMNO bandwagon. In 1961, consequently, three PMIP and three Party Negara state assemblymen in Trengganu defected to UMNO. The federal government promptly began allocating large sums of money for roads, bridges, community centers, clinics, and the like—at least twice as much money as was allocated for Kelantan. In the 1964 elections Alliance politicians in Kelantan campaigned on the thesis, "If you want to enjoy the same benefits as Trengganu, then vote for the sailing boat [the UMNO emblem]." PMIP politicians had little to say about development but merely mouthed the same old party line: "Vote for the star and crescent [the PMIP emblem] and you will elect a party that will safeguard Malay rights and uphold Islam."

The single most conspicuous and expensive Kelantan development project completed to date constitutes in fact a public monument to state-federal conflict. It is the new M$7,000,000 three-quarter-mile-long Sultan Yahya Petra Bridge across the Kelantan River at Kota Bharu. The Kelantan state government conceived the bridge project several years ago and assigned top priority to it. Since the Kelantan River neatly bisects the state and communications across the river have always been difficult, especially during the flood season when the ferries operate even less efficiently than in ordinary times, the bridge symbolizes genuine state-oriented development calculated swiftly to enhance the local economy. The PMIP government therefore requested the federal government to provide the necessary funds, an estimated total at the time of M$5,000,000. According to Kota Bharu report, the federal government ignored the original request and repeated follow-up requests. Alliance politicians, they say, noised it about that only an Alliance government could ever either undertake or complete the project. Several Alliance politicians, in fact, promised to cut off the tip of a little finger if the PMIP government itself succeeded. According to Kuala Lumpur report, the Kelantan government never drew up proper plans or properly presented those which it had;

it never consulted the Public Works department; and in any event, the bridge represented an extravagant expenditure of one huge sum on a single project, whereas there were dozens of smaller, more essential projects which needed to be undertaken first. Nevertheless, the Kelantan government pushed ahead with the bridge, calling in a Singapore firm to construct it and drawing upon state revenues to finance it. In April, 1966, it triumphantly inaugurated the completed bridge, a splendid example of engineering, although possibly rather more elaborate and costly than was absolutely necessary. The bridge is ornamented at its Kota Bharu end with a handsome fountain designed in replication of the state crest, and the total costs came to an eventual M$7,000,000. The bridge, incidentally, now carries approximately 1,000 vehicles a day, thus earning something over M$1,000 per day in tolls. It promises to return the costs of construction in perhaps ten to fifteen years. In building it, however, the Kelantan government has run up a M$6,959,652 state deficit (as of July 20, 1965), which it now hopes the federal government will pay off.

State-federal impasse over programs for opening up new lands for resettlement of landless farmers provides another example of the Kota Bharu syndrome. As a major part of its national development program the federal government is opening up many tens of thousands of acres of jungle and assigning ten-acre plots to carefully selected families. The government bears the original cost of resettlement, including the expense of clearing and planting the land, building houses for the settlers, and supporting them during the early years of the project. It later recovers its investment by collecting installment payments from the settlers once their crops begin to pay. The Kelantan state government, however, refuses to cooperate in the national program. It rejects the Kuala Lumpur formula whereby new lands must be assigned to Malays, Chinese, and others on a 60-20-20 basis, and states such as Kelantan, which have abundant undeveloped land, must admit settlers from other states. The PMIP insists that Kelantan state land can be assigned only to Kelantan Malays and no others, and certainly not to Chinese. It has embarked meanwhile upon its own land development schemes, doing so on the basis that after a private contractor clears the land of marketable timber (paying M$8 to M$12 per ton royalty to the state), the settlers themselves prepare the land for cultivation, plant the rubber and other crops, and build their own homes. They thus maintain themselves with no assistance from the state other than the construction of access roads, provision of seeds and fertilizer, and assignment of project supervisors.

In Kuala Lumpur one hears that the Kelantan schemes are incoherent, that the settlers live in shanty towns and develop ill planted stands of ill tended rubber, that schools, clinics, and community centers are makeshift, and that the incidence of discouragement and defeat on the part of the individual settlers is dishearteningly high. In Kota Bharu one hears that the Kelantan Malay farmer is a particularly rugged and resourceful type, much more hard-working than the Malays in other parts of the nation. On the new resettlement schemes, it is said, he develops into a prosperous pioneer without piling up a burdensome debt which must be paid off in installments over a long period of years. Some basic facts do emerge from the two versions of the story. The Kelantan schemes are by no means as well carried out as those elsewhere in Malaya. Nevertheless, the settlers do acquire new land and begin to earn a decent income, and they may also be acquiring a spirit of self-sufficiency. Up to the end of the year 1965, a total of some 6,544 families had been (or perhaps some were about to be) resettled on a total of some 62,987 acres of new land. The target for 1966 is 1,657 families on 16,598 acres of land is seven different schemes in various parts of the state. Statistically, at least, the program compares very favorably with that of other states.

Land development schemes are particularly important to Kelantan, where some 50,000 farmers are registered as landless and year by year, as a result of fragmentation through inheritance, land holdings are dropping further and further below the three-acre minimum needed to provide a decent family livelihood. Although the only real answers are more land or fewer persons, projects for irrigation and crop diversification hold out some hope for improvement. The government is now completing the federally financed M$11,700,000 Sungei Lenal Scheme for irrigation of some 23,000 acres of land to permit two rice crops per year rather than the usual one. It is applying to the World Bank for M$40,000,000 with which to finance the Kemubu Scheme to irrigate another 51,000 out of the state total of 185,000 acres of padi land. Even when these projects are complete, the prospect is that many Kelantan farmers will have to continue their present practice of supplementing their incomes by tapping rubber on foreign-owned estates and traveling to nearby Thailand or the west coast of Malaya to seek casual labor during the rice harvest. Various government-sponsored projects to induce rice farmers to shift to other crops on which the returns are potentially greater—peanuts and maize, for instance—have run afoul of the Malay preference for rice both as a crop and as a foodstuff. Private enterprise, however, has achieved significant success in introducing one new crop, namely, tobacco.

The Kelantan tobacco project is the work of one man and one company—Mr. L.C. Been of the Malayan Tobacco Company. Mr. Been, a Dutchman with experience in the tobacco industries both of

Indonesia and the Philippines, has personally persuaded Kelantan farmers to experiment with tobacco. As agent for the Malayan Tobacco Company he has demonstrated to them that their crop will fetch spot cash three months after planting. The Kelantan farmers, who have been slow to plant government-sponsored crops for which the market is uncertain, have become so enthusiastic about tobacco that the production of the individual farmer has to be strictly limited. The limitation is one-seventh of an acre per farmer—partly because this is the maximum amount which one family can care for efficiently, partly because the company is not prepared to buy unlimited quantities of local leaf which, at best, is only good enough to be used as a 5 per cent ingredient in the company's local output. At present some 14,000 Kelantan farmers are raising tobacco on a total of some 2,000 acres of land, and the company is buying and curing some 1,500,000 pounds of Virginia leaf at fourteen different "stations" scattered through various parts of the state.

The Kelantan tobacco project began in 1949 when Mr. Been induced a few farmers to grow tobacco on a total of some twenty acres of land. Mr. Been himself experimented, meanwhile, with various types of tobacco and fertilizer, gradually working out both the agricultural and the collecting and processing techniques. The present pattern of the industry is as follows. The Malayan Tobacco Company accepts, screens, and approves applications from the individual farmers; it provides seeds, and in fact actually plants the seed beds; it also provides insecticides and fertilizers on credit; it purchases the mature tobacco from the farmer, paying ten to thirty Malayan cents per pound, depending upon quality. The farmer himself carries the green leaf to the company station, where company employees grade and purchase it, dry it in company kilns (which are fired with old rubber trees), and then pack and ship the dried leaf to the company factory in Kuala Lumpur. The special advantage of tobacco as a Kelentan crop is that it can be grown in the rice fields during the dry season after the rice itself has been harvested, and that one-seventh of an acre of tobacco will yield as much profit as one full acre of rice—approximately M$150 per year after all expenses have been paid.

Pressure on the part of the newly awakened Kelantan farmers to acquire new land and opportunity has led the state government to conceive of one tremendous new project for opening up a total of 375,000 acres of land. The project, say its numerous critics, including officials in Kuala Lumpur, is likely to be little short of disastrous. The Kelantan government has made preliminary moves—some say commitments—to grant a concession to a Singapore Chinese firm which will undertake, in return, itself to finance a major resettlement program. The concession, say its critics, is reminiscent of the Duff concession of half a century or more ago. Kelantan's PMIP government, they allege, is pawning the state land reserves in order to pay for the Kelantan River bridge. In Kota Bharu the government claims that the terms of the concession are not significantly different from contracts negotiated by other states with Chinese contractors undertaking to prepare land for resettlement. State revenues from timber, it points out, have now jumped from M$1,000,000 to M$2,000,000 per year, and at a time when a major increase was necessary in order to offset the loss of about M$1,000,000 in annual revenue from the state's iron mines, which are now exhausted.

Neither resettlement nor bridge-building has generated nearly so much rancor in Kelantan as has one other aspect of the development program—the building of new mosques, suraus, community centers, and other projects of religious and social welfare. Elsewhere the federal government has supported such projects by grants of money from a special fund that is replenished out of profits from a national lottery. In Kelantan, however, the PMIP government has categorically refused to accept such "tainted money." It was not until several years ago that the traditional rulers of Malaya, meeting in royal council, worked out a formula which both the federal and state governments could accept. Lottery profits are now paid into a general account from which special funds can be siphoned off without giving offense to the more orthodox Muslim. The Kelantan state government is now beginning to draw Federal funds for construction, improvement, and repair of mosques, suraus, and other community facilities. It still experiences some difficulty, however, in convincing the ulamas and imams that the money is clean. It now engages rather ambivalently, furthermore, in explaining simultaneously that in the past it has been defrauded, that it has preferred not to make unnecessary outlays on buildings which are already quite good enough for a modest and economy-minded state, and that it plans to embellish all religious properties.

Emphasis upon state-federal conflict should not obscure the fact that Kelantan has experienced significant development in many important respects and that large federal grants have been made available. The city of Kota Bharu, for instance, now has three new multi-story government office buildings in which civil servants enjoy air-conditioned comfort after having been packed for years into inadequate and temporary quarters. The town also has a handsome new market (a state project), a new stadium (also a state project), and many evidences that development funds, whether state or federal, are generating private building and investment. One evidence is a big new headquarters for the PMIP. Another is an adjacent office building, built with pension funds to earn rental income from private business concerns. Despite its complaints about Kuala Lumpur's neglect and discrimination, the Kelantan government has in fact been drawing the standard per capita federal grant for ordinary administrative expenditures (about M$6,000,000 per year), as well as about M$10–15,000,000 per year for special development projects, and large additional amounts which federal agencies spend for such federal programs as health and education. Between 1961 and 1965, for instance, the federal government spent M$10,567,900 for new schools, and in 1966 it plans to spend approximately M$8,000,000 more.

EDUCATIONAL DEVELOPMENT

The national government has made great progress in educational programs in Kelantan in recent years. It may soon be able to provide the universal primary school education and the secondary school opportunity for 80 per cent of primary school graduates which is the current national target. Prior to 1957 there were no Malay-language secondary schools in Kelantan or anywhere else in Malaya. Now there are fourteen which provide a full six-year course, both in the English and in the Malay streams, and forty more which run for three years, plus four which conduct English stream courses only. The primary school system has experienced even greater growth and has approached the point of resolving one particularly difficult problem which is unique to the state of Kelantan—that of the *sekolah rakjat* (people's school).

In Kelantan, in the immediate postwar years, a great surge of nationalist sentiment and a sudden realization of the state's relative backwardness resulted in spontaneous educational development which may have done almost as much to retard as to advance the cause of true education. Suddenly everyone wanted schools, so in the cities, the towns, and kampongs there mushroomed little one, two, and three-room schoolhouses of thatch and bamboo where volunteer teachers dispensed learning of a sort to whoever showed up. The schools were unorganized and uncoordinated, there was no systematic curriculum, student attendance was casual, teacher qualifications were commonly from bad to nil, and finances were informal. Parents might occasionally contribute a dollar or two in cash, as well as whatever rice, coconuts, fish, or other comestibles they might have at hand and to spare. But enthusiasm continued sufficiently high to permit the existence of many institutions offering three to six years of primary education, usually in areas where no other school facilities were available. Some acquired more or less respectable buildings and staffs and registered up to 1,000 pupils. But over-all standards, naturally, were deplorable and classes tended to become clogged with over-age pupils who neither learned nor left.

In 1958 the federal educational authorities began gradually to impose their own control over the sekolah rakjat and to convert them into the standard government schools. At that time there were approximately as many of the former as of the latter (about 200 each), with the former enrolling the greater number of pupils. The government began to impose a standard curriculum, to pay teachers' salaries (approximately M$80 per month each), to require the students either to pass examinations or to leave, and to require teachers to attend the Kota Bharu Teachers College in order to acquire specified qualifications. As of the end of 1965 the government had in fact converted 108 of the one-time sekolah rakjat into standard schools. According to present schedule, it will complete the conversion of the remaining sixty-eight by the end of 1968. The process of conversion implies also the construction of new buildings to replace the grossly inadequate, unsanitary quarters which have previously been in use. With the problems bequeathed by the sekolah rakjat to cope with, in addition to many other difficulties, it will still require years of hard work for the Kelantan schools to catch up with those of the other states of Malaya.

CONCLUSIONS

It is the graduates of the one-time sekolah rakjat and of the standard government schools as well as those of the madrassah, the pondok, and the Arabic schools who will inherit the new Kelantan now being modeled by the capricious cooperation of the state and federal governments. Present indications are that the citizens of the new Kelantan will still be subject both to civil and to Islamic law, remaining, as they are today, rather more vulnerable to being hauled into the Shar'iyah Court for breaking the Ramadan fast than into traffic court for exceeding the speed limit. They may or may not remain disposed to regard the maintenance of the Sultan's court as an obligation as binding upon them as maintenance of a PMIP-dominated State Assembly or to regard Kuala Lumpur as the seat of the heretical who seem bent upon depriving Kota Bharu of its rights. There is no clear indication at present, however, that attitudes toward the Sultan, the PMIP, or the federal government are greatly altering. The PMIP lost certain constituencies in the last election, to be sure, and the

Alliance vote was nearly double that of 1959. But the total PMIP vote remained almost the same as before. Persons familiar with the east coast Malay mentality insist that swift political change is quite possible, but the sort of candidate who might soon steal votes away from either the PMIP or the Alliance, they say, would be more rather than less committed than are the present leaders to the imams and the ulamas. The east coast UMNO politicians themselves are distinguished from the PMIP less by liberalism of political or religious outlook than by affiliation with the party in national power which is capable of delivering patronage benefits.

In Kelantan, just as the PMIP says, religion and politics legally cohabit, and separation or divorce seem equally unlikely in the foreseeable future. Since all else, and particularly economic development, hinges both on politics and religion, the Kelantan system seems likely to continue to be one in which east coast citizens, including Malays, will feel both uneasy and uncertain. Yet the Kelantan situation is not without its very real advantages. Although there is greater incidence than elsewhere in Malaya of unemployment, underemployment, poverty, and severe hardship there is not so high an incidence of delinquency, crime, or other indicators of social unrest. Kelantan has its own built-in factors of self-correction, many of them directly related to religion. The ordinary Kelantan Malay-Muslim farmer-fisherman, young or old, and his wife, daughter, or sister are, in the good as well as the bad sense of the words, both pious and hard-headed.

Without belaboring the point, it is worth observing at the end as at the beginning that religion is the most important of various complicated factors which account for the fact that the State of Kelantan, as compared with the other states of Malaya, is both retarded and also relatively stable. In now stepping up the pace of development, the state is not achieving either the rate of speed or of acceleration of most of its sister states. Quite certainly, however, it is tampering with the traditional controls in a manner which, as elsewhere, may set off an unpredictable chain reaction. Whether for better or for worse, however, it may not be soon in coming. Even that prediction must be hedged with caution. In a deeply traditional and conservative society like that of Malay-Muslim Kelantan, even a little tampering and a little change can produce quite explosive results. Almost nobody in Kelantan anticipates any explosion soon. The great majority, of course, may be overly complacent as well as overly conservative and thus grievously wrong.

7.

THE PLATEAU OF PARTICULARISM:

PROBLEMS OF RELIGION AND

NATIONALISM IN IRAN

BY CHARLES F. GALLAGHER
American Universities Field Staff

Iran can be said to be in the Middle East but not fully a part of it. The high arid plateau lying north of the uprising barrier of the Zagros Mountains, which marks it off from the eastern part of the Fertile Crescent, is a distinct geographical region with a deep, inner unity belying the social, economic, and linguistic diversity which flecks the surface of the society. Similarly, Iranian history for more than two millennia provides the anomaly of having been played out on a repetitious checkerboard of triumph and disaster, imperial glory and near total annihilation, and through the most abject periods during which the almost obsessive idea of a lasting Iranian identity was somehow held fast. Often taxed with an absence of national will and purpose, Iran responds with an existentialist air of national being which has in the past confounded conquerors more surely than physical resistance. Far from being just a fragment of the Middle Eastern whole, or one of many desperate searchers after new national qualities, Iran stands apart as a mature entity resting on the tripodal base of a long and distinguished history, a shared endurance through many evil eras, and the persistence of a prestigious cultural tradition with solid and ancient roots in the national soil. It is by any cultural measure a nation, and it is from that perspective that it most interests us with respect to Islam. For Iran today, even though only imperfectly a nation-state in the modern political sense, is beyond doubt the most distinctive and self-assured national personality to be found within the Islamic scene; indeed, Turkey possibly apart, it might be argued that it is the only genuine one. The threads of geography, history, and cultural evolution have produced here on the Iranian plateau a national and religious particularism which deserves close attention because of the opportunity given to observe the interworkings of Islamic sentiment and national consciousness within a framework unmatched elsewhere in the Muslim world.

As soon as these protagonists in the continuing Iranian drama are set out, however, it becomes pertinent to recall that Islam, too, has been considered a nation as well as a religion by Muslims from the Prophet Muhammad down to modern pan-Islamists. In the eyes of the average Muslim, today as always, the Community of Believers is a reality with strong social bonds which at times have political overtones. The famous dictum that Islam is both *din* (religion) and *dawlah* (state) has become a part of Muslim literature and of the mystique of Islamic history, and it is true that evidence of its validity can be found at all periods of that history, beginning with the political organization of the Community in Medina after the Hijrah and continuing as recently as the international conferences of Muslims held to discuss the situation created by the abolition of the Caliphate on the part of the Turkish government in 1924.

Yet this formula is, despite its basic truth, an oversimplification masking complex realities which, although varying, have existed in one or another form throughout the course of Islam's existence. It hides the creative tensions which have so often crackled between the religious and political establishments. It ignores the slow and subtle changes which took place over long periods in the vast area of Muslim law, with particular reference to the tendency of administrative and commercial law to divorce themselves from the Holy Law (*Shari'ah*). Most of all, it overlooks the role played by that large body of men who began in the first Islamic decades to deal with religious issues and theological interpretations, and who gradually formed themselves into informal but readily identifiable groups of theologians (*'ulama*) and jurists (*fuqaha*). Classically the tension was expressed in the relationship between the ideal Caliphate and the various sultanates and power-states in being, with emphasis on the efforts of the theologians to reconcile ideal and actual conditions. In the 19th century the dominant motif became the position of Muslims living under foreign rule and subject to non-Muslim power, and today this theme has been superseded by the question of the reaction of Islam to modern ideologies like nationalism and socialism, together with the problem of its place as a socio-political institution, as well as a faith, in the organization of a modern nation-state.

Broadly viewed, the historical relations between religious and political elements in Islam have been expressed by two opposing currents: one, an independence of the religious institution from political power, with a tendency toward separation leading less to open opposition than to withdrawal from the affairs of state; the other, an interdependence which at times degenerates into simple dependence or ultimate amalgamation with the central power. Chronologically, the drift has in general been toward the latter alternative, although with numerous corrections, of course. A century after the inception of Islam the representatives of the first legal schools were often in positions of opposition to the state, but during the 'Abbasid Era after A.D. 750 the interpreters of religious matters increasingly became official clerics attached to the ruling body. This structure was made more formal in the 11th century by the establishment of religious colleges (sing. *madrasah*) like the official Nizamiyah in Baghdad; and by the time the Ottoman Empire was at its zenith it had turned into a full state bureaucracy with appropriate training institutions. Nevertheless, the principle of the autonomy of the religious institution was maintained and, as alert European observers noted in the 18th century, the legendarily all-powerful Ottoman Sultan deferred in all matters of religious concern—in many of which political content was not negligible—to the Mufti of Constantinople who, as *Seyh-ül-Islam*, was the authoritative jurist of the Empire. The members of the religious institution enjoyed the theoretical inviolability of their persons and their property and freedom from taxes, dispositions which contributed to the perpetuation of a tradition that the *'ulama* were the guardians of an order which was of the state and carried out by the state but, at the core, independent of it and morally superior to it. In this sense we can better understand the accomplishment of the theologians of the Islamic Middle Ages who, in an era of internecine warfare, usurpation of temporal power, and the proliferation of self-made, independent Muslim powers, bent their efforts toward preserving their vision of a Nation (*ummah*) above and beyond these petty states. These efforts at safeguarding the spiritual unity of the Community were largely successful but at the cost not only of diluting orthodox (*Sunni*) Islam by extending the boundaries of tolerance to an extreme degree, but also, and more importantly in the matter under discussion here, of heightening the tensions between the Islamic vision and the realities of the temporal states found in the Muslim World.

It needs to be remembered that these tensions ran between, on the one hand, the supranational solidarity ethos represented spiritually by the orthodox Muslim faith and politically by the concept of an indivisible earthly Community carrying out the precepts of that faith, and, on the other hand, the existing power states. Muslim Iran, as it first hesitantly manifested itself beginning with the Samanid revival in the 10th century and later in subsequent regional variations, was the locus of several such entities during the Middle Ages, and thus entered into this relationship. But when we discuss the question of the position of religious and secular power in Iran today, or, in effect, at any time since the 16th century, we are not touching directly on this basic tension, although it must be understood before the latter-day Iranian situation makes sense. We are dealing rather with a *unique* resolution of the tension that was historically achieved in Iran, based on a mutual reinforcement of both religious and political values on a parochial basis in opposition to universalism and communitarianism. For just as Iran is distinctive among Muslim national entities today, so Iranian Islam in its national, heterodox Shi'ite garb is very different from the Sunnism practiced by an overwhelming majority of Muslims from West Africa to Indonesia. This difference is found not so much in dogma or legal interpretation—even though quite significant differences do exist—as in the historical and political underpinnings which support Shi'ism in this country and which have given a special cast to both Islamic Iran and Iranian Islam.

What sets Iran formally apart from other Muslim states on the religious plane is that a specific sub-branch of the Shi'ite heterodoxy has been the national religion by decree since the beginning of the Safavid period (1502–1736). The Constitution of 1906 further establishes what is known as the *Ja'fariya Ithna'ashariyah*, or "Twelver"[1] version of Shi'ism as the religion of the state, and closely interlocks religious and political authority in its first two articles:

> (1) The official religion of Iran is Islam of the true sect of *Ja'fariyah Ithna'ashariyah*. The Shah must protect and profess this faith.

> (2) The Majlis, which has been formed by the blessing of the Imam 'Asr, may God speed His appearance, and by the grace of His Majesty the Shah, and by the vigilance of the Islamic *'ulama*, may God increase their example, and by the Iranian nation, may it at no time legislate laws that are contradictory to the sacred laws of Islam. . . . It is officially decreed that in each legislative session a board of no fewer than five men, comprised of *mujtahid*-s and devout *fuqaha*, who are also aware of the needs and exigencies of

---

[1] So named from the fact that it traces its origins to the Twelfth Imam (lit. "leader of the congregation," but in Shi'ite doctrine the infallible chief of the Shi'ite community), Muhammad al-Muntazar (the Awaited) who disappeared in 260/A.D. 873–74.

the time . . . be nominated by the *'ulama*. . . . It is their duty to study all the legislative proposals, and if they find any that contradict the sacred laws of Islam, they shall reject it. The decision of this board in this respect is binding and final. This provision of the Constitution is unalterable until the coming of the Imam 'Asr, may God speed His appearance.[2]

The Shi'ite version of Islam exists in one or another form in other areas—in Iraq where roughly half the population adheres to Twelver-ism, of which there are minorities in Lebanon, Syria, and Turkey; in the Yemen as the Fiver *Zaidi* sect; and in parts of India and East Africa where the *Isma'ili,* or Sevener sect has followers.[3] Iran, however, is

---

[2] *'Ulama* (sing. *'alim*), lit. "learned," is the general name given to the amorphous body of religious scholars everywhere in Islam. The *fuqaha* (sing. *faqih*), or jurisconsults, are specialists in matters of legal detail rather than broad inter-preters of the Holy Law. Special to the Shi'ite movement is the concept of the *mujtahid,* an interpreter of Shi'ite doctrine at the highest level. The quality of *mujtahid* is attained by recognition of the scholarship and piety of an individual from among the *'ulama* and conferred informally by general acceptance among leading members of the clergy or by sanction from already established *mujtahid*-s. There are not more than about a hundred *mujtahid*-s in Iran today. Particular to the eastern part of the Muslim World is the term *mullah,* used to designate lower-level clergy in general.

[3] The Fiver, or *Zaidi,* sect of Shi'ism is so named because it claims that the legitimate succession to the Caliphate devolved through Zaid, a grandson of Husayn, son of 'Ali, who was the rightful fifth Imam in their eyes. The Fivers, unlike the *Ithna'ashari* Twelvers, do not believe in a concealed Imam and have no esoteric dogma. The Imam of Yemen is the present head of the *Zaidi* community, which of all Shi'ite sects is the closest to orthodox Islam. The Sevener, or *Isma'ili,* sect arose out of a dispute about the legitimate successor of the sixth Imam, Ja'far al-Sadiq. Their preference for one of his sons, Isma'il, was not recognized by the Twelvers and a scission ensued. In fact, however, genealogical quarrels played a minor role in the spread of *Isma'ili* activity, which had other, social roots. The most extreme and divergent form of *Shi'ism, Isma'ilism,* used missionaries extensively to spread its message, preached revolt and political assassination, and was involved in several revolutionary uprisings in the Middle Ages. The term is misleading for the *Isma'ilis* were not known to their con-temporaries by that name, but as the *da'wah* (lit. "mission," from their evan-gelical tendencies), and it is not at all certain that the group which professed adherence to the Imamate of Isma'il in the 8th century can be correlated with the sudden appearance of *Isma'tili* missionaries preaching revolutionary doctrines in the second half of the 9th century. The Fatimid Caliphate which held sway in North Africa and Egypt from the 10th to the 12th centuries was *Isma'ili* in origin. *Isma'ili* dogma diverged not only from orthodoxy but also to a consider-able degree from all other forms of Shi'ism. It stressed esoteric numeralism based on sevens; a distinction between the true, inner (*batin*) meaning of knowledge and the simple, overt (*zahir*) reading of it; and a graded instruction in the secrets of the faith, with the whole truth known only by a select inner circle. *Isma'ilism* itself is associated with still more deviant off-shoots like the *Darazi* (Druze), *Nusairi,* and *Yazidi* sects, which are so syncretic and mystic at times that they can hardly be considered Muslim. In addition, the Assassin (*Hashshashin*) cult, combining drug-taking with terrorism, arose within the *Isma'ili* sect in the Elburz Mountains of Northern Iran with its headquarters at Alamut in the 11th century. It was only destroyed by the Mongol Hulagu Khan in 1256.

today the only country with a heavy Shi'ite majority, estimated at over 80 per cent. What is noteworthy in the Constitution is the clear attempt to give irrevocable official sanction to a distinctive sect through the most solemn legal procedure. The formalism of the Shi'ite position in Iran in recent times, when viewed in the light of evidence which suggests that there was no significant Shi'ite majority in the area making up the present state when Twelverism was officially adopted in the 16th century, has an air of defensiveness about it which rouses curiosity. How and why has one version of Shi'ism, which is not the extreme branch of the heterodoxy in terms of history activity, become so firmly identified with one country? Or does the fact that it is felt necessary to include such express stipulations in the basic national political document indicate that this identification is neither so complete not so natural as might be thought at first? Or again, are there reasons for stressing the relationship other than those which first make themselves apparent? While full answers to such questions may not emerge, hypotheses about the bases of this coexistence can perhaps be set up by looking at the historical development of the Shi'ite movement and the inner psychology of Shi'ism in the light of the Iranian role in Islamic history.

Shi'ism is the most complex and enduring deviation from orthodox Islam. It is a movement which has often cloaked socio-political grievances in the garment of theological dispute and given expression to dissent on the current scene by historicizing and sanctifying it in the guise of events long past. Political Shi'ism arose out of the support given to the fourth Caliph 'Ali (d., A.D. 661) by his followers during the first Muslim civil war. Its demands on personal commitment grew stronger after his defeat and death, and were intensified by the unsuccessful attempt of his son Husayn to regain power in 680 and by his ultimate martyrdom. The main area of Shi'ite activity was then southern Iraq, which administratively controlled large portions of what is now Iran; and Shi'ism there first exemplified the opposition of the Arabs in that region to rule from Syria. But this opposition was very soon mixed with the hostility of non-Arab, often Persian, "clients" (mawali), who felt themselves denied full membership in the young Muslim Community despite the intellectual and social accomplishments they had contributed to its formation. Gradually, resistance to 'Ymayyad rule in Syria (661–750) was in good part fixed around a political insistence on the legitimacy of the Caliphate of 'Ali and his descendants, thus calling into question the legality of the Community as then constituted. After the 'Abbasid Caliphate rose to power in Baghdad, with much 'Alid support which it soon disappointed, Shi'ism vegetated for some time. It held no notably distinctive doctrine apart from the difference over the Caliphate, and the majority of Shi'ites co-existed with their orthodox brethren without incident, mainly because the Persian lettered class and bureaucracy, which contributed so many adherents to the movement, were now more satisfactorily assimilated in the Islamic state and held important positions in the government. Indeed, under the rule of the Buwayhid Amirs (945–1055), Shi'ite Persians were technically in control of the reins of state. During the 'Abbasid period, however, the Shi'ite position underwent important changes. For one thing several different Shi'ite movements appeared, the most extreme of which was the Isma'ili (Sevener) sect, which in the late 9th century was found simultaneously in several distantly scattered regions, and whose turbulent later career in the form of the Fatimid Caliphate and of the Assassins in northern Iran and elsewhere played on already existing social unrest throughout the Islamic world.

The moderate Shi'ites at this time, however—who were later to become commonly known as the *Ithna'ashari* (Twelver) sect—were not involved in this agitation. In fact, they studiously refrained from any attempt to overthrow the existing authority at a time when it was quite weak and when they had numerous adherents in Baghdad and other nearby cities. And the Buwayhids allowed a Sunni 'Abbasid Caliph to remain on a powerless throne while they functioned as military governors. When such passivity is correlated with the fact that almost a hundred years before, in A.D. 873, the twelfth Imam of the Shi'ites had been "occulted"—that is, had disappeared from sight—it becomes clear that Twelver Shi'ism was consciously adopting an attitude of political noninterference which says much about its social make-up and its adaptability. There is little doubt that the *Ithna'ashari*-s, who contained in their largely urban ranks many wealthy merchants and land-owners as well as a substantial portion of the artisan class, felt closer to the Sunni *'ulama* and masses than to the *Isma'ili* revolutionaries, however much the similarities of Imamism appeared to link them with the latter and divide them from the former. In fact, what we find at this time is a Janus-like Shi'ism, one face of which is regional, restricted mostly to peripheral parts of the Middle East and North Africa which are often difficult of access, and associated with social discontent of a mainly agrarian nature directed against the increasing urbanization and centralization of the state and the economy. Fringe religious groups other than extreme Shi'ites were, of course, participating in this mass unrest, too, but the Twelvers were not. Quite to the contrary, their face of Shi'ism expressed the moderate socio-religious position of an aristocratic and bourgeois minority whose demands for social equality, originally based, to a great degree, on racial origin, had been more than satisfactorily met.

Because the aspirations of the heavily Persian-infiltrated intellectual and bureaucratic groups had been satisfied within a more genuine Islamic universalism, the Persian Shi'ites had by the mid-9th century a less vivid memory of their Sasanian heritage than had been the case a century or more before. Then, too, the Shi'ites as a class, and considering the non-Persian elements as well, given their commercial interests and their stake in the 'Abbasid enterprise, were unwilling to rock the Sunni Caliphal boat already in heavy seas for many reasons. Moreover, it is clear that at this crucial period in Islamic history there was a possibility that the Twelver Shi'ite community could have followed a path within the over-all Islamic framework, which could have led to a reintegration with orthodox Islam just as easily as it could have proceeded to eventual separation and mutual recrimination. It did neither at that time, however, and for this there were two principal reasons. The positive one was the emergence of Shi'ite theological doctrine for the first time during the Buwayhid Amirate, not on an important scale, but enough to hold the Twelvers back from the whirlpool of full consensus with the orthodox majority—which was always implicit in the coexistence of the 9th century—and lay down the groundwork for a separate intellectual existence. The negative counterpart, however, was the lack of a distinct political entity on which to found a polity that was in turn based on a specifically Shi'ite dogma.

It is well known that Shi'ite doctrine was late in arriving on the Islamic scene. Until the occultation of 873, the Imam had authoritarian responsibility for the Shi'ite community and for the interpretation of its law. Furthermore, reluctance to break with the universal Caliphate delayed the formulation of a fully separate identity. The Buwayhid period almost provided the political entity required for Twelver Shi'ism to burst into independent existence, but it just missed. The reasons for this are partly analogous to those already mentioned: the Caliphate was a useful vacuum facing serious social and economic problems, and it was easier to manipulate it from behind the scenes; the Shi'ite bureaucrats and professionals in the cities of Iraq and Iran at the time realized that little would be gained by attempting to substitute an 'Alid Imamate. The non-theological nature of Shi'ite reasoning at this period is an indication of the still cautiously political nature of the movement at the time. Nonetheless, the Buwayhid hegemony did permit the first spark of Shi'ite thought and provided a breathing space within which a truly Shi'ite version of Islam could begin to grow. In the end, the Buwayhid period was the first time that a religious particularism and a political particularism from the same part of the Muslim World (the Buwayhids originated in Tabaristan in the Caspian region of northern Iran) met and partially reinforced each other. In the end they failed, however, being unwilling to seize the opportunity to modify the course of Islamic civilization as they might well have tried to do.[4]

Apart from the general political situation and the still incomplete nature of Shi'ite formulations, however, there were other reasons for the failure of Shi'ite thought to develop rapidly at this time. The Buwayhids were an unsatisfactory temporal hitching-post, for one. They stemmed from an area which was all-in-all Iranian, but a remote and culturally backward part of the Middle East—a part which has contributed much to the history of revolt in Islam but little to its general culture. Furthermore, the durable bureaucracy in the cities of the 'Abbasid Caliphate had now been fully Islamified and was accustomed to using Arabic. The Persian element in this group was at the apogee of forgetfulness of its past and was now a full participant in an Islamic civilization knowing no racial barriers which, although using Arabic as its vehicle of expression, was no longer solely Arab property. Consequently, it was not from such groups that the great revival of Persian culture and letters was to spring, but from the semi-independent principalities and frontier states of northeast Iran, Khurasan, and Transoxiana beginning in the first half of the 10th century. It was this renaissance which ultimately provided the "matching pillar" to serve along with Twelver Shi'ism as the basis for an Iranian national corpus.

Little need be said about the quality of this cultural rebirth, which began with the lyricism of a poet like Rudaki, the first Muslim literary figure to express himself in Persian, and gave to the world the epic *Shahnama* of Firdawsi (d., A.D. 1020). Over the ensuing centuries it made immeasurable contributions to all branches of Islamic culture in the persons of such outstanding figures, to name only a few, as the historians Bal'ami and Rashid al-Din, the astronomer al'Tusi, the mystic poet and Sufi master, Jalal al-Din al-Rumi, and the greatest poets in the Persian language, Sa'di and Hafiz. It came to a climax with the incomparable painter Bihzad in the 15th century. The five centuries or so ending around 1500 witnessed a dual phenomenon, then, in the re-emergence of a definite Persian consciousness which slowly but surely took deeper root with each succeeding century, while at the same time it was sustaining Islamic civilization as a whole in some of the most difficult moments the latter faced. In fact, when the logical

[4] For cogent interpretation and speculation about the entire problem of Shi'ite behavior in 'Abbasid times—still very insufficiently studied—see *L'Elaboration de l'Islam*, Colloque de Strasbourg, Paris: Presses Universitaires de France, 1961, a symposium of the Centre d'Études Supérieures spécialisé d'Histoire des Religions de Strasbourg. In particular the articles "La changeante portée sociale de quelques Doctrines religieuses" by Claude Cahen, pp. 1–22, and "Government and Islam Under the Early 'Abbasids" by Sir Hamilton Gibb, pp. 115–27.

question arises as to why it is only in the 16th century that an embryonic Iran first appears with its own version of Islam, some part of the answer must lie in that duality: the energy expended by Persian elites for both Persian culture and Islamic civilization, and the steadily worsening state of Muslim political and economic institutions from the 11th century on, as the result of the incursion of Turkish and, later, Mongol nomads into the Islamic heartlands. During the first half of its renaissance, Perso-Islamic culture was occupied in the essential but enormous task of civilizing the Turkic-speaking peoples on its northern and eastern borders, as well as those who were making their way to the center of the empire: Ghaznavids, Seljuks, Turkomans, Khwarizm-shahs, and the like. It is a commonplace that the Turks received their Islamic upbringing in a primarily Persian atmosphere, but that the religious sophistication and diversity of their teachers tended to escape them, except for the activist, popular, and mystical dervish movements which later took root in Anatolia. At this time, though, the introduction of Seljuk Turkish power into the 'Abbasid Caliphate (from 1055) meant a reaffirmation of Sunni orthodoxy and a further delay in the process set in motion in the preceding century through which Shi'ism was beginning to structure itself.

These obstacles to the deployment of a more vigorous activity among the moderate Shi'ites—for they had no effect on the violent predilections of the *Isma'ili* supporters during the same period—were compounded by other factors. One was the total collapse of the Caliphate and the devastation of Iran, Iraq, and much of western Asia during the Mongol holocaust from 1220 to 1260; and the other was the spread of Sufi mysticism as an important social and political force. Sufism had existed from very early periods of Islamic history in the form of an intuitive, personal approach to religion, and it prospered as such in partial reaction to the austerity of orthodox Sunni formulations of the 10th century and later. In fact, the formula of Sufi-orthodox synthesis, at which al-Ghazzali (d., A.D. 1111) finally arrived in a remarkable attempt to hold the two currents together, only led in the end to a dilution of orthodox norms in many areas of practice and to a final capitulation by both orthodox *'ulama* and Muslim rulers before the vitality of popular practices.

What interests us more directly, however, in trying to trace the evolutions of the Iranian religious past and its eventual encounter with Shi'ism, is the institutional evolution of Sufism in this area in the 13th and 14th centuries. Remarkably diverse though the appeal of Sufism has been at different times, it is undeniable that in a declining age such as the latter part of the 'Abbasid Caliphate much of that appeal lay in its otherworldliness and the garden of retreat from mundane worries which it offered its adepts. This facet of the Sufist personality was in full swing before the 13th century, but the complete breakdown of existing social and political institutions in much of western Asia following on the Mongol invasions, while not eliminating this, brought out another, more societal aspect of its nature. This post-Mongol social evolution of Sufism was characterized by the spread of a more active type of mystic fraternity and secret association, natural in an era when Islamic territory was for the first time occupied by a heathen invader utterly disdainful of its traditions. However, as Mongol power waned and Mongol remnants were absorbed into Islamic civilization, particularly in Iran, the Sufi organizations which arose from the rubble of a shattered society acted as socio-political organisms, as volunteer or vigilante groups, or as associations for the maintenance of local or regional order. With the orthodox establishment in disarray, such groups, usually associated with a Sufi *tariqah*, or "way," making up an extensive cross-country network with all its affiliated lodges, meeting houses, schools, and such, were often the only authority in being, and they brought a deeply needed quality of social and cultural cohesion. In other areas of Islam, and in later times, the Sufi movement played an eminent role in galvanizing popular resistance to the threat of foreign conquest; but in the Iranian case, where invasion came earlier and was traumatic in effect, the main task and the most notable accomplishment of Sufism was to help heal a convalescing society and to begin reconstructing its battered social fabric. It is significant that in both Anatolia and in Iran it was out of organizations of this type directed by Sufi *shaykhs* in the 14th and 15th centuries that there arose the nucleus of the two principal Islamic states of the next several centuries. In the first case, one of the *ghazi* freebooter states of Asia Minor, organized along militant Sufi lines, developed finally into the Ottoman Empire; in the other, it was a Sufi-Shi'ite synthesis practiced in Azerbaijan by the *shaykhs* of Ardabil attached to the Suhrawardi *tariqah*, wherein the origins of the Safavid state and ultimately of modern Iran are to be found.

As noted above, during much of this same period—from the Mongol invasions on to 1400 or so—a specifically Iranian culture within the general Muslim framework, but now very much cut off from the Mamluk state in Egypt and the Levant, was engaged in the second of its two great civilizing enterprises: that of converting the pagan (now sometimes Buddhist) vestiges of the Mongols to Islam and of domesticating the conquerors and assimilating their rulers, the Ilkhans, to local culture. This was done with finesse and care, but the religious hesitancy of the times is shown in the fact that the Ilkham ruler Ghazan (A.D. 1295–1304), brought up in Buddhism, was converted to Sunni

Islam shortly after his accession, and his successor Oljaitu Khodabanda —already bearing a mixed Mongol-Persian name—professed Shi'ism. For the first time in Iranian history since the Arab Conquest, one can see a clear convergence of course at this juncture. While local Sufism, intermittently tinged with Shi'ism, was maintaining the basic under-pinning of the society, secular cultural forces of a proto-national nature, expressing themselves in the Persian idiom, were reaching a new height of creativity in literature and the arts. It was now natural that these two streams should finally come together.

Nevertheless, the rise of the Safavid state raises important questions. If Sufism, which cut broadly across Sunni-Shi'i lines and was not necessarily identified with any sect, was an integral element of the Safavid construction, why did Iran take a clear Shi'ite form in the 16th century? The outcome in Anatolia, where many similar forces were at work, turned in favor of Sunni orthodoxy, although after a long strug-gle and at the price of leaving an active *Alevi* Shi'ite minority as an almost perennial problem in the hinterlands. Without attempting to judge the Ottoman case here, it would appear proper to look for answers about Iran in the long-range historical and psychological foundations of Shi'ism and Iranianism.

The essential features of Shi'ism which have distinguished it at all times from Sunni orthodoxy are its tendencies toward a hierarchy based on the hereditary principle (as opposed to an elective egalitarian-ism based on the Community as a whole); the intensity of its personal devotion to a charismatic leader, first 'Ali and then the successive Imams (in contrast to the emphasis on communitarian empathy in Sunnism); and a deep feeling of minoritarianism marked by rejection and bitterness at the overthrow of 'Alid Caliphal authority (as com-pared to the broadly tolerant feelings of a victorious majority).

The basic principles of the pre-Islamic empires of the Achaemenids and the Sasanians in Iran approximate the first two of these character-istics of Shi'ism. It was in Iran that the very idea of empire as such was first conceived, sounded on the autocratic rule of a remote and semi-divine sovereign whose subjects were considered his personal property. The Zoroastrian religious institution also prefigured a central aspect of Shi'ism in the interidentification of the kinghead and the cult to the degree that the ruler symbolized the national religion and it had no existence without him. It was this interlinkage which brought speedy disaster to Zoroastrianism when the Sasanian state collapsed in the Arab invasions. Although Iran provides the outstanding example, it is worth recalling that the other principal focus of Shi'ism in Islamic territory has been in the Yemen among the *Zaidi* sect, an area which reflects the old, pre-Islamic South Arabian tradition of hierarchical society and established kingship and is quite different from the rest of the peninsula. As to the bitterness which is a marked feature of Shi'ism, it can be seen how easily this was mutated and transferred to groups like the *mawali* clients and the Persian bureaucrats who felt themselves a dispossessed minority within Islam in its formative decades. It can also be seen how this sense of rejection, contained for many centuries without passing into action in the case of the Twelvers at least, could and did encourage the growth of masochistic tendencies among the Shi'ite masses, reflected today in stylized mourning and weeping and also in flagellatory practices. Finally, we see a convergence in the growth of a willed distinctiveness on the part of a minority, which held itself to be "separate and better," again interiorized in the first Islamic centuries but given fuller reign when political conditions proved propitious.

In these ways the philosophical bases of Iranian empire and the psychological substrata of Shi'ism prepared the ground for the Safavid creation, which eventually produced a new compound: the national Islamic state. Those qualities of Sufism which had made it a superb agent for the maintenance of social solidarity at grassroots level in troubled times—its personalized commitments, its theological tolerance, and even its intellectualization of religion—were negative contributions to Iranian national political needs in the 16th century, needs which were centripetal, simplistic, nonintellectual, and relatively intolerant. Thus, when the first Safavid ruler Isma'il entered Tabriz in 1502 to be crowned Shah, he decreed Shi'ism the state religion despite having been informed that two-thirds of the city's population was orthodox.

The 16th century in Iran may be read as a continuing process of religious and national fusion. At the beginning, the Ardabil *shaykhs* were hardly Persian except for their birthplace, and the Iranian population was far from uniformly Shi'ite. During the century one Safavid ruler even turned briefly to Sunnism, possibly for reasons of personal spite toward his family; but by the turn of the 17th century, when Shah Abbas the Great moved the capital from Qazvin to Isfahan in the heart of the country, it could be said that *irani* was on the way to equaling *shi'i* and vice versa. The great catalyst in this process was the hostility of Sunni states on the eastern and western frontiers of the Safavids: the Uzbeks on the Khurasanian marches, who were minor opponents, and the Ottomans, who were the major antagonist in Mesopotamia and on the Anatolian-Iranian border. The unremitting Ottoman enmity, marked by bitter vituperation of a kind which showed how the heterogeneous Ottoman state, which claimed Islamic universality, was threatened on both religious and political scores by a specifically religious nationalism, did more than anything else to intensify the sense of being Shi'ite in Iran, and ultimately to transform the conflict into one between states. By 1640, when more than a century of warfare with the Ottomans ended for a time, there was little doubt among Persians about their national identification. The cultural richness and the material prosperity of the reign of Shah Abbas (1587–1629) had strengthened the feelings they already held about their Persianness, and the zealotry of the Shi'ite clergy, which was not slow to take advantage of its official position to persecute opponents, had soldered the country and its faith into one being. It was a nation, however chaotic its organization and however imprecise its definition of itself, to be compared with those few other nations which were taking their first steps elsewhere at about the same time.[5] The parallel is striking with the process undergone during the 16th century in Europe, where a budding nationalism connected with Anglican religious separatism was fortified by warfare with an empire of universalist pretensions founded on an orthodox Catholic faith. The Ottoman Empire played much the same role vis-à-vis Safavid Persia as the Spain of Philip II did toward Protestant England, and it is worth noting that thereafter the kinds of problems faced by essentially non-national empires, like the Spanish and the Ottoman, differed sharply from those confronting states in which well-defined feelings of identity were backstopped by a nationally integrated and generally accepted religious sect.

Fusion and synthesis were not the only leitmotivs during the era of the Safavids and their successor dynasties, however. Almost imperceptibly over this long period, which continued from the 16th through the 19th century, the balance of influence, although not power, was shifting within the religio-national framework. In an early flush of enthusiasm, the first Safavids laid claim to the vacant Imamate for themselves, in violation of Twelver doctrine; but there was no general acceptance of this contention, something which indicates that the Shi'ite clergy were from the start in a fairly strong position. Later Safavids and the Qajars (1779–1925), who followed them after an interval of instability, were increasingly circumspect. They contented themselves with more normal Islamic relations with the clergy, whom they patronized and whose learning and advice they respected. There were aberrations during these three centuries, to be sure, and the usurper Nadir Shah (1736–47) even made an extraordinary attempt to

[5] For a discussion of how the discovery of the national self eventually affected the Arabs in the Middle East, see Albert Hourani, "The Changing Face of the Fertile Cresent in the XVIIIth Century" in *A Vision of History*, Beirut: Khayat's, 1961.

convert Twelver Shi'ism into a fifth orthodox school [6] with special privileges in Mecca. Such schemes came to nought, however, and the drift of the times is clear.

For a century before Nadir Shah's rule and for more than a hundred and fifty years after his death, the growing weakness of the ruling institution, beset with internal rivalries and implicated from 1800 on in the sense of shame engendered by the national inability to resist foreign encroachment by Russia and Britain, contrasts with the relative solidity of the religious hierarchy. The enduring accomplishment of that body was to impose formal Twelver Shi'ism within Iran through continuing victorious confrontations: first with Sunni orthodoxy, then with Sufist groups which came under attack around 1700, and finally, in the 19th century, with modern syncretisms like the Bahai movement. Thus, royal authority was downgraded, although it should be added that this did not diminish its capricious arbitrariness, and this was balanced by a firming up of Shi'ite orthodoxy, which by the 19th century had put the *'ulama* in the strongly entrenched position they maintained until the nationalist revolution of Reza Shah began its program of forced-draft modernization after 1925. The contrast with the impotence of the Sunni clergy in other Muslim areas at the end of the 19th century, who were coming under reformist attack along with their rulers, is striking enough to raise the question why this should be so.

In part this situation existed because the Shi'ite clergy were such an intimate element of the national machinery. They were more deeply involved in the state fabric of Iran than were Sunni *'ulama* elsewhere, even in the Ottoman Empire, which outdid other Sunni areas in the control it exercised over religious appointments. To the extent that the clergy as *shi'a* symbolized a vital aspect of Iranian national consciousness, they inevitably suffered from the spread of foreign influence in the 19th and early 20th centuries, all the more because the urban bazaar classes on which they relied for a counterweight to the political power were hard hit by Western commercial intrusion. Still, in comparison with the political wing of the state, the clergy's prestige was less damaged—the Qajars considered themselves a military dynasty but were nonetheless impotent against the Russian nibbling away of

[6] The four orthodox schools (sing. *madhhab*), or rites, of Islam are the Hanafi, Maliki, Shafi'i, and Hanbali legal codifications made in the early Islamic centuries by famous scholars and jurists who gave their names to the schools founded by them. Except for the Hanbali, they differ little among one another on the whole, and their points of divergence mainly concern questions of personal law, marriage, divorce, and inheritance, or details of ritual. All are accepted within Sunni Islam, and an individual belonging to one school may, for example, in most areas choose to be married under the provisions of another.

national territory—and they simultaneously offered a pole of attraction for those who were most disgruntled with foreign pressure and disgusted with the inefficient despotism of the monarchy. It is for these reasons that the clergy may be found during the Constitutional Crisis of 1906, and thereafter in the transitional period leading to the rise of Reza Shah, both among the "progressive" groups demanding constitutional rule, order, and progress, and in the "reactionary" camp which looked on any change as dangerous to a divinely established order. Indeed, during the following generation the Shi'ite 'ulama were divided into several groups. They were subject to pressure from illiterate masses, who responded to a rigorous fundamentalism, as well as from more sophisticated urban merchants, craftsmen, and lower middle-class supporters, who looked to them for solutions to contemporary problems which involved more than just haranguing and inveighing against heretical enemies. At the same time, as important but adjunctive participants in the ruling elite, they were as a group undecided whether to submit to the authority of the Qajar Shahs under all circumstances, or to take initiatives on their own which might range from attempts to impose a higher morality on the royal power (or on some of their own members) to efforts to guide the nation themselves. It was a compromise between such attitudes which produced the Constitution as a whole and the provisions in it relating to the position of Shi'ism in particular.

The tenuous and ambivalent relationship of the Shi'ite clergy to the power structure in Iran stems historically from the bases of Shi'ite theology and its concept of legitimacy. The sources of Twelver Shi'ite Law are the Qur'an, the Traditions of the Prophet Muhammad and of the Twelve Imams, the consensus of the Imams, and reason.[7] The authoritative role of the Imams up to the occultation of the twelfth Imam in 873 is as crucial as the void subsequently left by them and their designated lieutenants after 940.[8] From that date on, through the absence of any specifically nominated successor, Twelver Shi'ism is guided by a general agency of the 'ulama as a whole, who as mujtahid-s are entitled to make a reasonable interpretation (ijtihad) of the Law until the rightful, hidden Imam reveals himself and inaugurates a new

[7] These differ from the sources of the Law in orthodox Islam, which are: the Qur'an, the Tradition of the Prophet Muhammad (Sunnah handed down in the form of hadith narratives), the consensus of the Community (ijma'), and analogical reasoning (qiyas).
[8] The period from A.D. 873-74 to 940 is known as that of the "lesser occultation," during which the Shi'ite community was guided by a specific agency of those designated by the last visible Imam. After 940 the age is that of the "greater occultation," and in the absence of any specifically designated successors the guiding force is the general agency of the 'ulama.

era for mankind. Several consequences ensue from this doctrine, the most important of which is that all forms of government existing today are temporary and of dubious validity. The main purpose of government is to maintain the *status quo* until justice and righteousness return with the concealed Imam.

The position of the Shi'ite clergy is ambivalent in another way, however. The *'ulama* have extensive rights of interpretation, although always within the total frame of reference of the truth as fixed by the original Imams and Shi'ite doctrine. The *mujtahid*-s have a greater authority than their Sunni compeers, who are restricted by the Sunni doctrine of the acceptance of the authority of the four orthodox schools and of *taqlid*, that is, the acceptance of the fact that the right to interpretation has ceased and is no longer possible. Thus, the Shi'ite jurisconsults are in the happy position of speaking with the legitimizing authority of the Imams, whose very absence (as early Shi'ite organizers found) can be advantageous. However, unlike the Sunni case where power relationships between religious and political forces in Islam have been working themselves out for thirteen centuries, the structure of Twelver Shi'ism within a political context has been able to express itself only since 1500 in the limited area of Iran, under special national conditions which have influenced the development of Shi'ite doctrine as well as those power relationships. The full expansion of the Shi'ite science of *usul*, the study of the sources of the Law and their arrangement into coherent doctrine, did not take place until the 18th century, and the principle of *ijtihad* was correspondingly tardy in receiving widespread recognition. The vital fact, then, that Shi'ite theology—quite contrary to the Sunni case—had only recently matured and was functioning with a certain vigor at exactly the time when Western intellectual influences were first felt and when the political structure of Iran, indeed its very existence, was threatened, helps to explain in another way the divisions and inconsistencies in the clerical position in modern times.

The confused period from the Constitutional Reform of 1906 to the coup of Colonel Reza Khan in 1921, which finally led to his proclamation as Shah in 1925, merely underscored the already existing situation. With the continuing decline of the monarchy, the Shi'ite *'ulama* were forced to take political stands which revealed their deep divisions. One Shi'ite cleric, Sayyid Zia al-Din Tabatabai, was instrumental in the coup which first brought Reza Khan to power as Commander-in-Chief (*Sardar-i-Sepah*) of the Army, and many others were influential members of the Fourth Majlis (Parliament) which convened in 1921. But it was primarily Shi'ite opposition inside and outside the Majlis which made Reza Khan abandon the idea of imitating Kemal Atatürk and proclaiming a republic. While the practical results of his auto-cratic, centralized reign would likely have been the same whether he had been presidential dictator or absolute monarch, the choice of a monarchical solution both says something about Shi'ite influence and has been of great importance in shaping more recent developments in Iran under the reign of Reza Shah's son, the present Shah.

The true history of modern Iran begins with the nationalist revolu-tion engineered by Reza Shah, who ruled from 1925 to 1941, and carried on thereafter, by more complex means and with greater subtlety, by his son, Mohammad Reza Pahlavi, who came to the throne in 1941. It is after 1925 that the divergence of paths between the new nationalism and the national religion becomes apparent. The national-ism of the Pahlavi period, although obviously born in the ferment of the 19th century, differed sharply from the deep but inchoate sense of national identity with which Iranians have been imbued at all times, but especially in the last several centuries. We have seen how that feeling of national identity on the whole happily encompassed—and was in turn encompassed within—a sect which was, and is, both a spiritual and a political movement. But after 1925, for the first time, modern-style nationalism, which does not digest another political religion so easily, began to make its mark on a widening circle of urban Iranians and to undermine many of the foundations of Shi'ism by appealing to old emotional needs and diverting psychic drives into new channels.

That the divergence was not apparent at first—and is still not clear to a good many Shi'ite leaders—has been demonstrated by their participation in both regimes, despite a stream of measures which have steadily restricted their influence within the state. To some extent this collaboration can be attributed to a Shi'ite fear of worse reactions to be expected were all-out secularists of the left (the Communists, the Tudeh, the National Front, and the like) to gain power. For some of the clergy, too, participation meant a genuine will to share in the modernization of a Shi'ite state by agreeing to a revision of certain religious practices and attitudes which from 1925 on were often labeled reactionary and obscurantist. But the religious establishment has also been drawn along willy-nilly in many cases by the lack of a definite Shi'ite tradition of opposition to a state still officially Shi'ite although by now broadly secular in outlook. The only recourse open to the clergy, aside from the grumbling and muttering that has accompanied much of its preaching and private conversation in recent years, is the kind of open defiance of the political leadership of the Shah which occurred in 1963, when the question of women's voting rights triggered an open split between the two establishments and led to sanguinary riots in several cities. On that occasion the Shi'ite clergy, in the person of the outstanding *mujtahid* in the religious center of Qum, laid down a challenge tantamount to declaring the regime illegal by resurrecting the right, granted to the clergy in the Constitution still in force, to pass on the validity of governmental acts which, as in the case at hand, violated Shi'ite legality in their eyes. This quasi-insurrection of the *'ulama* was broken at a high price socially, and some of the leading religious opponents of the government were sent into exile; but the physical victory of the Shah's regime does not mask the fact that when the leading clerical opponent of the sovereign said to him, "It is not you who decides what is right; it is I and the *'ulama*," a serious parting of the ways—ways shared uneasily at times but with much profit to the nation for more than four centuries—seemed now to have come, with consequences that will only gradually unfold.

This parting of the ways was not recognized early in the rule of Reza Shah because the young nationalist regime was doing those things which most Iranians wanted. The concentration in the 1920's on a strong military to repel the foreign aggressor, on measures of sanitation and public health, and on the establishment of a modern bureaucracy, interested Persians more than the judicial and educational reforms which were constricting the sphere of religious influence.[9] The Pahlavi synthesis, moreover, going beyond that of the Safavids, introduced as a subsidiary factor of pride the idea of the renewal of the Persian Empire in the broadest historical meaning of the term, via a glorification of the pre-Islamic past and a neo-Achaemenidism in art, architecture, and official mythology.[10] This added dimension of Iranian historical consciousness, which is still an important constituent today and to which many nationalist intellectuals respond positively, gave greater weight to the political side of the equation and facilitated a secularist trend which might not have been so pronounced if there had been a direct attack on religion alone. It may be doubted that a

[9] For details on reform and social change in the Reza Shah period, see Joseph Upton, *The History of Modern Iran: An Interpretation*, Cambridge: Harvard University Press, 1960, and Amin Banani, *The Modernization of Iran, 1921-41*, Stanford: Stanford University Press, 1961.

[10] The name chosen by Reza Shah for his dynasty sets the tone of the period. Pahlavi, or Parthian, refers back to the Persian Empire which followed the Achaemenids and preceded the Sasanians (c. 249 B.C. to A.D. 226). The crucial link in this neo-Persian mythology is the claim that the Sasanian royal family was united with that of the Prophet through the marriage of a daughter of Yezdegerd III, last Sasanian ruler, with Husayn. This may be a (deliberate) confusion of the more historically probable marriage of a noble Persian woman with Husayn under the sponsorship of Salman, the Persian "companion of the Prophet" who, as an authentic figure in the eyes of Massignon, helped mold the sons of 'Ali along the lines of his Iranian background.

frontal clash was ever the intention of Reza Shah, despite a few incidents which seem, like much in his career, to have been the result of personal pique. Certainly it is not the tactic of the present Shah. Rather, Pahlavi policy today, which is the expression of the Pahlavi synthesis in this domain, has been to promote the welfare of Iran, as understood by both father and son in reference terms of modern nationalism, by strengthening the dynasty at the expense of the clergy; that is, by redressing the imbalance which had endowed the religious establishment with prestige at the end of the traditional era, when it was dealing with a discredited and inefficient political authority.

By keeping this policy goal in mind we are better equipped to follow the zigzags and seeming contradictions of Pahlavi actions in the past forty years. Thus, although Reza Shah reduced the legal and juridical authority of Shi'ism, no attempt was made to disestablish religion, and the Constitution was not tampered with. The secularization of education, from the primary level up, was carried out in the decade between 1925 and 1935 and capped by the founding of Teheran University at the end of that period; but republicanism was carefully eschewed. European clothing was prescribed for men and the veil banned for women, but enforcement of these decrees was lax in the countryside where the majority of Iranians lived. Moreover, polygamy and the special Shi'ite institution of "temporary marriage" available to travelers (unknown to orthodox Islam and denounced by it as equivalent to prostitution) were left unchanged. All in all, the activities of most of the lower-level *mullah* preachers in the towns and villages went unaffected by reforms which were instituted from the top and primarily directed at the power structure of the religious establishment. What has finally begun to touch the ordinary cleric in recent years is the accumulated weight of secularist feeling inculcated in the generation which has grown up since the first period of educational and social reforms. This feeling has been translated into a vague but nevertheless conscious belief that traditional Islamic values as taught by traditional Islamic preceptors are, if perhaps not wholly incompatible with Iranian progress, at least largely irrelevant to it.

Reza Shah dealt from a position of strength during most of his career. When his son succeeded him, however, the new Shah looked around—after the smoke of Allied occupation in World War II and Russian pressures subsidiary thereto had somewhat cleared—and found that he needed to conciliate all elements of power within the nation before he could effectively begin to reign, let alone rule. From this realization came his acceptance of *'ulama* support in the early years and even at later times, such as after the Iraqi Revolution of 1958, when the throne felt itself menaced, at least by example, from without. Yet basically, the history of Mohammad Reza Pahlavi's quarter-century as Shah has been that of a consolidation of power. This process has led him from a position of cooperation with and acquiescence to the clergy at the beginning of his reign to one of outright confrontation when pushed to it by the *'ulama* as in the 1963 crisis, and, more importantly in recent years, to a gradual appropriation of Shi'ite symbols of legitimacy. Appropriation is a valuable weapon in the hands of the Shah for the preservation, if not the enhancement, of his own legitimacy in the eyes of the masses, for whose benefit he ostentatiously visits the national religious shrines, orders several thousand copies of a rare 16th-century Qur'an printed for distribution to religious centers, attends all important religious ceremonies, dedicates religious monuments, and so on. The manipulation of religion has nothing to do with whether or not the ruler is, as he claims, a somewhat mystic believer; it is a normal gambit in a national political struggle, just as are his reported plans to rationalize and regulate the clergy by incorporating them into civil service functions and by establishing state-controlled theological institutes. Minor efforts have actually already been made along the latter lines, but so far they have been only spotty and ineffective.

Under conditions of such rapid social, political, and economic transition as have prevailed in Iran in recent decades, other forces have naturally been unleashed. The battle is not only between national modernization as desired and understood by the Shah and the more ambiguous positions of the still divided clergy; nor, to be sure, is it a simple contest of power between them. The Shah is far from representing the only nationalist elements in the country, nor do the *'ulama* embody the only religious forces. The growth of extremist, frustrated religious fringe groups of a fundamentalist and activist kind has been in Iran—as in Egypt, Pakistan, and elsewhere in Islam—one of the most marked reactions to imposed modernization. Such groups as the Fidayan-i-Islam, the followers of Ahmad Kasravi, and others have been active since World War II in the fields of sporadic violence and political assassination. At other extremes there are nationalists of the right and the left: the latter secular and Marxist-oriented; the former including geographically pan-Iranian elements and historical Iranists like the Iranvij Society. All these fringe groups, however, despite the deep split between the religious and the secular among them, huddle under the umbrella of Iranian patriotic nationalism. Thus, the Fidayan, who call for an Islamic state under a purified form of Shi'ism, also seek the spread of national Shi'ism and Iranian aggrandizement at the expense of Shi'ite territory in Iraq, while the pan-Iranians look for their territorial expansion in Afghanistan and even Soviet Central Asia.

Too, the Fidayan, just like the adherents of the Iranvij group, claim to be working for the restoration of a "pure" Persian language. In this respect, extremist Muslim forces in Iran should be distinguished from those, like the Muslim Brotherhood in Egypt, which preach fundamentalist Islam and admit nationalism (of any kind, Arab or Egyptian) if it is useful for an Islamic state. Because this difference exists, and because the umbrella of patriotism is natural to the minds of so many Iranians, it gives greater leverage to the Shah (or whatever legitimate national power might be applying it) in putting the emphasis on a strong nationalism which has, almost in passing, a national religion embedded in it. The nationalism may proceed to increasingly secular positions, but the national religion will coexist with it as little more than a national cult, or a form of national tradition which ceremonially sanctions whatever deeds are done, with its blessing, on behalf of the nation.

Moreover, the corollary of the emergence of multiple groups among both the nationalist and the religious elites is that the struggle to influence the direction of the country's future has undergone permutation and is now acted out primarily among competing groups of nationalists with divergent theories, rather than, as in Reza Shah's day, between reformers of a general type and religious traditionalists. We note that nationalist groups like the National Front, an offshoot of the Mossadegh movement of the early 1950's and now a much-reduced body of intellectuals of the left-center in opposition to the present regime, took no part in the religiously motivated disorders of June, 1963. In this, they underlined the fact that their only quarrel is political in nature and is a matter of who will manage the modernized state. They thereby also illustrated that the religio-national synthesis is moribund if not dead. On the other side of the fence, although religious elements do not show the same concentration of energy on rivals within their own camp, this is for the good reason that they sense how close the battle is to being lost, and because of their consequent disarray. This disarray is expressed on occasion among extremists in tactics of terror, whereby they try to show that the government in their view is no longer justly Islamic and that the synthesis has no meaning, and also to reproach the orthodox Shi'ite 'ulama for their passivity and inactivity.

Recent conversations held by the present writer with a broad spectrum of Iranian intellectuals, religious and not, touched on the question of whether the ethical basis of Iranian life today is Islamic in essence. Although a minority made a vigorous defense of the proposition that it is—and practically none disputed that this is the case for the mass of the population, which has almost no conception of the abstract existence of the state as such—most either denied a close connection between Islam and modern Iran as a political entity or chose to ignore the problem as unimportant. Manifestly the regime cannot act on such premises, and it is not doing so. The religious maneuvering of political authority today has two main justifications. The first is that the experience of this century has demonstrated to the satisfaction of the present holders of power, i.e. the Pahlavi establishment, that its own brand of nationalism can bind the official religion of the state to it in a symbiosis in which nationalist factors effectively control religious factors. At the same time, a true fear of the void into which the society might be plunged through too drastic an extirpation of its religious values, together with sound political acumen, hold the regime back from the more radical steps it otherwise might be tempted to take. The personal position of the Shah, which is of considerable but not overwhelming importance, is complex and, despite his own writing on the subject, unclear in the broadest political sense.[11] It can, however, at least be supposed that the regime feels that no steps need be taken at the moment when religion, as managed by it, serves the national purpose, as conceived by it, as well or better than it ever has before.

The second justification lies in the particularist quality which Iranian society has shown at most times in its long history, as a result of which it evolved rather early into a nation with a sense of identity. This evolution in itself poses problems; after a solid, historical identity has been created, what does one do with it? Not many countries have yet had to face this problem in world history outside European civilization: Japan has, and perhaps China, but certainly none of the Muslim states, among which Iran occupies in this respect a singular position, almost—as some Iranians put it—a lonely place. Thus the Islamic Alliance in which Iran has been showing much interest recently, along with Saudi Arabia, Jordan, and some other conservative Arab states can be construed as not only a political move directed at regimes deemed unfriendly, such as the United Arab Republic, but also as a tentative expression of a desire to establish contacts of solidarity which will help it break out of an isolation which is both national and religious. There are other signs of this, many of them minor, but one sees how such efforts do not come easily to a people long steeped in feelings of their own uniqueness and cultural pre-eminence; and in the

---

[11] See *Mission to My Country* by H.I.M. Mohammed Reza Pahlavi, New York: McGraw-Hill, 1961. Many useful insights into the personality of the Shah, including direct observations by him, appear in various Reports written by E. A. Bayne for the American Universities Field Staff, and in his *Four Ways of Politics*, New York: American Universities Field Staff, 1965, pp. 251–310.

main moves of this kind have had little resonance among the mass of Iranians. The truth of the matter is that when Iran succeeded in joining together religion and history in the 16th century, it seceded from the Muslim Middle East for most practical purposes; and it is this secession which is perhaps slightly regretted by an aware minority today, even if they are unsure what to do about it.

Possibly the main focus of Iranian religious history—which is a crucial issue for the future as well—should be on this. It is the question, really, of how adaptable Shi'ism is after all. It can be argued that the facilities of *ijtihad* leave room for considerable theological and intellectual mobility, and it could also be held that the relative recentness of Shi'ite doctrinal development holds out the promise that it may achieve much more in the near future. The continuing elaboration of *usuli* principles of reasoning applied to doctrine could well produce significant accomplishments. Furthermore, should we forget the political astuteness which Shi'ism displayed in the difficult times of the 'Abbasid Caliphate when it did not show its hand unnecessarily? In a difficult transitional period like the present one in Iran, it might appear advantageous, now as then, to the collective mind of the religious establishment to allow secular political authorities to take the responsibilities and the risks of modernization while the *'ulama* practice the traditional Shi'ite prerogative of *taqiyah*, or dissimulation of one's true beliefs in time of danger.

Against these possibilties, however, stand not only the stubbornly traditional interpretations of Shi'ite Law practiced by many *mujtahid*-s, but also the critical fact that Twelver Shi'ism has developed in recent centuries within a quite restricted geocultural compass. It is inevitable that this has had a serious impact on its intellectual horizons, in much the same way, for example, that Lutheran Sweden or the Dutch Reformed Church in South Africa exhibit the stultifying effects of physical and cultural restrictions. A faith with an ultimately significant message for mankind, like the original Protestantism of Luther and Calvin, can kindle the fires of the spirit and spread to all peoples; but one which is reduced to the role of a prop for a political apparatus in one country normally has little to offer. The problem of Iranian Shi'ism today is exactly this: that it lacks the ecumenical nature and the catholicity of orthodox Sunni Islam, which can appeal to every man. It is perhaps not too much to suggest that a great Sunni reformist like Muhammad 'Abduh, although writing in Egypt, was asking himself what was "Good" for men anywhere at any time within the framework of Islamic righteousness, while one suspects that most Shi'ite jurists today are condemned to be more concerned with what is "Good" for Shi'ism in Iran (and perhaps Iraq), or for Iranians, or at best for the Shi'ite Community as a whole, set off as it still is from the main body of Islam. In the end it is that most precious quality of Islamic religious thought and the civilization which stems from it—its vast powers of spiritual and cultural integration applied to the most diverse societies and types of men—which seems to be missing in Shi'ism as practiced today.

In so far as Iran itself is concerned, it is hard to avoid concluding that as a modernizing and self-confident national body embarked upon an irreversible process of development—and indeed far into it when compared with many nearby countries—the nation has outgrown the need for Shi'ism in the sense of what Shi'ism once meant to it. As a linchpin of national identity and as a mechanism of balance for national integrity, it is no longer necessary. But it is unlikely to the highest degree that a transitional society like Iran has outgrown, or will for some time outgrow, the need for an orderly summation of the deep religious impulses which still move very large segments of its people. The dilemma today of what has been called the "Two Irans" is that the peasantry and a sizable body of the urban masses do not and cannot understand this first fact, which is essentially political; and that, conversely, the large and growing number of secularist or agnostic individuals among the elite and the bourgeoisie fail to recognize the second fact, which transcends politics. Beyond the Safavid synthesis and the even wider Pahlavi synthesis, Iran at some time in the future will have to work out a true reconciliation of all the spiritual and material roots of its society if it is to achieve in the future what its past has the right to demand of it.

8.

THE POLITICAL USES OF RELIGION:

AFGHANISTAN

BY LOUIS DUPREE

American Universities Field Staff

Afghanistan, long considered one of the more backward Islamic countries, is moving ahead today at an almost frightening pace. Changes in all spheres—economic, political, and social—have been phenomenal since World War II. In economic matters there has been the creation of an infrastructure of roads, airports, river ports, and telecommunications; an expansion of export trade (particularly with the barter nations of the Soviet Union, Eastern Europe and, recently on a much smaller scale, the People's Republic of China); increasing development aid from both the Soviet Union and the West (especially the United States, but including West Germany and the United Kingdom); and the encouragement of regional economic development with an eye to producing items which cost much hard currency: cement, textiles, clothing, light machinery, petroleum-oil-lubricants. In the political arena Afghanistan has maintained its neutrality in the Cold War and improved its relations with neighbors Pakistan, Iran, the Soviet Union, and China; it has also shifted from oligarchical rule with a military power base to a constitutional monarchy with the same military base of power plus free elections to form a two-house parliament. In the social sphere we see the voluntary abolition of *purdah* (isolation of women) and the *burqa* or *chowdry* (the veil— although many women, especially in urban areas, still continue to wear it), the adoption of laws establishing a free press and political parties, and a revision of judicial codes and administration. Educational facilitics have increased, and there is a gradual breakdown of ethnic discrimination in the upper echelons of government.

In addition Afghanistan had its first student riots in October, 1965, a sure sign of incipient political competitiveness if not of maturity in developing nations.[1] The smashing of the long plate glass windows of USIS, another sign of political growth, has yet to occur, however. It is not that pitfalls are absent or will easily disappear, but to understand the progress and the pitfalls, let us examine the cultural patterns which influence the processes of change.

Afghanistan, in spite of advances in education, is primarily a *non-literate* society. Although the nation and the Muslim culture have a long literate tradition, few Afghans (about 5 to 10 per cent) can read and write. A non-literate society contrasts with a preliterate society in that the latter never had a script, whereas the former has a literate culture but a fundamentally illiterate society. Most of the post-World War II changes listed above have affected primarily the literate segments of Afghan society, few filtering down to the non-literate population. (No formal census has been taken in Afghanistan, but estimates of the population cluster between 12 and 15 million persons.)

Although Islam is a sophisticated religion with a logical theological base, few non-literates in Afghanistan know the philosophical niceties of the religion they practice. Tinged with many pre-Islamic beliefs and rituals which often range beyond the limits imposed on man by Islamic dicta, village and nomadic Islam becomes, in essence, non-Islamic or, at best, a local, bastardized version of Islam. For example, the *Pushtun-wali* (the traditional, unwritten code of the Pushtuns on both sides of the Durand Line [2] separating Afghanistan from West Pakistan) emphasizes blood vengeance (see Appendix A). The local customs and informal legal codes of nomadic and mountaineer groups often offer violent solutions to internal problems. Harsh environments breed harsh individuals, and the ideal personality type in Afghanistan is the warrior-poet, a brave fighter who can also deliver flowery orations at tribal councils or *jirgahs*.

The Nuristanis of eastern Afghanistan, forcibly converted to Islam in the 1890s, perform a spring sacrifice which relates directly to their pre-Islamic days when they were called "Kafir," or heathen, by their Muslim neighbors.

Although forbidden by Islam, saint cults abound throughout the

[1] Louis Dupree, "Democratic Trouble in Kabul," *Foreign Report: The Economist,* London: November 25, 1965, pp. 4–7.
[2] Louis Dupree, "The Durand Line of 1893: A case study in artificial political boundaries and culture areas," T. Cuyler Young, (ed.), *Current Problems in Afghanistan: Thirteenth Annual Near East Conference,* The Princeton University Conference, Princeton, 1961, pp. 77–94.

Muslim world. Pilgrims flock to the *ziarat* (tombs) of saints to ask for intercession with Allah for specific favors. In Afghanistan, for example, a saint's tomb near Jalalabad specializes in curing insanity; another near Charikar cures mad dog bites; and in the valley of Paiminar, just north of Kabul, sit forty-odd shrines, all dedicated to fertility. Women desiring children visit Paiminar to buy amulets from the caretakers of the tombs, each guaranteeing a son or daughter, as the case may be. At one tomb, women actually fondle the bones of *shaheed* (Afghans killed fighting the British) and eat a pinch of earth, reflecting a very primitive belief in impregnation by mother earth.

Many other examples could be cited. Black magic, shamanism, and types of voodoo (including sticking sharp objects in dolls) are practiced, particularly in northern Afghanistan, and witches, usually old women past childbearing age, exist throughout the country.

A non-literate society breeds inward-looking attitudes that prevent individuals from accepting the impersonal and achievement-oriented measures of a nation-state in the Western sense. In a modern nation-state, individuals have rights protected by the government; the government, in turn, demands that certain obligations be accepted by the people in return for the guaranteed rights. The key is reciprocity. On both sides, rights and obligations must be legally definable and, more important, practically functional and operable.

In Afghanistan, as in all other non-literate societies, rights and obligations revolve about the local group, usually based on kinship. A man's occupation, class or caste, and position in the power elite are often determined before his birth. In addition, his choice of mate is limited, and his responsibilities in warfare, mutual aid, and blood vengeance tightly defined. Each kin generation succeeds in perpetuating the inward-looking society unless outside influences penetrate to destroy or, more desirably, to modify the given cultural patterns so that the changes affect the largest number of persons in the lightest possible manner.

Another way of describing an inward-looking society is to say that a man is born into a set of answers. For every question, a logical answer must be available within the ethos of the culture. In Afghanistan these answers usually come from the local brand of Islam. "Why did the crops fail?" "No rain." "Why no rain?" "Because Allah willed it." "Why?" "Because someone (or we) has broken the laws of Islam." (In truth, most men and women break the tenets of their religion daily in one way or another.) Unanswerable questions are simply not asked. Each member of the group knows the whys of birth, puberty, marriage, and death, and group rituals for each of these life crises reinforce individual beliefs in the system.

These predeterministic beliefs of the non-literate segment of Afghan society, however, violate a basic Islamic tenet. The term "Islam" means "submission," but not an unquestioning fatalism, as characterized by the phrase "Inshallah"—"if God wills." In the real sense a man submits to Allah of his own free will only after examining the religion, its rituals, and its interpretation of man's relationship to other men, to nature, and to God. By accepting Islam, he agrees to follow the principles of Islam as revealed to the Prophet Mohammad.

The belief in a predestined will of Allah, however, has been fostered for centuries by religious leaders with vested interests in the maintenance of such beliefs. In modern times, these traditionalists have opposed secular education for, in the past, they controlled the educational institution. They have fought land reforms because, under the *waqf* system (and often through direct land grants) they controlled large tracts of land. They have schemed against judicial reforms, for they were the ultimate judges of right and wrong in courts. They have torpedoed attempts to create secular nation-states, for in classical Islamic political theory, church and state cannot be separated because a government rules as caretaker of God's Community on earth.

Another facet of the inseparability of church and state is mentioned by Stirling who, writing on Turkey, points out that Islam in Turkey did not wither away when Atatürk separated church and state in 1928, but continued to grow within the Turkish cultural patterns in spite of official pressures that discouraged many non-functional Islamic practices.

> The relaxation of this official pressure (in 1950) caused what looks like a revival, but it is in fact, so to speak, the religious stream emerging from an underground section of its course. But more fundamental than these oscillations, *the process of secularization continues*, perceptibly in the villages, vigorously in the towns. This is not so much a matter of the decreasing performance of religious rituals, but of a decline in the number of socially important activities to which religion is relevant, and a change in the way of thinking to a less theoretic view of the universe.[3] [Italics added.]

Therefore, Islam, like most other religions, must be considered at two distinct levels: the essence, or universal philosophy; and the action component (including the various bastardizations of local Islam), the carrying of Islam into the daily lives of the masses by the interpretations of the religious leaders, both traditionalists and modernists. Before analyzing the mundane aspects of Islam in action, however, let me state that the major difference between Western philosophies and

[3] Paul Stirling, "Religious Change in Republican Turkey," *The Middle East Journal*, Vol. XII, No. 4, 1958, pp. 395–408.

Islam is attitudinal. Westerners are born into an outward-looking society, into a set of questions, and each answer only poses additional questions in an endless round-robin of seek and find, seek and find. In contrast, as stated previously, the non-literate Muslim is born into an inward-looking society, into a set of answers—an attitudinal set which conditions the action dimensions of community religious practice.

THE ROLE OF THE VILLAGE MULLAH IN AFGHANISTAN

Two types of religious leaders exist in the nonliterate milieux of the towns and villages outside the major urban centers of Afghanistan: government-paid mullahs, who usually double as teachers or judges; and "folk" mullahs, often illiterate and relatively untrained, usually part-time religious leaders, being farmers first. Several examples will give the flavor of the day-to-day roles of these two generalized types.

The Tajiks of Midanam (the fictitious name of a village in north-central Afghanistan) are primarily Shi'i muslims, but the central government assigned a Sunni mullah to serve the mosque-school compound. Whether or not he served as the "eyes and ears of the king" could not be determined.

The mullah held two daily classes in the *maktab* (mosque school), one for boys and one for girls. Attendance was irregular and not compulsory. The mullah taught the boys the Qur'an, which they intoned noisily by rote in Arabic, although even the mullah understood but little Arabic; an old woman taught the girls the Quran with a few side hints about housewifery. The mullah, a political appointee, wielded a sizable amount of covert political power, and without his tacit consent our anthropological work would not have been possible. The Afghan government representative with us attended prayers at the mosque at least twice daily, and the mullah permitted our whole party, including my wife, to bathe inside the mosque compound, an act of near technical heresy.

The mullah of Midanam, then, had three important functions: educational, religious, and political.

Later in 1950–51, we lived in the Sunni Pushtun village of Mifamam (again a fictitious name) in south-central Afghanistan, which had no government-appointed and paid mullahs, but rather two farmers who doubled as part-time mullahs. Both had families and both were illiterate. Both had committed large sections of the Qur'an to memory. The village had fewer than a hundred souls, and the two mullahs competed for bodies to add to their congregations. They both claimed to have been touched by Allah; the villagers respected both but considered them a little crazy. The mullahs wanted more than anything to perform a miracle—to heal the sick, or make barren women give birth to sons—so that they would be considered *pirs* or saints and be buried in an honored tomb. To this end they sold amulets (*ta'wiz*) to their fellow villagers. If their amulets succeeded, the mullahs would become famous and peasants all over the area would come to do homage and buy amulets. These mullahs desperately wanted to be different; they were illiterate men obsessed with the drive for power and they attempted to achieve this power in the only way open to them. The Pushtun villagers devoutly prayed the prescribed five times a day, even if at work in the fields or excavating for our expedition. They accepted as normal the mullahs' being touched by Allah. The nearest government mullah lived in the sub-provincial capital and was a large landowner. He owned several fields in the village of Mifamam, and was the butt of many local jokes.

The two respected, unpaid, part-time mullahs of Mifamam served an important religious function—more so than the government-appointed mullah in Tajikistan or the land-owning mullah of the sub-provincial capital. The people respected both the Mifamam mullahs and looked on their competition as normal. Their amulets also made them function as doctors or magicians, just as many of our general practitioners with their pills and antibiotics are obviously both doctors and magicians.

The village mullah is moved by the amorphous, emotional god who moves us all at one time or another. He is the epitome of the "folk society" preacher or evangelist who emotes in the culturally approved manner, and thus induces what we call a state of religious experience. He emphasizes the emotional reality of the basic beliefs—nothing less, nothing more. The local, god-touched mullah is accepted only as long as his—and I use the term unblushingly—*mana* is effective. His role is strictly religious, and he reinforces the basic beliefs of Islam by leading group worship.

The government-appointed and -paid mullah teaches formal doctrines and the Qur'an by rote, but the village mullah touches the hearts of the people. If he touches them often enough and his amulets and charms seem effective, he may become a local saint at death. Favors will be asked of Allah in the name of the dead saint; thus, his power and status may continue to grow after death. An unscrupulous government appointee, on the other hand, cannot be expelled from a community; his role is secular as well as religious and he helps the central government maintain political control.

Several incidents from other areas of Afghanistan are worth recording. At another Pushtun village, near the town of Panjwai, a government-appointed mullah gave us considerable trouble while we excavated a prehistoric mound. He exhorted the villagers not to work for an infidel (me) because I was digging up and defiling Muslim dead. As proof he pointed to several prehistoric burials we had uncovered. Overnight our three carefully exposed skeletons were stolen, under the eyes of a guard, and unceremoniously reburied in the flood plain near the village. We endured this insult with the stoic, inscrutable dignity of the Occident. The mullah, however, persisted in his persecution. He claimed that all bones we uncovered were from Muslim burials. I showed him cow mandibles and teeth, and he consistently repeated, *"Adam ast"* ("This is man"). He threatened to force the workmen off the site if we did not desist in our flagrant disregard of the Muslim dead. In desperation, I drew a line around a trench we were digging and announced that whoever stepped over the line would be forcibly removed from the site. The mullah immediately squatted over the edge of the trench, and tossed small stones and clods of dirt at the workmen. I threw him bodily off the site. The workmen and spectators laughed. The mullah left, shouting curses on the heads of all born and unborn Duprees, and announced that the sub-governor of Panjwai would have me arrested. He left to visit the governor. He returned later during the day, and the smooth about-face he exhibited should be studied by our State Department spokesmen. The sub-governor told me later he ordered the mullah in no uncertain terms to leave us alone, for we were doing good work for Afghanistan. This is a far cry from the first half of the 19th century, when an Afghan mullah could start a *jihad* at the drop of an English footstep on the frontier.

In central Afghanistan we lived for a short time near a nomadic Pushtun group which specialized in raising Afghan hounds. No mullah traveled with this band. A leader said, "We need only our guns and Allah." This was the one group which refused to let us visit their tents, even though several of the men worked for us as laborers at a cave site.

In other tribal areas, I watched mullahs leading young men in prayer. These young men laughed and made fun of the mullahs behind their backs, making obscene gestures which no good Muslim could possibly call sacred.

From the foregoing a question emerges: how important are the basic beliefs of Islam in the everday lives of Afghan villagers and tribesmen? I think they are very important, but sectarian differences have lost significance because the generalities of the concepts have encouraged local flexibility. Fundamentally, Islam is a literate religion with a sophisticated liturgical literature, although most of its followers are illiterate.

The study of the relative value of literate religion in daily interactions should not be considered a sacred cow which cannot be butchered, or the analysis of religious institutions will remain the opiate of the anthropologists. Religions, then, should be analyzed in their functional, day-to-day aspects as well as at the theological, philosophical level.[4]

THE ROLE OF ISLAM IN THE DEVELOPMENT OF MODERN AFGHANISTAN

The struggle to create a modern state began in 1880, when Abdur Rahman became Amir of Kabul, and extended his influence—if not actual control—throughout most of what we today call Afghanistan. By the time of his death in 1901, Abdur Rahman had seized most religious properties (*waqfs*) and placed both the lands and religious leaders involved under government supervision.

Under Abdur Rahman's son, Habibullah (1901–19), the religious leaders regained much of their political power, but Habibullah's successor and third son, Amanullah (1919–29), dramatically changed everything. He attempted to secularize and Westernize Afghanistan by introducing, among other things, constitutional and administrative reforms, by forcing the people to wear European clothes in Kabul, by taking the veil off the women, and by initiating co-educational schools.

Amanullah's grand plans failed because he underestimated their impact on a traditionalist, inward-looking, non-literate society. In addition, he failed to appreciate the necessity for a stable base of power in order to create a modern nation-state. Drastic changes such as those proposed by Amanullah needed either a broad base of popular support or strong military backing. He had neither, for, earlier in his reign, Amanullah disbanded most of his military establishment in order to divert more funds to his modernization programs. Furthermore, Afghanistan lacked the necessary literate class to support socio-political reform movements.

In all fairness, external factors did contribute to Amanullah's down-

---

[4] For more details, see Louis Dupree, "Religion, Technology and Islam," pp. 370–81; L. P. Vidyarthi (ed.), *Aspects of Religion in Indian Society*, Meerut, 1961. Also published in *Journal of Social Research*, Vol. IV, Nos. 1–2, 341–354, Ranchi.

fall. To accelerate his programs, he agreed to accept Soviet assistance. Naturally, the British objected to this real or imagined threat to the security of British India. The fine hand of the British appears to have been present in the revolt against Amanullah, probably through Deobandi-trained mullahs spreading propaganda in the tribal belt, accusing Amanullah of being anti-Islamic.[5]

Conservative religious elements gained power once more with the rise of General Mohammad Nadir Shah to the throne of Kabul as King Mohammad Nadir Shah in 1929. The new king, a distant cousin of Amanullah, chose to make haste slowly. The 1931 Constitution, a legacy of Nadir Shah (he was assassinated in 1933), established Afghanistan as a Sunni Muslim state, with the Hanafi Shariat (school of Islamic Law) supreme. But the Afghan government never adequately implemented the provisions for independent legislative action and the introduction of democratic processes.

Religious leaders representing strong vested interests continued to be powerful during the first twenty years of the region of King Mohammad Zahir Shah, son of Nadir Shah. A succession of uncles (Sardar Mohammad Hashim Khan, 1933–46, and Sardar Shah Mahmud, 1946–53) ruled Afghanistan while the young king reigned, a patrilineal, patrilocal, and patriarchal pattern which fits nicely into the modes of Afghan society. When a boy's father dies, the paternal uncles take over the father's rights and obligations.

In 1953, however, new forces began to take shape in Afghanistan, and since then religious leaders have lost much of their secular power. They fought several rear-guard actions against encroachment upon their religio-secular prerogatives and transference of these prerogatives to secular authorities.

Two examples will suffice. First, during the Afghan national holidays (*Jeshn*) in August of 1959, the government of Prime Minister Mohammad Daoud Khan, who had seized power from his uncle in a bloodless 1953 coup, informally ended *purdah* (the isolation of women) and the *chowdry* or *burqa* (Afghan version of the veil). The king, cabinet, high-ranking military officers, and members of the royal family stood before the march past of the army and the fly past of the air force as they had in past years —but with a radical difference. Their wives stood beside them unveiled. The thousands of villagers and tribesmen (including many religious leaders) in the crowd were stunned, some genuinely shocked. Amanullah had tried the same thing, but without the support of the army. In addition, he had issued a royal *firman* (proclamation) which made unveiling obligatory. The 1959 un-

[5] Louis Dupree, "Mahmud Tarzi: Forgotten Nationalist," *AUFS Reports*, South Asia Series, Vol. VIII, No. 1, January, 1964.

veiling, however, was technically voluntary. The king did not issue a firman, and only high government officials were actually forced to display their unveiled wives in public, to set an example for the masses.

The immediate result of the voluntary unveiling could have been easily predicted. A delegation of leading religious leaders in the country demanded and received an audience with Prime Minister Daoud, whom they accused of being anti-Islamic, of having succumbed to the influence of the Isai'ites (American Christians) and Kafirs (heathen Russians).

Prime Minister Daoud, normally not a patient man, waited until the mullahs vented their spleens, and then calmly informed the delegation that the removal of the veil was not anti-Islamic, and that if the venerable religious leaders could find anything in the Qur'an which definitely demanded that women be kept in purdah, he would be the first to return his wife and daughters to the harem. Daoud knew he stood on firm theological ground, for several young Afghan lawyers had carefully checked the Qur'an. Chief among the legal advisers was Musa Shafiq, member of a distinguished religious family. Shafiq received his legal education in Afghan theological schools, Al-Azar in Egypt (fountainhead of Muslim legal learning), and Columbia Law School, so he is expert in all manner of secular and religious law. In addition, the young lawyers know that that purdah and the veil were not originally Islamic customs, but had been copied from the urbanized Byzantine (Anatolia) and Sassanid (Persian) Empires after their conquest by the Arabs. Over the centuries, however, purdah had acquired the aura of religious sanction, without any justification in Islam except for later questionable interpretations after the fact.

The Afghan religious leaders who criticized Daoud had believed in the sanctity of purdah all their lives, and secular logic had little place in their thinking—true in any religion where generations accept a custom as a religious doctrine. So the disgruntled mullahs went into the bazaar and began to preach against the godless government of Daoud. Knowing this would happen, Daoud's secret police tailed the religious leaders and arrested about fifty of them as they exhorted the crowds to action.

Incarcerated, the religious leaders spent about a week in Afghan jails, where they were systematically brainwashed by the young lawyers with religious backgrounds. I hasten to add that Afghan jails are not designed to rehabilitate prisoners, but to punish wrongdoers. The young lawyers impressed three points on the mullahs. First, the removal of the veil would be strictly voluntary, and the government did not plan to interfere in the process, and those women who wished 'to wear the burqa (or whose male relatives forced them to wear it) would not be prosecuted. Second, purdah and the veil are not originally Muslim customs, but adapted by urbanized Muslims in order to protect their beauteous properties from prying eyes. And third, an Islamic state exists with the sanction of Allah and if Allah had been displeased with Daoud's actions, He would have withdrawn the sanction and the government would have fallen. Obviously, Allah approved the removal of the veil, because Daoud still ruled. Therefore, the mullahs (the logic continues), in opposing the voluntary removal of the veil and preaching against Daoud were not only guilty of treason—but heresy! The weight of this logic (plus a week's stay in Afghan jails) moved the mullahs to accept, if not freely agree with, the voluntary abolition of purdah and the veil.

Many women still wear the veil in Afghanistan, particularly in urban centers, but more come out each year. The voluntary abolition of purdah served a very practical function. It released a potential 50 per cent increase in the labor force. Today, women work in all government and many commercial offices in Afghanistan. Women teachers teach in coeducational classes; women doctors and nurses serve both sexes.

Village and nomadic women had seldom worn the veil previously, for their hard work in the fields and with the flocks had precluded such frills—a fact which again emphasizes the urban aspects of the veil. However, in villages growing into towns, many upper- and middle-class women now wear the veil for the first time, for they look on the head-to-toe garment as a sign of sophisticated citified ways.

The second example concerns the Qandahar riots of December, 1959, which began over payment of land taxes and quickly developed into general anti-modernization destruction. The people of the Qandahar area had been made exempt from land taxes by Ahmad Shah Durani (1747–73) for their services to his cause. Subsequent amirs, however, whether they exercised control from Kabul, Qandahar, or Herat, attempted to collect land taxes from the Qandaharis. Each year the same sequence of events occured. The amir, governor, or other administrative head invited the large landholders or their agents to come to the government center in Qandahar, usually in the winter, the off-agricultural season. When those concerned assembled in the administrative compound, the governor read a proclamation demanding payment of taxes. The landowners and agents immediately repaired to the *Masjid-i-Jami Kherqa Mobarak* (Mosque of the Sacred Cloak of the Prophet) and declared *bast* (sanctuary). Anyone can enter a mosque or a shrine and declare bast, and cannot be touched by law or enemy while he remains inside the holy grounds. For a week or so the crowd would live in the compound, and their friends and families would bring food, clothing, and bedding. The bastis spent their time praying and socializing. The government would give up and the land-owners and agents would go home until the next year.

Flushed with several quick secular successes over the religious leaders, the Daoud regime decided the time had come to start collect-ing land taxes from the Qandaharis. The governor sent out the usual summons and the usual crowds duly appeared. The governor read the usual proclamation demanding the payment of taxes, and the crowd left the compound for the nearby mosque. But the government had introduced a new ingredient. A line of armed Afghan soldiers stretched directly across their line of march. At first startled, the crowd then refused to take the soldiers seriously. Joking and laughing, the delinquent taxpayers moved forward. Someone threw a rock. Other rocks followed. An officer ordered the soldiers to fire over the heads of the people, but they kept coming. The next volley ripped into the crowd, killing and wounding several. Stunned, the people dispersed and ran. They recovered quickly, however, and anger replaced stunned fear.

Encouraged by ultra-conservative religious leaders, who saw a chance to strike at the heart of Daoud's progressive programs, an anti-modernist cloudburst immediately descended on Qandahar. Religious-ly inspired hatred of all things "modern" and "progressive" surged through the streets. Wealthy landlords—including, it must be re-membered, many influential religious leaders—brought in the infamous *pa-luch* (barefoot boys) of the bazaars, who, traditionally, will support any cause for a price. The mobs attacked several visible manifestations of modernization. A girl's school went up in flames and several girls were manhandled. The mob fire-gutted the local movie house. The fuchsia-colored, air-conditioned Cadillac of a local US-AID official was overturned and burned. An American technician, wandering through the streets to warn all Americans to stay indoors, was inadvertently slightly wounded with a knife. Even the pa-luch leader later expressed regrets for this incident, and the mob did not attempt to scale the clearly marked compounds of the US-AID community.

The Daoud regime in Kabul, shocked but not completely caught off guard by the sequence of events, reacted swiftly and effectively. Lorryloads of troops from the mobile Central Forces (Kabul) immedi ately reinforced the Qandahar garrison, followed by tanks. The riots, which had flared quickly, died quickly, and the government imposed martial law in the area.

Such mobility would have been impossible for security forces a decade or so ago, but now even the wealthy and relatively independent

Qandahar landlords could see the handwriting on the mud wall. They paid their taxes.

In addition the government spread the rumor that land reforms would be introduced in the near future. Panicked, the larger landholders began to sell land (obviously not their best) to peasant farmers and bazaar shopkeepers. No one knows exactly how much land changed hands because the cadastral survey has not been completed, but I personally know two previously landless peasants who purchased forty and twenty *jiribs* (two jiribs equal one acre) of land in the Panjwai just west of Qandahar. These two peasant farmers had been saving money for many years and dug it up from hiding places to make their lifetime dreams come true.

Daoud's regime came to an end because of the closure of the border with Pakistan between 1961 and 1963 over the complex "Pushtunistan" issue, involving the status of several million Pushtuns on the Pakistani side of the Durand Line. Although many applauded Daoud's downfall, his decade of achievements cannot be lightly dismissed. Among his most important accomplishments was that the king now ruled as well as reigned. Afghanistan was becoming a constitutional monarchy.[6]

Probably the most important event in 20th-century Afghanistan was the promulgation of a new Constitution, one which uses Islam as a positive, dynamic weapon in helping create a nation-state, and not as mere window dressing, as does the Pakistani Constitution of 1962.[7] Neither did the Afghans try to create a completely secular constitution which ignored Islam, as did several post-World War II Arab states, such as Tunisia.

The writers of the Afghan Constitution interpreted as fact that *'ijtihad* (or legal decisions based on knowledge and reason) held supremacy over the Islamic hardening of the legal arteries which occurred about a thousand years ago, when *qiyas 'aqli* (logical deduction by analogy) and *qiyas shar'i* (legal deduction by analogy) made it possible for a Muslim judge to reach a decision (or *'ijam*, consensus) without recourse to previous legal decisions or changed social conditions. The result had been a legal straitjacket which constricted Muslim judges for a thousand years.

At the *Loya Jirgah* (Great Council of Notables) held in September, 1964, to pass the Constitution, many arguments in interpretation arose, usually generational in nature. Traditionalist-oriented fathers argued with their modernist sons on several occasions.

[6] Louis Dupree, "The Decade of Daoud Ends," *AUFS Reports*, South Asia Series, Vol. VII, No. 7, May, 1963.
[7] Louis Dupree, "Constitutional development and cultural change," Parts I–VIII, *AUFS Reports*, South Asia Series, Vol. IX, Nos. 1–4 and 7–10, 1965.

The men writing the Afghan Constitution, however, emphasized modern social thinking and conditions. The following articles make the Constitution an essentially secular document, but within the framework of Islam, as interpreted by modernists. Article 69 (which establishes the supremacy of secular over religious law):

> Excepting the conditions for which specific provisions have been made in this Constitution, a law is a resolution passed by both Houses, and signed by the King. In the area where no such law exists, the provisions of the Hanafi jurisprudence of the Shariah of Islam shall be considered as law.

Article 102 (which establishes supremacy of secular over religious courts):

> The courts in the cases under their consideration shall apply the provisions of this Constitution and the laws of the state. Whenever no provision exists in this Constitution or the laws for a case under consideration, the courts shall, by following the basic principles of the Hanafi jurisprudence of the Shariah of Islam, and within the limitations set forth in this Constitution, render a decision that in their opinion secures justice in the best possible way.

In similar ways, the essence of Islam permeates all of the 1964 Constitution, and the articles describing the organization and power of the executive, legislative, and judicial authorities emphasize the supremacy of the secular without divorcing the mundane from the values embodied in Islam.

In addition, Article 2, Paragraph 2 guarantees freedom of religion to non-Muslims "within the limits determined by laws for public decency and public order." The constitution does establish that "Islam is the sacred religion of Afghanistan," a much milder statement than that of earlier constitutions. For example, the 1931 Constitution stated, "The religion of Afghanistan is the sacred religion of Islam, and the official and popular school of religion is the Hanafi School" (Article 1). The 1964 Constitution merely established that "Religious rites performed by the state shall be according to the provisions of the Hanafi Doctrine" (Article 2, Paragraph 1).

Little overt religious discrimination exists in Afghanistan, and more is present between Sunni and Shi'a Muslims than between Muslims and non-Muslims. Both Hindus and Sikhs, for example, celebrate their holy days without disturbance, and Afghan Muslim government officials now make opening speeches at such festivals. Hindu temples, Sikh *gudwaras*, and Jewish synagogues all exist and thrive in the urban centers of Afghanistan. But few in minority groups, including Shi'a

Muslims, can as yet aspire to high government positions under the overwhelmingly dominant Sunni society. Steady progress toward civil equality is being made, however.

Meanwhile, the government continues its policy of using certain important religious places to further the cause of nationalism and the creation of a nation-state. For example, the reconstructed Jami Masjid in Herat also has a large monument to the heroic nine-month defense of the city against a numerically superior Persian army in 1837–38. Also, the raising of the sacred banner at the tomb of Hazrat Ali in Mazar-i-Sharif to commence forty days of religious festivities on March 21 (the Afghan New Year) has become the occasion for nation-building speeches by the prime minister and other high government officials. Since 1959, when purdah began to die with the sanction of government, many Afghan women have attended religious ceremonies without veils, dressed in Western clothes but wearing discreet head-shawls. At the 1966 raising of the banner in Mazar-i-Sharif, most of the women present were unveiled.

CONCLUDING REMARKS

The goal of every developing society is to create a nation-state with mutually acceptable and functioning rights and obligations toward government and governed. The chief ingredient for such a system is a qualitatively literate middle class which can function as the base of power. Literacy alone does not provide a panacea. A man must use the tool of literacy intelligently and effectively. To me, this means man's ability to define, discuss, and activate his rights and obligations toward his fellow men, his state, his world, and the universe at large, in the light of whatever religious beliefs he might hold.

Clashes often occur in the minds of literate Afghan secular leaders, most of whom were brought up in religious traditions which they now reject. Unlike the non-literate villagers and tribesmen, Afghan literates, especially those educated in foreign countries, have been exposed to sets of questions outside the circle of traditional answers. Islam, however, can be conservative and traditional or liberal and progressive, depending on interpretation. The essence of Islam (equality of man before Allah and individual submission to the principles of Islam after a freely willed examination) remains the same.

Modernization involves a change in attitudes, for without such change technological innovations merely reflect the amount of outside aid penetrating a country. If a man believes a tractor runs because of the will of Allah, and not because of proper preventive maintenance, the tractor will sit dormant at the first sign of mechanical trouble. Women will continue to die because of the will of Allah instead of from childbed fever, and large dams and paved roads will have little social effect.

Afghanistan, for all its initial economic, political, and social backwardness just after World War II, has used Islam as a weapon for development, and the new breed of religious leader, young, Western-trained and outward-looking, reflects this change. Many serve in the two-house parliament (*Shura*) and stand among the staunchest supporters of the king's reform programs. One, the Maulana Irshad, is Secretary of the Lower House, the all-elected *Wolesi Jirgah*.

In addition one interesting, unplanned by-product of the new constitutional system has been the election of a group of traditionalist-oriented religious leaders to the *Wolesi Jirgah*. Since no organized clergy formally exists in Islam, these leaders previously exercised their power in geographic zones or among specific ethnic groups. Having been elected to the *Wolesi Jirgah*, however, they now, for the first time, form an organized, politically oriented group with an institutionalized platform from which they can launch their conservative interpretations.[8]

If the present rate of progressive movement slows down and the vocal left- and right-wing elements combine to harass the government to the point of constitutional collapse, the traditional leaders may say, "See. We told you so, Allah is against these reforms. Return to the old ways. Allah knows best."

But for the present, the modernists ride high, and interpret Islam in the light of modern social thinking. The government continues to secularize all institutions without destroying the fabric of Islam as a system of belief and a guide to individual actions. It simply wishes to keep religion out of partisan politics, even though many religious leaders do actively participate.

The government, however, hopes to prevent religion from becoming a political issue. *Inshallah*, the modernists will succeed.

[8] Recent minor triumphs of the traditionalists in parliament are discussed in, Louis Dupree, "Afghanistan: 1966. Comments on a comparatively calm state of affairs with reference to the turbulence of late 1965," *AUFS Reports*, South Asia Series, Vol. X, No. 4, July, 1966.

APPENDIX

The Pushtun code of honor, *Pushtunwali,* has never been accurately recorded. I have recently been collecting versions of it. Briefly paraphrased, the code generally places the following obligations on a Pushtun:

1) To avenge blood.

2) To fight to the death for a person who has taken refuge with me, no matter what his lineage. (Example: if a man, rich or poor, kills a man in another lineage, he can force anyone outside the slain man's lineage to help him simply by killing a sheep in front of an individual's hut or tent.)

3) To defend to the last any property entrusted to me.

4) To be hospitable and provide for the safety of the person and property of a guest.

5) To refrain from killing a woman, a Hindu, a minstrel, or a boy not yet circumcised.

6) To pardon an offense on the intercession of a woman of the offender's lineage, a Sayyid (descendant of the Prophet), or a mullah. (An exception is made in the case of murder; only blood or blood money can erase this crime.)

7) To punish all adulterers with death.

8) To refrain from killing a man who has entered a mosque or the shrine of a holy man so long as he remains within its precincts; also to spare a man in battle who begs for quarter.

This is a stringent code, a tough code for tough men, who of necessity live tough lives. Professor Carleton S. Coon, noted authority on the Middle East, called the Pushtun country the "Land of Insolence"; in the 1890's, Amir Abdur Rahman Khan called it Yagistan, "the land of the unruly." The barren land of the Pushtun forces him into an active life, and better insolence then indolence!

Honor and hospitality, hostility and ambush are paired in the Afghan mind. These are best summed up in the three most important elements of the *Pushtunwali:*

(1) *Nanawati*—the right of asylum, and the obligatory acceptance of a truce offer.

(2) *Melmastia*—the obligation of hospitality and the protection given each guest.

(3) *Badad*—blood vengeance, but blood money is acceptable if the two families involved agree.

The values of the Pushtun and of the Muslim religion, modified by local custom, permeate in varying degrees all Afghan ethnic groups.

Conclusions

The salvation sought by the intellectual is always based on inner need, and hence it is at once more remote from life, more theoretical, and more systematic than salvation from external distress, the quest for which is characteristic of nonprivileged classes. The intellectual seeks in various ways, the casuistry of which extends into infinity, to endow his life with a pervasive meaning, and thus to find unity with himself, with his fellow men, and with the cosmos. It is the intellectual who transforms the concept of the world into the problem of meaning. As intellectualism suppresses belief in magic, the world's processes become disenchanted, lose their magical significance, and hereforth simply "are" and "happen" but no longer signify anything. As a consequence, there is a growing demand that the world and the total pattern of life be subject to an order that is significant and meaningful.

Max Weber
The Sociology of Religion

CONCLUSIONS

BY KALMAN H. SILVERT

American Universities Field Staff

Religions espouse universal values, but they often serve the ends of human isolation. Industrial societies depend on specialization and differentiation, but their continued ability to change and thus to survive depends on their nurture of broadly universal human relations. These observations are not intellectual tricks. They are but a statement of simple empirical truisms. To sanction all human acts in terms of a single set of values by ranging all authority monolithically upward to divine sanction serves to divide man from man. That is, paradoxically, human societies become "particularized" in the name of universal truth supported by hierarchical authority. On the other hand, to permit an individual many varied roles and functions in a complex society with differing, interrelated structures of authority is to offer him the possibility of broader, richer, more humanly "universal" social relations.

What may not be so obvious, however, is that dogmatic belief systems are not necessarily supportive only of authoritarian social relations, and that specialized social institutions are not supportive only of plural and open structures. Religious beliefs are necessarily absolutist; religious institutions may assist in applying such beliefs to the strengthening of relativistic social systems. Analogously, industrial work attitudes may be based on specialization, the reward of merit, and impersonal social relations; they can be employed to maintain totalitarian political systems. It is the mix of the universal and the particular, the absolute and the relative, and the socially differentiating and the socially integrating which defines the elements both necessary and sufficient for diagnosing the interplay between churches and states in the processes of modernizing social change.

Too much thinking about church-state relations emphasizes the integrating, total embrace of religious belief; too little thought is given to the relation between these global belief systems and the many varieties of individual and group action. With regard to modern secular society, too much is made of the breakdown of the extended family, estrangement of the worker from his product, and the loss of individual identity. But much too little is made of the integrating effects of identification with national community and broad social classes, and of the new freedoms promised by the ability to occupy many differing roles that permit varied structures of loyalty and communication.

An appropriate relationship between differentiating and integrating institutions and values may well be the key to self-sustaining social change. But in this dialectic of the analytic and the synthetic, agreement is always more easily reached on the component parts than on the shape of the total structure that is made more than the sum of its parts by the very addition of the styles, methods, and idea systems of the integration itself. Social modernizers find no difficulty in espousing industrialization, extended communications and educational systems, urbanization, and public health programs. Their task becomes much thornier when they must solve such problems as relations between modern and traditional social groups, the containment of contention within national legal systems, and the creation of convincing national ideologies with supra-class appeals. Religious leaders, exactly to the contrary, are comfortable when dealing with matters of truth and morals, those generalizations not subject to empirical verification from which they can deduce ideal patterns of universal human behavior. Their troubles begin when they attempt to translate their truth statements into a non-ideal world increasingly employing validity tests and not truth as the measure of the good as well as the viable. However, religious and political men share a common difficulty in attempting to describe a general social synthesis, as distinct either from a supernatural synthesis or a partial tactic of social manipulation or influence.

Religious and political institutions move all too easily into antagonistic positions as the secularizing effects of the modernization process begin to take hold. Their enmity—usual but not inevitable—is rooted in the fact that they are natural institutional competitors for the role of synthesizer amidst the growth of differentiation. The specialized function of the modern nation-state is generalization. The nation-state is the institutional setting designed to contain class conflict, interest disputes, and those other manifestations of necessary diversity, and to prevent them from shaking society to pieces. When the nation-state is functioning positively it helps to turn conflict toward system continuity and the maintenance of ordered adjustments to change. To the extent to which religious institutions insist on their right and duty to proclaim a truth basis for general social relations, they are in the same terrain as the nation-state with its claims to overriding temporal authority. The coincidence of church-state conflict and modernization thus requires no elaborate theoretical explanation. The general patterns of resolution of the conflict are also quite clear.

In all democratic national societies competition between church and state to define the total social situation is resolved by dividing their spheres of legitimacy. The state institutionalizes relative secular values of order, adjustment, and rationalization. The religious agencies devote themselves to postulations of truth and explications of the moral normative order outside the umbrella of the system of legalized political sanction. The nature of the authority of each institutional sphere is also clearly defined in terms of differing origins and jurisdictions. The religious law, for example, is seen as stemming from revelation; secular or political law is the product of human decision, although hortatory support may be sought by claiming consistency with a natural order. The ultimate sanction of the religious order is found only in the supernatural, while the ultimate sanction of the state is expressed through an enforcement process in the here and now. Because the other-worldly must pre-exist man's quest for it, religious knowledge and authority is exegetical, an uncovering. Secular law may legitimately be thought of philosophically as at least potentially a truly original and creative act, as well as an extrapolative one. The jurisdiction of religious authority extends to the community of believers involved; the jurisdiction of states is as much a product of consensual acceptance as is that of religious institutions, but its extension is territorially defined. It is with these distinctions, as well as others, that modern democratic nations have justified the separation of churches from states. But in the search for these postulations, it is clear that the social characteristics of states and churches more often than not lead to clashes as the unitary organic quality of traditional society reluctantly cedes to the plural relativism of modern organization.

The democratic pattern of conflict resolution by separation is not the only alternative historically at hand, however. Totalitarian regimes take on the truth quotients of religions, finding a device of great utility in the addition of religious to political sanctions. Such states, typified by Nazi Germany, are not theocracies, of course, for the religious institutions are made entirely subservient to the political authority. There are no cases of religious groups manipulating very highly specialized and institutionally differentiated modern societies. But indeed there are societies close to modern organization in which religious leaders have assumed enormous and effective political power in defense of their traditional prerogatives, thus creating quasitheocratic forms. Some of the case studies in this volume describe examples of this kind of last-ditch but sometimes long-term defense.

It is not historically "necessary," then, that the resolution of church-state conflict in modernizing situations take a given, single path. But if the way of effective separation is not followed, then the entire development process is confounded by the resultant confusion between absolute and relative truth, religious and secular authority and sanction, and the socially universal as opposed to the religiously universal. Judging social matters by dogmatic prescription impedes that self-correction without which change becomes tortured maladjustment instead of enthusiastic exploration.

This analysis explains why all the authors in this book, in examining the general question of the religious institution and modernization, had eventually to rest their discussion on church-state relations. Professor Neusner treated socialism and Zionism as major themes in the development of contemporary Judaism. Messrs. Du Bois, Sanders, and Rusinow analyzed the political dimension to reveal the differing ways in which the Catholic Church is seeking adjustment to rapid social change. Sanders described a Catholic group in Brazil attempting to employ the authority of the state to revolutionize a population while consciously rejecting the immediate attempt to "Christianize" it. Rusinow studied the processes of church-state separation after a long era of easy and classbound identification between religious and secular authorities. And Du Bois described early stages of the church-state struggle as the new "nations" of Africa sprout their first independent governments. Precisely the same preoccupations governed the analyses of Schaar, Gallagher, Dupree, and Hanna concerning modernization in the Islamic world.

The case studies, the introduction, and these conclusions reaffirm the earlier findings of social scientists who have worked on the general theory of the political sociology of religion. Additionally, the eight studies in this book demonstrate that what such early nationalists as the American Founding Fathers knew, the political and religious leaders of recently modernizing nations are learning all over again. This confirmation is not a task unworthy of the relativist, who always wants to know how far his relative truth extends.

The cases presented here also clearly suggest that the separation of church and state not merely removes inhibitions to development, but affirmatively promotes modernization by opening areas of civic freedom, thereby immediately fostering economic and other forms of modernism. It has been commonly argued that Ascetic Protestantism fomented development by encouraging the processes of capital accumulation and inculcating certain values of work and denial directly affecting economic behavior. There is another possibility; or it is perhaps but an added one. That is, that such political theorists of the early Protestant period as Locke and Hobbes postulated a secularized natural law directly affecting institutional relations in such a way as to permit the freeing of individuals for their more rational recruitment into nation-building tasks. To argue that all men are equal before the natural law no matter what their formal religious convictions is also to argue that religious labels should not impede individuals from full participation in public life and affairs. Modern man's freedom from the stigmata of religious ascription is another one of those painfully won victories over the accidents of birth that inhibit persons from adjusting their individual abilities to the general social need and their own preferences. We need not labor the obvious relationship between ordered recruiting to economic, social, and political roles from as wide a public as possible, and the most effective use of the human resource in development.

Most studies of development emphasize the importance of land and capital, and at best "labor," the human element, is treated in studies of education or is dealt with in nonhumanistic terms as a gross input. That is unfortunate, for it is in the sweeping panorama of human organization that the primary solutions are to be found: in the freeing of man to benefit by his education, to apply his training and his skills to his land, to make his rational decisions concerning what to spend and what to save. The search for freedom is promoted by the formal separation of religious from secular authority. But that search comes fully to fruition only when the separation of churches from states is part of a larger separation between the comfort of amoebic unity and the joy of the individual human good made compatible with the good of humanity.

INDEX